AN AFFRONT TO THE GOSPEL?
The Radical Barth and the
Southern Baptist Convention

American Academy of Religion
Academy Series

edited by
Susan Thistlethwaite

Number 56
AN AFFRONT TO THE GOSPEL?
The Radical Barth and the
Southern Baptist Convention
by
Elizabeth B. Barnes

Elizabeth B. Barnes

AN AFFRONT TO THE GOSPEL?
The Radical Barth
and the Southern Baptist
Convention

Scholars Press
Atlanta Georgia

AN AFFRONT TO THE GOSPEL?
The Radical Barth and the
Southern Baptist Convention

by
Elizabeth B. Barnes

Library of Congress Cataloging-in-Publication Data

Barnes, Elizabeth B., 1938
  An affront to the Gospel?

  (AAR studies in religion ; no. 56)
  Bibliography: p.
  1. Barth, Karl, 1886-1968. 2. Southern Baptist
Convention—Doctrines. 3. Baptists—Doctrines.
I. Title. II. Series: Studies in religion (American
Academy of Religion) ; no. 56.
BX4827.B3B34 1987   262'.7   87-12725
ISBN 1-55540-100-7 (alk. paper)
ISBN 1-55540-101-5 (pbk. : alk. paper)

Printed in the United States of America
on acid-free paper

CONTENTS

PREFACE

This thesis seeks to advance the efforts of contemporary theological thinkers to critique our Protestant Christian tradition in the interest of finding a methodology that is true to the Gospel and faithful to the creative encounter between church and world. Special attention has been given to the part of the Southern Baptist Convention, my own denomination, in that endeavor. Accordingly, some attention has also been given to the current debate between conservative and moderate thinkers within the Convention.

Argument is made that, underlying the failure of modern theology to heal the theology-ethics hiatus and the church-world dislocation, is an ancient understanding of faith and theology promulgated principally by Anselm of Canterbury and endorsed by the church through the centuries. This notion characterized by the Latin phrase *fides quaerens intellectum*, faith seeking understanding, has steered theology in the direction of the abstract and theoretical. Karl Barth's work in particular is studied in this light.

It is time now, I have argued, to develop another methodology which I have termed *fides quaerens rationem reddere*, faith seeking accountability which understands. This methodology situates theological reflection immediately in the dual context of the church's worship and the concrete experience of the poor of humanity and para-humanity (nature). Thus, it is theology conducted in a new and different manner for which I am arguing. The work of the early Barth offers directions for this endeavor.

There are many whose contribution to this work and the insights contained within it I wish to acknowledge. Principally, the teaching and example of Frederick Herzog at Duke University have shaped the formation of these insights in crucial and indispensable ways. Robert T. Osborn served to enable my understanding of Karl Barth's ecclesiology, and I am indebted to him for his excellent guidance.

My family has been my undergirding strength through this entire process, and each one of them I extend my deep love and gratitude. To them I dedicate the completion of this work, for they have joined me in it.

Elizabeth Barnes
April 23, 1987

CHAPTER I

BAPTIST FAITH AND ECCLESIOLOGY

Introduction

In the summer of 1981, the tragic Atlanta murders occasioned a quest to determine the church's response to that tragedy. Research conducted by me that summer, particularly with the *Atlanta Constitution*, disclosed conditions of poverty, discrimination, and racial hatred in Atlanta that the Southern Baptist Convention and other churches had for the most part, for whatever reasons, failed to perceive as their pressing concern and responsibility. Why? Although various factors contributed as penultimate causes, the core problem, it seemed, was one: The church, while accepting engagement with social justice concerns as an implied task, has not commonly seen that task as one which cannot be separated from the heart of the Gospel and message of Jesus of Nazareth. Hence, social action has been understood as diaconate, good works which the church is to do *also,* in addition to its primary function of proclamation. The Southern Baptist Convention's complicity in this understanding of the church's nature and tasks has led me to a review of those distinctive teachings which Baptists regard as the essence of their doctrine, a review which will suggest where further thought is needed and reorientations indicated.

Developments Affecting the Emergence of the Baptist Pattern of Congregational Polity and Associational Autonomy

Robert T. Handy lists three developments in the nineteenth century which converged to fashion that distinctive Baptist church pattern which is characterized by radical individualism, congregational polity and the associational principle.[1] The first is the evangelical understanding of Baptist belief which emerged in the Great

Awakening; the second is Baptist Separatism and its emphatic individualism, especially that of Isaac Backus; and third, the Jeffersonian Baptists, particularly John Leland, and the influence of Enlightenment thought which they introduced.[2]

From these influences and others in the late eighteenth and early nineteenth centuries came what Handy, following Alfred N. Whitehead, calls a "gospel of individualism." Puritanism's early stress on an intense, personal, religious experience had been balanced by the Calvinist emphasis on divine sovereignty and a high doctrine of the church. In time, however, the focus on individualism strengthened and the balance weakened. A significant factor in that weakening was the Enlightenment. Handy asserts that Enlightenment philosophy was "enshrined" in the documents of the new American republic and that prominent Baptist leaders, notably John Leland, a staunch admirer and supporter of Jefferson, were influential interpreters of that philosophy for their faith. Romanticism, too, in its own way, encouraged individual freedom and at a critical juncture reinforced a philosophy with which it otherwise was in sharp disagreement. A fourth influence, Handy and others agree, was the frontier experience. Self-reliance and freedom were the lessons taught by the frontier and absorbed by Baptists. Liberal political economy and its stress on the freedom of the economic individual and of the marketplace from political control were a fifth significant influence. "The sense of corporate responsibility for human welfare was . . . largely dissolved, and major currents in economic, political, and social thought supported the trend toward individualism."[3] Prominent Baptists like Francis Wayland supported the emergence of a "clerical laissez faire" which eroded "earlier corporate Christian concerns for the larger structures of the church," eventuating in a near equation of the Gospel of Christ and the gospel of individualism.[4]

Pervading and surpassing all other influences was the singular influence of the Enlightenment.[5] "Its impact on religion was immense"; churches restated their theologies "with varying degrees of accommodation to the Age of Reason," Handy notes. "The emergence of Enlightenment trends in the late seventeenth and early eighteenth centuries was one of those seminal shifts of thought and feeling of which the consequences were widespread and are still influential. . . . Impelled by the brilliant advances in the science of its time, which seemed to be sweeping mystery from the world . . . Enlightenment thinkers proposed to discover the truth about God and the world by utilizing their rational faculties in the examination of Nature. . . ."[6] The Age of Reason, itself a time of overwhelming faith, was, Stromberg maintains, characterized by a "remarkable faith that the world is a rational one and man a rational creature, from which among other things it follows that man has a rational religion."[7]

Francis Wayland was such a Baptist rationalist who, according to Maring, "could prove the existence of God or the divine inspiration of the Scriptures by sheer logic."[8] Highly esteemed by his denomination and influential on it, Wayland understood the Bible as the record of God's moral law which, when understood and obeyed, resulted in conversion of the individual soul and, consequentially, of all reality. An intimate union of rationalism, individualism, naturalism, and confidence in knowledge surfaces in Wayland's writings. *Occasional Discourses* espouses a confidence in "the progress of knowledge" which reveals the "indissoluble connection between moral and physical laws of nature" and humanity's "powers of discovery."[9] The Bible itself is seen as but an amplification of the truths of natural religion.

Stressing Wayland's individualistic bent, Maring notes that this famous Baptist makes no reference to the collective people of God. "Since he viewed the Old Testament chiefly as a system of law and a demonstration of man's failure, he did not appreciate fully the significance of Israel as a covenant community. . . . He conceived the true church as an aggregate of saved individuals."[10] At other times Wayland referred to the need for Christian philanthropy and the "world's renovation," but it appears that the conversion of individuals was the method and goal.[11]

Frugality, hard work, and enlightened self-interest were other themes espoused in Wayland's writings. The principles of the Gospel, he believed, could make one rich and, indeed, formed the theological base for such a quest, since "Our own interest and the interest of men everywhere, are, by the ordinance of the Creator, one."[12] Because self-interest and that of others are one, Wayland could write in *Elements of Moral Science:* "Every human being is, by his constitution, a separate, and distinct, and complete system, adapted to all the purposes of self-government, and responsible, separately, to God, for the manner in which his powers are employed. . . . He need assign no other reason for his conduct than his own free choice. Within this limit, he is still responsible to God; but . . . he is not responsible *to man,* nor *is man responsible for him.*"[13]

Maring notes that Wayland was opposed to the church's involvement in political life, seeing the remedy for the world's ills in salvation of the soul and the change of heart which derives from that change. In reference to the passing of the Kansas-Nebraska Bill, Wayland stated, "I am opposed to uniting this, or anything else, with the preaching of the gospel. . . . The Christian view is to look up to God, and to arouse the Christian feeling in men. To abolish slavery is a good thing, but it is not religion. . . . I have no faith in any other means for curing the evils of the present time. . . . What is needed is a general revival of religion. Nothing else will save us."[14]

"Giant With His Hands Tied Behind His Back"

Because the world was to be conquered, but not by political means, and not by the modification of individual freedoms, but by the conversion of souls alone, Maring says that the church, as Wayland described it, was "a giant with his hands tied behind his back."[15] The individual joining the church was not committed beyond his or her own autonomous interest, and those agencies which might have aided the church in living out its ministry were not allowed that function. Maring concludes therefore that, although Wayland was respected in his day as a seminal thinker, ". . . the fact that he was in a position to influence Baptists is tragic."[16]

Winthrop Hudson concurs with Maring that Jeffersonian and Enlightenment individualism left on Baptist faith and life an indelible mark. From those sources and others already mentioned came what E. Y. Mullins identified as the constitutive principle of Baptist church life, the principle of soul competency. According to Hudson, this principle became the apologetic for the pattern of church life further developed in the early decades of this century, Hudson observes, "It has become increasingly apparent that this principle was derived from the general cultural and religious climate of the nineteenth century rather than from any serious study of the Bible."[17] Further, ". . . it served to dissolve any real concept of the church."[18] Hudson goes on to say that the adoption of the principle of soul competency as the central doctrine of the Baptist faith had the practical effect of making "every man's hat his own church."[19] Hudson, Maring, and others have questioned whether a corporate notion of the church was then possible.[20]

Paul Harrison contends that the radical individualism and principle of soul competency embraced by Wayland, Backus, Leland, and others of their day, represented a nineteenth century distortion of the primary intent of those early Baptists who framed the English and American confessions of faith. For those founding fathers, the dignity and competency of the individual were clearly derivative from and secondary to the sovereignty of God. Freedom of conscience and religious liberty were social corollaries of the freedom of God's Spirit; the freedom of God, then, was the cardinal concern of the Free Church fathers. However, as individualistic forces in the eighteenth and nineteenth centuries pressed in upon them, later Baptists, Harrison states, "slipped off their theological base." What the Free Church founders wished to teach was that the Word of God can be a lively word only as it is spoken within a tradition which affirms, as well, the freedom of men and women. Subsequent emphasis on soul competency, however, "crystallizes attention upon the possibilities of men rather than upon the power of God." This, Harrison insists, is the Free Church's most serious weakness.[21]

Harrison agrees with Handy and Maring that the chaotic though creative socio-religious milieu of the eighteenth century nurtured a mixture of liberal democracy and Baptist theology. Sorting out all of the threads of influence, however, is a task yet to be achieved. As Harrison notes, "The ideas of the Independents of Cromwell's army, the writings of John Locke, the theological thought of the Puritan Separatists, and the courageous writings on religious liberty of Thomas Helwys—all contributed to the present theological milieu, and greater efforts are necessary to clarify the existing confusion."[22]

Harrison's claim that, in every decade of Baptist history since the early nineteenth century, the principle of soul competency has been reaffirmed as a basic distinctive doctrine of Baptist faith,[23] is abundantly confirmed by Baptist literature to the present. In 1908, E. Y. Mullins' classic *The Axioms of Religion* espoused the "elementary . . . universal . . . and self-evident" truth of the principle of individual soul competency,[24] and William R. McNutt, Professor of Practical Theology at Crozer Theological Seminary from 1928–1944, wrote in 1935 that the major contribution of Baptist thought to Christian theology has been "the creative idea that the individual is competent in all matters of religion. . . . He has no inescapable need of church to bring him salvation or mediate to him divine

grace. . . ."[25] "Competency," McNutt declared, "resposes authority in religion within the individual. It sets each man on a
throne which holds absolute sway over his own realm. And he may
not, for any reason, abdicate; he rules by divine right and appoint-
ment."[26] Indeed, McNutt went so far as to say that the Baptist
doctrine of the church *originates* from the doctrine of soul competency which is its "mother" and "directive life principle."[27]

McNutt and Mullins were joined in their emphasis on soul
competency in 1951 by Edward A. Pruden who, while denying that
this doctrine is more important than more orthodox doctrines such
as the sovereignty of God or justification by grace through faith,
finally upheld its primal significance as the one doctrine which
Baptists have historically felt constrained to emphasize.[28] Finally, in
the decade of the eighties, strong reaffirmations of the centrality of
the doctrine of soul competency have been made by Baptist leaders.[29]

Individual Salvation and a "Spiritual" Church

From the distinctive Baptist doctrine of soul competence follows the correlative doctrine of individual salvation. The salvation of
the individual soul and the nurturing of its one-to-one relation with
Jesus Christ means, in turn, that the church is a "spiritual" reality—
i.e., it is concerned above all with the individual and his or her
"spiritual" life. The church's primary task, then, is an evangelistic
one, the winning of souls to Christ.[30] *Annuals of the Southern
Baptist Convention* have consistently affirmed and reaffirmed the
primacy of evangelism and missions and the spiritual essence of the
church.[31] Classic studies of the Baptist dedication to individual
salvation and of the social consequences deriving from that singular
focus show that the tradition of the primacy of evangelism conceived
as individual conversion is strong and long-standing.[32] Indeed, it is
"the primary characteristic" of Southern Baptists.[33] There is in-
grained in Baptists a wariness of "soap and soup" salvation and a
belief that it detracts from soul-winning.[34] Henderson notes that
opposition to the Christian Life Commission, the social service
organization of the Southern Baptist Convention, surfaces regularly
in Baptist state newspapers and at the annual convention. A resolution was submitted in 1965 to disband the CLC for its suggestion
that Southern Baptists needed to acknowledge their guilt for racial

injustice.[35] Though the resolution failed to pass, that move to dissolve the CLC represented the thought of an element of the Southern Baptist constituency that is seeking now to control the denomination; more will be said about this current struggle within the Southern Baptist Convention in the conclusion to this chapter.

An Alternative Baptist Conception of the Church

An articulate Baptist minority is questioning now the adequacy of a doctrine of the church committed preeminently to individual salvation. Samuel S. Hill, Jr. has stood in the vanguard of that growing number.* "To the considerable extent that the essence of Christianity was viewed as the conversion of individuals, reality was reduced to two constituent units, God and the individual. . . . That was the pivot of all the doctrines. . . ."[36] Not surprisingly, then, issues of social concern have been, and are likely still to be, considered matters of significant social and human import, even of political moment, but not appropriately a major task of the church whose primary calling is a "spiritual" one, Hill argues.[37]

Francis M. DuBose and Bob E. Adams assert that, at least for some, a new understanding of evangelism includes a social action focus.[38] Carl W. Tiller quotes from a 1969 commentary in the *New Zealand Baptist:* "Baptists are traditionally committed to evangelism. . . . But we have, also, an obligation beyond evangelism and towards social righteousness. . . . It is not a passion for souls that distinguishes the true Christian. It is a passion for souls plus a passion for social justice."[39] William Pinson has spoken eloquently for a new understanding of the church's nature and essential tasks. Insisting that the Baptist choice is not between evangelism and social ministry, he argues that the church is called to care for the whole of human need, "and that calls for evangelism *and* social ministry."[40] Pinson's norm is "the biblical mandate to minister." He writes, "The Bible is shot through and through with explicit commands to help people who hurt or who are in difficulty. . . . When true to their biblical mandate, churches are concerned about whole people."[41] Concern for the total life of persons calls for political involvement and group action.[42] C. Brownlow Hastings joins Pinson in calling for a new sense of corporate responsibility.[43] Hill and Torbet, as well, herald the need for Baptist involvement in matters of social and economic concern. An ecclesiological reassessment is imperative, they stress, and a zealous and courageous stance demanded, if Baptists are to realize "their Christian social mission to a world torn by dissension, wounded by injustice, and weakened by hunger."[44]

No more prophetic or eloquent Baptist voice in this century has spoken out for a new ecclesiology concerned with social justice than that of Martin Luther King, Jr. His speeches, sermons, and books have unmasked Christian hypocrisies, exposed Christian failings, and shamed Christian ignorance and pettiness. Contrary to the notion that "Get a man's heart right and all else will fall into place," King wrote, ". . . it is an immoral act to compel a man to accept injustice until another man's heart is set straight."[45] Contrary to the idea that the church's realm is merely or evenly primarily a spiritual one, King wrote, "It is not enough for the church to be active in the realm of ideas; it must move out into the arena of social action."[46] "How often the church has had a high blood count of creeds and an anemia of deeds!"[47] Always cognizant of the church's failure to actualize its ethical commission, in his "Letter from Birmingham Jail" King castigated the eight Christian and Jewish clergymen who had failed to understand that ethical imperative and act accordingly. In *Stride Toward Freedom*, King answered those who accused him of a "social gospel" devoid of roots in salvation. Seeing no valid separation of otherworldly and temporal concerns, he wrote:

> Certainly, otherworldly concerns have a deep and significant place in all religions worthy of the name. Any religion that is completely earthbound sells its birthright for a mess of naturalistic pottage. Religion, at its best, deals not only with man's preliminary concerns but with his inescapable ultimate concern. When religion overlooks this basic fact it is reduced to a mere ethical system in which eternity is absorbed into time and God is relegated to a sort of meaningless figment of the human imagination.

But that is not all, King insisted:

> . . . a religion true to its nature must also be concerned about man's social conditions. Religion deals with both earth and heaven, both time and eternity. Religion operates not only on the vertical plane but also on the horizontal. It seeks not only to integrate men with God but to integrate men with men and man with himself. This means, at bottom, that the Christian gospel is a two-way road. On the one hand it seeks to change

the souls of men, and thereby unite them with God; on the other hand it seeks to change the environmental conditions of men so that the soul will have a chance after it is changed.[48]

Towards a More Adequate Baptist Ecclesiology

While it is true that Baptist statements calling for social justice have never been completely absent from denominational literature,[49] an ambiguity prevails in Baptist thought regarding the place of social concern in the church's understanding of its nature and tasks. This portion of this chapter will seek to analyze points of conflict and ambiguity and to locate possibilities for growth.

Prominent Baptist thinkers are now finding the distinctive doctrines of their faith questionable, at least in some aspects. Such notions as local church autonomy and soul competency are raising questions of definition and origination. As already shown, analysts of the Baptist tradition have identified Enlightenment roots for such ideas. Harrison notes that there are those who think that the notion of soul competency reflects John Locke more than the New Testament. So, too, extreme emphasis upon individual freedom contradicts the concept of the gathered church.[50] Thinkers like McNutt, Wayland, Dillard et al. have promulgated rationalist notions only lightly baptized with Christian understandings.[51] DuBose and Adams, too, have identified natural law, albeit as a pre- or subconscious function in much of Baptist thought, while the conscious function is scriptural exegesis. They see a need for a concerted Baptist effort to analyze and understand tacit and explicit conceptual and theological bases for social action.[52] Hays and Steely acknowledge that the effects of an insistence on individual religious experience and freedom have often militated against a proper concern both for the needs of other persons and for the corporate integrity of the church.[53] H. Wheeler Robinson does not hesitate to charge Baptist churchmen with capitulation to an eighteenth century philosophy of society. He sees reflections of Rousseau in the fact that talk of the work of the Holy Spirit is carried on "as if it occurred in a social vacuum, in order that a number of unitary products might subsequently be brought together to form a Church."[54]

Other Baptist leaders have faulted various Baptist denominations for their lack of consensus on virtually all matters except those of soul competency and local church autonomy. These leaders call

for a reorganization of denominational structure.[55] Accommodation
to culture, as well, is cited as a serious deterrent to Baptist social action.
Glenn Hinson critiques his denomination: "Southern Baptists have
been shaped in great part by their culture. Indeed, they excel in
accommodating themselves to it. As the 'old' South passes and the
'new' comes into being, they will have to struggle, along with
others, to develop and maintain a critical stance. They tend to favor
'cheap' grace, but the Lord they claim to follow talked about 'costly'
grace. This may be the most critical issue in the end."[56] David W.
Sapp asserts that prophetic statements related to the economy have
most often defended the status quo and have approached affirming
capitalism as a uniquely Christian economic system.[57]

Enlightenment influence, lack of ecclesiological consensus,
problematical denominational structure, cultural Christianity: these
are partial causes of Baptist inadequacy in meeting social ministry
responsibilities. More pressing than all of these, however, and en-
capsulating them all, is the need for a more adequate doctrine of the
church.[58] H. Wheeler Robinson calls for a "nobler church-consciousness" which can only come, he insists, through a new conception of the church itself.[59] Winthrop Hudson alleges that Baptists have not had an adequate "churchly understanding," one which
recognizes that God's unique purpose in Jesus Christ has been to
create a people of God, a Body of Christ, not a band of solitary
Christians. Hudson charges that Baptists have held a "nonchurchly
understanding" rooted in the notion that God's purpose has been to
create individual Christians for fellowship with God in Christ, which
means, finally, that there is no church. Hudson challenges his
denomination to face the theological implications of this view and to
deal with them accordingly.[60] Hastings concurs: "It is unrealistic to
believe that a gospel designed primarily for individual regeneration
is, *ipso facto*, applicable to the evils entrenched in social institutions."[61]

It is, then, a new theology of the church's essential nature and
tasks that Baptists of all persuasions need. So long as social justice
action is seen merely as an implication of the Gospel rather than a
part of its *substance*, the church will continue to fail to join God in
caring for the whole of creation and the entirety of human life. This
thesis holds that *social justice is not a corollary of faith; it is of its
very essence.* James E. Wood, Jr., Executive Director of the Baptist
Joint Committee on Public Affairs in 1978, was squarely on target
with his call for a theological base for social action which affirms its

essentiality to Christian faith itself and to the church's nature and mission.[62] (Neither Wood nor I use "essence" in any idealistic sense.)

In summation, the church, and not least the Southern Baptist Convention, has often understood the ecclesia as "an aggregate of saved individuals" and salvation as an affair of the soul alone. The primary task of the church, logically, then has been the evangelistic one of winning souls to Christ through proclamation of the Word. Disclosing God in Christ to receptive hearts who then hear and believe has been construed as the primal mission of the church. Even as Samuel Hill argues, matters of social concern have been, and are likely still to be, on such a view, deemed issues of significant social and human import, even of political moment, but not appropriately as major concerns of the church whose primary calling is a spiritual one.[63] The lack of a sense of communal responsibility in a church with an inadequate understanding of its corporate oneness is correlative to the notion of individual salvation and a spiritual church.

Behind all this, however, this thesis hypothesizes, lies an issue of critical theological moment which demands rigorous reassessment and evaluation. Even as Wood et al. have stressed, *the need for a theological base for social action is where the root problem lies.* That problem, in turn, this thesis proposes, involves the church's understanding of faith. *How the church conceives the nature of faith will determine how it conceives theology and the doctrines with which theology concerns itself.* It is at this point that the accepted formula of faith seeking understanding, *fides quaerens intellectum,* and the notion of theology derived from it are seen as critical issues to which much rigorous thought needs to be given. The Southern Baptist Convention, and the church generally, have operated within that theological understanding *(fides quaerens intellectum)* and methodology. *Fides quaerens intellectum* has traditionally defined for the church the nature of faith and, hence, the nature of theology. This thesis proposes, instead, faith seeking accountability which understands, *fides quaerens rationem reddere.*[64] Analysis of Anselm's formula of contemplative union discloses that faith is there understood as that which most characteristically desires understanding or knowledge. Understanding is rational cognition given by divine Reason to human reason, enabling movement toward the *visio Dei.* Faith's object God is rational and faith's subject humanity is rational; implicitly, at least, it is suggested in this view that the divine-human relation is, at its core, that of Reason-reason. Knowing God engenders love of God and trust in God. Doubtless, many of those who hold to the faith seeking understanding formula will contend that it is the other way around, that love for and trust in God engender the desire to know God. That, however, is simply another way of stating the formula; either way the desideratum is knowledge. Theology, hence, is rational reflection on Scripture and creed in the quest for understanding and knowledge.

We need to inquire into the meaning of the first term, faith. Faith perceived as belief in and acceptance of the Scriptures (and the creed), whatever else is included such as love, trust, and commitment, makes sense as faith seeking understanding, *fides quaerens intellectum*. On the other hand, faith perceived as awakened accountability to God and others, informed by the witness of the Scriptures, whatever else is included such as understanding and knowledge, makes sense as faith seeking accountability which understands, *fides quaerens rationem reddere*. Theology, on this view, is *discipleship* first, in social location with the poor to whom God is actively faithful. Avowing God's action first, we are also to join God in acts of faithfulness to those excluded ones. Reflection and reason are an integral part of that faithfulness, but a conscious reflecting and reasoning *with* those who have formerly been excluded in the exegetical, hermeneutical, and reflective moments in theology. Extension also needs to be made to the otherkind[65] *for* which we reflect and reason, the para-human creation which God also loves. Accountability is to oppressed humankind and to oppressed nature; it is accountability to God and to all whom and which God values.

Faith seeking accountability which also understands will see God's transformative action in history as primary and humanity's co-action as response to claim in accountable relation to God and others, including the others of nature. Social justice issues, environmental responsibilities, and issues of world peace will then be seen as more than correlative to, implicate of, the Gospel. *Fides quaerens rationem reddere* will see these as lodged in the heart of God, and thus in the heart of the Gospel. With this hypothesis, then, a doctrine of the church can emerge which understands the church's essential role as more than that of proclaimer, though it is certainly that; the church as provoker/transformer for the realization of God's truth can then be seen as a fuller understanding of what it means to proclaim the Word of God. In a world where God is present, opening up paths of justice and peace, it will be seen that social justice, ecological responsibility, and peace action are *of the essence of the Gospel*. For the Southern Baptist Convention, as for the church generally, these concerns have most often been viewed as *implications* of the Gospel for which *application* needs to be made. Faith seeking accountability which understands, *fides quaerens rationem reddere*, shows that neither implication nor application adequately designates the import of these concerns; it is *more*.

The next chapter will examine the formula *fides quaerens intellectum* as expounded by Anselm and Barth and the methodology which Barth derived from his understanding of that formula. Karl Barth's theology of the Word of God has been, perhaps, as influential as any modern theology on Baptist thought. Effort will be made to establish in that chapter and those following the assertion that, while *fides quaerens intellectum* fails to retain early insights of Barth's which might have developed into a view akin to that of *fides quaerens rationem reddere*, attention to Barth's Safenwil years offers directions toward reclaiming and further developing in regard to the Southern Baptist Convention and in some measure for the church as a whole, an ecclesiology which embraces social justice, ecological responsibility, and peace action as of its essence.

Reflections on the Current Debate Within the Southern Baptist Convention

The Southern Baptist Convention is currently embroiled in a struggle between conservative and moderate factions which define the nature of the Baptist faith and practice in incompatible terms. While Winthrop Hudson, Paul Harrison, and others have questioned the validity of the distinctive Baptist principle of soul competency and have suggested its liability for the failure of Baptists to develop a strong church-consciousness, new light is being focused now on the wisdom of early Baptist thinkers like E. Y. Mullins who insisted on the indispensable value of this doctrine for the life of the Free Church.

Though critics may indeed be correct in locating Enlightenment roots and nineteenth century individualism as partial sources, and distorters, of this distinctive Baptist affirmation, it is important to recognize that there is strong biblical support for this doctrine as well. Its cruciality is being recognized anew today at a time when control of church doctrine is being attempted within a denomination that has historically resisted such control.

Paul Harrison's focusing on the primary intent of the early Baptists who framed the doctrine of soul competency helps us to reclaim its value and wed it to a communal consciousness which does not obviate the individual's freedom of interpretation but incorporates it within a doctrine of the church as the communal Body of Christ. The founding fathers, Harrison notes, understood God's sovereignty and freedom as central and the individual's competency and dignity as derivative from and social corollary of the freedom of God's Spirit. The understanding and intent of those early Baptist forebears was that of a living Word of God freely spoken within a tradition requiring as well the freedom of men and women to receive and interpret that Word. It is *this* which Southern Baptists need again to affirm in the Free Church heritage and develop in richer ways than our theological ancestors have done. Soul competency, freedom of interpretation which is the priesthood of the believer, and a corporate Body of Christ functioning as a unity for God's work of proclamation, peace, justice, and love, can correct errors in nineteenth century understandings of the church and late twentieth century ones as well.

NOTES

/1/   Robert T. Handy, Foreword to *Baptists in Transition: Individualism and Christian Responsibility,* by Winthrop S. Hudson (Valley Forge, PA: Judson Press, 1979), p. 8.
/2/   Ibid.
/3/   Handy, Foreword to *Baptists in Transition,* p. 12.
/4/   Ibid., p. 13.
/5/   Among those works documenting the Enlightenment's effect on religion and the church are: Gerald R. Cragg, *The Church and the Age of Reason: 1648–1789* (Grand Rapids: William B. Eerdmans Publishing Company, 1960; second printing, 1967); Peter Gay, *The Enlightenment: An Interpretation. The Rise of Modern Paganism* (New York: Alfred A. Knopf, 1975); Paul Hazard, *The European Mind: The Critical Years (1680–1715)* (New Haven: Yale University Press, 1953); Henry F. May, *Protestant Churches and Industrial America* (New York: Harper & Bros., 1949); Roland N. Stromberg, *Religious Liberalism in Eighteenth-Century England* (London: Oxford University Press, 1954).
/6/   Handy, Foreword to *Baptists in Transition,* p. 17. This same disdain of mystery is mentioned by Cragg. See *Church and Age of Reason,* p. 281; and this same substitution of Enlightenment faith for traditional theologies is noted by Peter Gay in *Enlightenment: An Interpretation,* p. 22.

/7/   Stromberg, *Religious Liberalism*, p. 9.

/8/   Norman H. Maring, "The Individualism of Francis Wayland," in *Baptist Concepts of the Church*, ed. Winthrop Still Hudson (Chicago: Judson Press, 1959), p. 138.

/9/   Ibid., pp. 142, 143. Henry F. May also documents this dependence on natural religion in Wayland's thought. See *Protestant Churches and Industrial America*, p. 14.

/10/   Maring, "Individualism of Francis Wayland," pp. 146, 148. "The object of the church of Christ on earth is very simple," wrote Wayland, "it is the conversion of souls." See *Notes on the Principles and Practices of Baptist Churches* (New York: Sheldon and Co., 1859), p. 182. Similarly, it is "the promotion of holiness in the souls of its members, and in the souls of the men by whom they are surrounded. It is, in a word, to advance the kingdom of Christ, and to prepare themselves and others the better to meet the solemn awards of the day of judgment." See *The Limitations of Human Responsibility* (Boston: Gould and Lincoln, 1838), p. 122.

/11/   Francis Wayland, *Sermon to the Churches* (New York: Sheldon, Blackerne & Co., 1858), p. 130.

/12/   *Occasional Discourses*, p. 122, quoted in Maring, pp. 145, 146.

/13/   Francis Wayland, *Elements of Moral Science* (Boston: Gould and Lincoln, 1852), pp. 200, 201.

/14/   *Memoirs*, p. 294, quoted in Maring, p. 168.

/15/   Maring, "Individualism of Francis Wayland," p. 169.

/16/   Ibid.

/17/   Winthrop S. Hudson, "Shifting Patterns of Church Order in the Twentieth Century," in *Baptist Concepts of the Church*, ed. Winthrop Still Hudson (Chicago: Judson Press, 1959), p. 215.

/18/   Ibid., p. 216.

/19/   Ibid.

/20/   Edwin S. Gaustad, "The Backus-Leland Tradition," in *Baptist Concepts of the Church*, p. 113, has noted the same radical individualism in Isaac Backus (1724–1806) and John Leland (1754–1814). Though Gausted sees value ·in the affirmation of individual freedom, he opines: "If it took Backus thirty-two years to understand 'one Lord, one faith, one baptism,' perhaps he ran out of time before understanding 'that ye may all be one.'"

/21/   Paul M. Harrison, *Authority and Power in the Free Church Tradition: A Social Case Study of the American Baptist Convention* (Princeton: Princeton University, 1959), pp. 18, 19.

/22/   Ibid., p. 25.

/23/   Ibid., pp. 21, 22.

/24/   Edgar Y. Mullins, *The Axioms of Religion* (Philadelphia: Griffith and Rowland Press, 1908), p. 50.

/25/   William Roy McNutt, *Polity and Practice in Baptist Churches* with a Foreword by Douglas Clyde MacIntosh (Philadelphia: Judson Press, 1935; reprint ed., 1948), pp. 21, 22.

/26/   Ibid., p. 24. McNutt's contemporary James Dillard claimed for the Baptist doctrine of soul competency principal credit for the First Amendment to the Constitution. See James Edgar Dillard, *We Southern Baptists: 1937–8* (Nashville: Southern Baptist Convention, 1937–8), pp. 7, 8.

/27/   Ibid., pp. 21, 22.

/28/   Edward Hughes Pruden, *Interpreters Needed: The Eternal Gospel and Our Contemporary Society* (Philadelphia: Judson Press, 1951), p. 54.
/29/   See C. Brownlow Hastings, *Introducing Southern Baptists: Their Faith and Their Life* (New York: Paulist Press, 1981), pp. 23, 24; Herschel H. Hobbs, *The People Called Baptists and the Baptist Faith and Message* (Shawnee: Oklahoma Baptist University, 1981); Presnell H. Wood, "Guest Editorial: Southern Baptist Responses to the Twentieth Century," *Baptist History and Heritage* 16 (January 1981): 1, 2.
/30/   Numerous Baptist works either favorably or critically describe with varying degrees of comprehensiveness this sequence of ideas. Among them are W. R. White, *Baptist Distinctives* (Nashville: Sunday School Board of Southern Baptist Convention, 1946); Harold W. Tribble, *Our Doctrines* (Nashville: Sunday School Board of Southern Baptist Convention, 1936); Maitland M. Lapping, *Baptists in the Protestant Tradition* (Toronto: Ryerson Press, 1947); Brooks Hays and John E. Steely, *The Baptist Way of Life* (Macon: Mercer University Press, 2nd rev. ed., 1981); Samuel S. Hill, Jr., *The South and the North in American Religion* (Athens: University of Georgia Press, 1980). (Samuel Hill is an Episcopalian. He was for several years, however, a prophetic Baptist voice for a socially committed church and a doctrine of the church which understands the covenant community in those terms.)
/31/   Only a few of these are the *Annuals of the Southern Baptist Convention* of 1963, 1966, and 1970. Excerpts from these are: "It is the duty and privilege of every follower of Christ and of every church of the Lord Jesus Christ to endeavor to make disciples of all nations. . . . The church should not resort to the civil power to carry on its work. The gospel of Christ contemplates spiritual means alone for the pursuit of its ends." 1963 *Annual*, pp. 278, 281; "The Foreign Mission Board is to do everything possible to bring all men in other lands around the world to a saving knowledge of Jesus Christ as rapidly as possible. . . ." 1966 *Annual*, p. 60; "The Executive Committee of the Southern Baptist Convention has clearly emphasized the primacy of evangelism. . . . Therefore, be it *Resolved*, that we the messengers of this Convention rededicate ourselves and lead our churches to rededicate themselves to the task of witnessing to the unsaved and the unchurched. . . ." 1970 *Annual*, p. 71.
/32/   See Kenneth K. Bailey, *Southern White Protestantism in the Twentieth Century* (New York: Harper & Row, 1964); John R. Earle, Dean D. Knudson, and Donald W. Shriver, *Spindles and Spires: A Re-Study of Religion and Social Change in Gastonia* (Atlanta: John Knox Press, 1976); John Lee Eighmy, *Churches in Cultural Captivity: A History of the Social Attitudes of Southern Baptists* (Knoxville: University of Tennessee Press, 1972); Samuel S. Hill, Jr., *Southern Churches in Crisis* (Boston: Beacon Press, 1966–1967); George D. Kelsey, *Social Ethics Among Southern Baptists, 1917-1969* (Metuchen, NJ: The Scarecrow Press, 1973); Liston Pope, *Millhands and Preachers: A Study of Gastonia* (New Haven: Yale University Press, 1942).
/33/   Steven T. Henderson, "Social Action in a Conservative Environment: The Christian Life Commission and Southern Baptist Churches," *Foundations* 23 (July–September 1980): 245.

/34/ Ibid., p. 247.
/35/ Ibid.
*See footnote 30.
/36/ Hill, *South and North*, p. 25.
/37/ Ibid., pp. 140, 141.
/38/ Francis M. DuBose and Bob E. Adams, "Evangelism, Missions, and Social Action: A Southern Baptist Perspective," *Review and Expositor* 79 (Spring 1982): 353.
/39/ Carl W. Tiller, *The Twentieth Century Baptist: Chronicles of Baptists in the First Seventy-Five Years of the Baptist World Alliance* (Valley Forge: Judson Press, 1980), p. 3.
/40/ William M. Pinson, Jr., *The Local Church in Ministry* (Nashville: Broadman Press, 1973), p. 17. In *Applying The Gospel: Suggestions for Christian Social Action in a Local Church* (Nashville: Broadman Press, 1975), p. 11, Pinson writes: "Christians need to become as concerned about dirty air and water as we have been about dirty books and movies. . . . We need to become as concerned about what the poor have for supper as we have been about who is eligible to partake of the Lord's Supper."
/41/ Pinson, *Local Church*, pp. 13, 15.
/42/ Ibid., p. 20.
/43/ C. Brownlow Hastings, *Introducing Southern Baptists: Their Faith and Their Life* (New York: Paulist Press, 1981), p. 30.
/44/ Samuel S. Hill, Jr. and Robert G. Torbet, *Baptists North and South* (Valley Forge: Judson Press, 1964), p. 126.
/45/ Martin Luther King, Jr., *Stride Toward Freedom: The Montgomery Story* (New York: Harper & Bros., 1958), p. 198.
/46/ Ibid., p. 207.
/47/ King, *Stride Toward Freedom*, p. 207; *Strength To Love* (New York: Harper & Row, 1963), p. 26.
/48/ King, *Stride Toward Freedom*, p. 36.
/49/ See, for example, the *Annuals of the Southern Baptist Convention* for 1925, 1963, 1968, 1979, and 1982. Strong endorsements of world peace, economic justice, and racial equality are included, particularly in the Christian Life Commission's 1968 "Statement Concerning the Crisis in Our Nation," pp. 67–69, and its 1979 "Statement of Social Principles for Christian Social Concern and Christian Social Action," pp. 140f.
/50/ Harrison, *Authority and Power in the Free Church*, p. 26.
/51/ McNutt and Wayland have been discussed in preceding paragraphs. Dillard wrote, "The fundamental assumption of our American government is the competency of our people to work out their own political destiny. This is analogous to the Baptist fundamental of the competency of the soul in religion." *We Southern Baptists*, p. 8.
/52/ DuBose and Adams, "Evangelism, Missions, and Social Action," p. 359.
/53/ Hays and Steely, *Baptist Way of Life*, pp. 7, 49.
/54/ H. Wheeler Robinson, "The Strength and the Weakness of the Baptists," in *A Baptist Treasury*, ed. Sydnor L. Stealey (New York: Thomas Y. Crowell Co., 1958), pp. 187f.
/55/ Hudson, *Baptists in Transition*, p. 83.

/56/ E. Glenn Hinson, "Southern Baptists: A Concern for Experiential Conversion," *The Christian Century,* June 7–14, 1978, p. 615.

/57/ W. David Sapp, "Southern Baptist Responses to the American Economy, 1900–1980," *Baptist History and Heritage* 16 (January 1981):7.

/58/ Agreeing with Harrison, Ernest Alexander Payne writes, "Baptists have probably suffered as much as any Christian community of recent years from the general slackness, casualness and confusion regarding the doctrine of the Church, and have departed as widely as any from the traditions of their fathers." *The Fellowship of Believers: Baptist Thought and Practice Yesterday and Today* (London: Carey Kingsgate Press, 1952), p. 11.

/59/ Robinson, "Strength and Weakness," pp. 188f.

/60/ Hudson, *Baptists in Transition,* pp. 19f.

/61/ Hastings, *Introducing Southern Baptists,* p. 124.

/62/ Wood writes, "There is . . . an urgent need today for a theological foundation of human rights which may be identified with the essence of Christian faith. There must also be a theological basis on which the church's support of human rights can be seen as essential to the church's mission. While relatively few people would argue today against human rights or against efforts to implement them throughout the world, there are those in positions of leadership within the Christian world community who maintain that the struggle for human rights is not really related to the mission of the church. . . . In a profound sense, respect for human rights is deeply rooted in biblical faith and is an essential part of the gospel." "Baptist Thought and Human Rights," *Baptist History and Heritage* 13 (July 1978):51, 52.

/63/ See p. 13.

/64/ I am proposing in this work *fides quaerens rationem reddere* (faith seeking accountability) as a counterpoint to *fides quaerens intellectum* (faith seeking understanding).

/65/ Claude Y. Stewart, Jr. has coined the term *otherkind* for nature. Dr. Stewart used the term in classes at Southeastern Baptist Theological Seminary as early as the fall of 1978. See his dissertation work *Nature in Grace: A Study in the Theology of Nature* (Macon, Ga.: Mercer University Press, 1983).

CHAPTER II

FIDES QUAERENS INTELLECTUM: KARL BARTH'S ANSELMIAN METHODOLOGY

This thesis proposes that Karl Barth's theology is developed according to an Anselmian methodology drawn from Barth's study of Anselm's formula—faith seeking understanding—and described in his book of 1931, *Anselm: Fides Quaerens Intellectum*. While there are intimations of a nascent praxis methodology begun and employed in the Safenwil years present still in the *Church Dogmatics*, the theory-over-praxis method adopted with the Anselmian turn predominates and shapes Barth's theology, a fact which holds especial significance for his doctrine of the church. Nonetheless, the praxis orientation is not entirely obliterated and holds important potential for Barth's ecclesiology. It is mainly the Anselmian method, however, and its implications for Barth's ecclesiology which will be examined in this chapter. Scholarly evaluations of Barth's work will be attended to at those points where those assessments intersect with Barth's choice of method and the ecclesiology resulting. It is proposed that difficulties in arriving at an adequate notion of the church derive at least in part from the employment of the Anselmian method by Barth himself, on the one hand, and in part from the utilization of a corresponding method by those who offer their critiques, on the other. Standing in the same spot with Barth methodologically, or, if not that, acquiescing in a similar perspective, his critics see weaknesses partly uncovered, but also partly created, by that joint methodological stance or view. Hence it is part of the burden of this chapter to show that there is a problem in Barthian scholarship generally. There are those like T. F. Torrance who accept the Anselmian method and read the *Church Dogmatics* from that angle without objections to what is read there and with no substantial identification of problems. Others like Jürgen Moltmann and G. C. Berkouwer read Barth in light of the same Anselmian perspective but object that Barth's theology is thereby divorced from history.

The challenge, however, I propose in this thesis, is to examine the turn toward Anselm on the foil of what happened in Safenwil and what that means for Barth's doctrine of the church as it appears in the *Church Dogmatics*. Allowing Barth's early praxis methodology to inform what is encountered there, the reader discerns possibilities of alternative interpretations emerging.

In his early pastorate in Safenwil, Barth employed a methodology vitally connected with the poor of his parish with whom he acted to gain economic justice, and with whom he worshipped and reflected. Knowledge of God happened in the midst of discipleship and what Frederick Herzog terms *social location* with the poor.[1] Acting with God on behalf of the poor and worshipping God were for the young Barth correlative moments. Barth's theological reflection included both as ingredients of an epistemological whole, and Scripture and Creed were read in the light of this action and worship. The young Barth assumed that God is world-transforming Person more than self-disclosing Person, and thus that God locates the divine action *with* the poor to whom justice has been denied, transforming unjust structures into just ones. For that reason, the church and theology are also located primally with the dispossessed, and their essential function is transformative rather than disclosive. Social location with the poor, then, and not with the academy and abstract reason, is indicated for both church and theology. Knowing realized in accountability to God and a suffering humanity is the yield—not abstract cognition but concrete, reasonable accountability, e.g., a discipleship which knows.

The final pages of this chapter will seek to show what that focus can mean for understanding Barth's theology and his ecclesiology particularly. It will be advanced that the praxis methodology employed in Safenwil and inchoately present in the *Church Dogmatics* connects church and world in a way which, perhaps, others have not perceived and has the potential for relativizing a tendency in Barth's theology toward the abstract and theoretical.

Anselm and Fides Quaerens Intellectum

In his preface to the first edition of *Anselm: Fides Quaerens Intellectum,* Barth writes of his love for Anselm and of his superior regard for his theology. In the preface to the second edition, Barth acknowledges his debt to Anselm in the formulation of his own theological methodology. As soon as he had completed *Fides Quaerens Intellectum,* Barth says, "I went straight into my *Church Dogmatics.* . . . My interest in Anselm was never a side-issue for me . . . in this book on Anselm I am working with a vital key, if not the key, to an understanding of that whole process of thought that has impressed me more and more in my *Church Dogmatics* as the only one proper to theology."[2] That process of thought will surface with an examination of Barth's exposition of Anselm's formula—faith seeking understanding.

Intelligere—understanding, Barth points out, issues in Christian joy. Understanding one's faith, the early Church Fathers contended, results in beauty and the joy of the *ratio* of faith. Anselm, thus, wishes both to understand and to enjoy. His principal concern, however, is with theology, the *intellectus fidei.* While *probare* and *laetificare* are desirable, it is the *intelligere* of faith which is most desired and which Anselm is concerned to uncover. Barth writes, "What we are speaking of is a spontaneous desire of faith. Fundamentally, the *quaerere intellectum* is really imminent in *fides.* It is not the existence of faith, but rather and here we approach Anselm's position—the nature of faith, that desires knowledge. *Credo ut intelligam* means: It is my very faith itself that summons me to knowledge."[3] It will be helpful to remember that Barth is expressing his own views in tandem with his explication of Anselm. *Fides Quaerens Intellectum* is a book written in deep admiration for the thinker and the thought which he expresses.

Barth insists that reason and rational knowledge are not accorded a higher place than faith and revealed truth. Barth comments that "knowledge . . . ranks higher than faith only in a very relative sense. . . . Just because he is *intelligens,* the Christian, of all men, has to learn to discern with agonizing clarity what is conceivable by him about God himself. So we shall have to interpret the medial character of knowledge in Anselm's sense by saying that knowledge stands between faith and vision in the same way as we might say that a mountain stands between a man looking at it from the valley and the sun. *Intelligere* is a potentiality for advancing in the direction of heavenly vision to a point that can be reached and that is worth trying to reach. It has within itself something of the nature of vision and it is worth striving for as similitudo of vision, just because it leads men, not beyond, but right up to the limits of faith."[4] Grace is the aide of reason, giving to reason the capability of understanding faith. Finally, grace is the gift which makes highest thinking possible. It is the "actualization of that power to know which was originally created in man."[5]

Intelligere cannot be explicated apart from considering the content of what is understood, Barth points out. The basic notion is one of reflection, reflection upon "what has already been said in the *Credo*." It is here that believing and understanding come together. Still, *credere* is merely the embryo of *intelligere* and the latter represents an advance beyond that initial cognition. *Intelligere* requires reading and pondering—the Creed. Indeed, this active intellection is indispensable for understanding the Creed; one does not simply receive with faith and belief the deeper truths of the Credo, the understanding that faith desires and seeks. "Rather he must seek it in prayer and by the persistent application of his intellectual powers."[6] The Creed holds the content of that which is believed in faith and understood through reflection.

Anselm's notion (and Barth's) of an outward and inward text further validates the necessity of *intelligere*. The believer hearing or reading the scriptural text does not immediately discern its inner truth. Both special effort and special grace are required for an understanding of the inward text. It is the theologian's specific task to explicate that inner text.[7] That the inner text may be understood through reflection on the Creed, is, as Barth notes, the "possibility of theology." Faith is knowledge of, and faith in, the content of that which is preached. That is to say, the Creed is heard through preaching; it is believed, and finally, understood. Theology is itself a "science of the *Credo*." Faith is inextricably related to acceptance of the *Credo* of the church, and *intelligere* is nothing more nor less than the understanding of that *Credo*. "Thus the knowledge that is sought cannot be anything but an extension and explication of that acceptance of the *Credo* of the church, which faith itself already implied."[8]

Barth finally identifies and equates the Faith and the *Credo*. Denying, even questioning, the Creed is tantamount to denying the Faith altogether. The theologian who essays to question the Creed is neither scientific nor faithful to his or her trust. Barth's picturesque language describes his disdain and scorn for such a one whose "denials would *a priori* be no better than bats and owls squabbling with eagles about the reality of the beams of the midday sun."[9]

How, then, does proof fit into this picture? Proof, Barth explains, is incidental to knowledge. The highest attainment of knowledge logically is proof. Still, Anselm is not interested in proof for proof's sake: as noted earlier, Anselm is also desirous of beauty and joy. He wishes, too, to answer reasonably those who scoff and those who are plagued with doubt. Thus, in achieving understanding, Anselm gives a *ratio* for the hope that is in him, realizes joy and beauty, and at the same time, proof. Proof cannot be understood in any of the common modes usually associated with that notion, Barth insists. Anselm at no time was searching for the basis of believing or disbelieving, i.e., of accepting or rejecting revelation. All along, it is *knowledge* which Anselm seeks. Barth sees Anselm's purpose as one of marrying faith and reason, of destroying "the appearance of a *repugnare* between ratio and *fides*." He writes, "It was and remains quite impossible for Anselm to allow his faith to come to peaceable terms with lack of knowledge."[10] Barth states that with Anselm's formula for God—*Quo maius cogitari nequit*—the One than whom nothing greater can be thought—a name was found, or rather God revealed a Name, which "makes room" for the Christian God of revelation.[11]

With the quest for knowledge as Barth affirms it in Anselm's scheme, a tendency is established in Barth's theology which encourages reading him from an abstract and theoretical angle. Problems immediately emerge for the church. If knowing is the goal, dissemination of knowledge, the content of the Creed, becomes the church's primary task, and application of that knowledge to concrete reality an implication of it. Even application, however, is hampered by starting with Anselm's presuppositions, as further examination of the faith seeking understanding method and its impact on ecclesiology will show.

Barth's turn toward *fides quaerens intellectum* is evaluated both positively and negatively by those who assess Barth's work and its import. Their critiques, though problematical themselves, offer perspectival foci which help to isolate crucial implications of Barth's methodology for his doctrine of the church.

Positive Critiques of the Anselmian Method: David Mueller

David Mueller, T. F. Torrance and George Hunsinger are three Barthian scholars who have evaluated Barth's turn toward Anselm positively. It will be instructive to attend to their expositions and conclusions regarding that turn. Thereby, problems in Barthian scholarship itself will be shown to be a substantial part of the difficulty in assessing the significance of Barth's Anselmian orientation.

David Mueller notes that, for Barth, faith is the possibility of all knowledge of God. Mueller stresses that Barth, with Anselm, insists that theology is conducted always in the context of faith and the church and centers on the givenness of revelation in the *Credo*. He agrees that "Anselm taught Barth how theology should be done."[12] Mueller identifies Barth's crucial methodological problem as one of attempting to explain why faith seeks understanding; Barth strove to explain, Mueller states, how the movement from faith to theology is made. Barth's answer, of course, was the clarification of faith through reason. Again, the movement of faith seeking understanding is understood as faith's characteristic nature, faith itself summoning the faithful to knowledge. Mueller writes that with Barth, "We must understand Anselm's concept of faith," and his great desire not to confuse faith with irrationality or illogicality.[13] In the quest for rational and logical faith, then, one begins with the Scriptures and traditional church Confessions, the expressions of the church's Credo. These constitute the individual Christian's norm for his or her own "true" faith. Mueller wishes to say that Barth's perception of the progression of faith to understanding in Anselm is that of one which begins in an intellectual act in which even unbelievers can participate, but which moves "beyond this logical understanding of the truth affirmed to an understanding of the reality behind the words."[14] A move from faith to faith is made, from seeing through a glass darkly to seeing face to face, fully realized in the eschaton.

The *Church Dogmatics* consistently upholds the theological presupposition that God has acted in Jesus Christ to reveal and disclose God. Faith seeking understanding, though never absolutely, can and does issue in "the true knowledge of God."[15] Theological statements, because of God's initiatory act of disclosure, can be analogous to their object. Mueller affirms with Anselm and Barth the revelation through divine grace and the process of faith seeking understanding which can make theology "the most beautiful of sciences."[16] It should be transparent, Mueller insists, that Barth rejects the commonplace interpretation of Anselm as a rationalist, first because Anselm begins in faith and with the Credo, and second, because Anselm intimately associates prayer with the theological task. For Anselm "true knowledge" never is received apart from

God's prevenient grace, and the progression to understanding which attains "true knowledge of God" must be prayed for continually as its power lies "beyond the powers of human reason."[17] "Moreover, were it not for the fact that God made himself known to man once and again and again through his grace, faith could never comprehend God."[18] Faith depends upon revelation for "true knowledge of God," and "fuller knowledge" deriving from *fides quaerens intellectum* is that "true knowlege of God," says Mueller, following Barth.[19] Citing the *Church Dogmatics* 4, 1, Mueller notes that *Anerkennung, Erkennen,* and *Bekennen* denote for Barth that "Faith understood as acknowledgement is above all else a cognitive act" in which "the act of acknowledgement is primary and the act of cognition flows from it as its necessary consequence."[20] The process of recognition following from the primary moment of acknowledgement, Mueller explains, is the same methodology emphasized in Anselm. It is one in which "faith becomes articulate or understood"; Barth, like Anselm, strove against "an anti-intellectualist view of faith. 'Without an increase of knowledge, there can be no increase in faith.' (4, 1, p. 764)."[21]

It may be that Mueller's Baptist heritage predisposes him not to read Barth critically at this point. He states, "Anselm taught Barth how theology should be done."[22] There is no questioning of whether what Anselm taught Barth was indeed how theology should be done, but merely a felicitous acceptance of that fact. Mueller does not challenge the commonplace datum that faith naturally seeks understanding as its primary *desideratum*. Nor does he question theoretical reason's primary role in the acquisition of "true knowledge of God." Nowhere does the realization appear that the idea of confusing faith with something irrational and illogical and the mortal fear that it strikes in the hearts of so many theologians suggest a Greek passion for logical necessity rather than a wish to be accountable in discipleship. As with Anselm and Barth, too, Scripture and Confession are the sole criteria of the theological task; no praxis criterion is apparently deemed useful.

The "true knowledge of God" becomes, in Mueller's treatment, a virtual catch-phrase; it is for this reason only that it has been quoted so often in preceding paragraphs. He simply asserts that faith seeking understanding is the route to "true knowledge of God." What true knowledge of God might be and whether the genuine road to it is the Anselmian-Barthian one is, once again, unquestioned. That true knowledge might be less purely cognitive, more like discipleship than intellection, is not adequately recognized. Mueller's failure to question Barth at this important juncture derives, at least partly, from his own uncritical dependence upon Barth. Faith seeking understanding's sole criteria of Scripture and Confession seem to obtain for Mueller as for Barth.

It is important to interject a crucial point in this thesis. The issue here is not whether in the Anselmian-Barthian method reason is solely theoretical or not; there is no effort here to say that it is. Trust, love, and discipleship are genuine concerns of these theologians. What *is* at issue is the *weight of priorities* and how they interact. This thesis holds that trust, love, discipleship, *and* reason are embraced within the greater frame of claimed accountability arising from social location with those with whom God is located; location, not cognition, is the first order of business. A praxis methodology which recognizes that situating theology in the context of the poor and their struggle for justice, and that locating with— thinking and acting with—the poor is hermeneutically vital to understanding God, is a methodology of accountability which then understands. Instead of *fides quaerens intellectum*, faith seeking understanding, this method is *fides quaerens rationem reddere*, i.e., faith seeking accountability which, in accountability, understands. This was Barth's movement in Safenwil. Socially located with the disadvantaged who filled his pews, Barth read Scripture and Creed with eyes informed by their lived experiences.

Chapter III will examine Barth's early apprehension of this methodology. In social location with the poor, the theologian engages in a co-cognition with God that is not a logical construct which alone discloses knowledge and comprehension of God, but a logically reasonable accountability to God, realizing God's purposes in a co-acting and a co-knowing that is genuine discipleship.

Mueller's failure to identify the inadequacies inherent in *fides quaerens intellectum* supports the hypothesis projected in the preceding chapter. Baptists have not generally examined what faith perceived as accountability which understands means for a Baptist ecclesiology. *Rationem reddere* calls for a corporate church body acting and reflecting with those with whom Jesus Christ acted and reflected, and acts and reflects. Socially located with the poor, the church is enabled to see social justice, global peace, and responsibility to all of God's good creation, as constitutive of faith's innermost core.

Positive Critiques of the Anselmian Method: T. F. Torrance

T. F. Torrance hails Barth's *Anselm: Fides Quaerens Intellectum* as the breakthrough to an understanding of what theology really is which carried the Swiss theologian beyond his liberal predecessors and their teaching. With the Anselm study Barth perceived that revelation is at heart the "impartation of rational truth" through Jesus Christ, the Word, Torrance declares. Because the object of theology, God, is rational, theology and faith are rational. Indeed, it is for this reason that theology is a rational science which penetrates into "an understanding of the inner rational nature of the object of theological knowledge."[23] The inner rational nature of theology's object, God, requires, thus, a rational, theo-logical method appropriate to that nature. *Anselm: Fides Quaerens Intellectum* was for Barth the clarification and solidification of "the fundamental nature of theological method."[24] The passage from dialectical theology to scientific exaction had been made with the turn to the "objective, inner necessity or logic that must inform the whole structure of theology."[25]

Torrance agrees with Anselm that faith by its very nature seeks to understand. The divine self-disclosure gives to faith seeking understanding true knowledge of God. Theology's primary task, hence, is to draw out of the implicit understanding given in faith an explicit understanding in intellection. Essentially cognitive, faith is conceptual and intellectual (although Torrance hastens to add that faith is not "simply" intellectual, since it is mediated through trust and love, even as Anselm and Augustine insisted). Because God's Word in Christ is given in preaching and thus received through hearing, the *analogia fidei* is made possible. Jesus Christ, the "Author of our knowledge," gives himself as the object of our understanding through language. Thus, theology moves from what is given to it in Christ into a "clearer knowledge." That is why believing precedes understanding and cannot be separated from it. "In this event theology may be spoken of as the activity of the reason within the knowledge bestowed on man by God, operating within the limits of noetic investigation required by the nature of the given object."[26] Noetically, then, the theologian moves from faith initially given by God in Christ into "deeper and clearer knowledge through understanding of the inner and necessary relation between the knowledge of faith and the inherent rationality of that which is believed, the very Truth and the Being of God himself."[27] The theologian knows that human knowledge of God is "in accordance with the Being of God himself" and stands under "the compulsion of his Being, as an obedient creature before the Creator, who lets God be to him the One who, in his sheer objectivity as God, prescribes for man the manner and the limits of his knowing of God. . . ."[28] It is thus that the theologian penetrates into the inner rationality which is theological understanding.

Said differently, reason operates on a threefold level: first, noetically, reason conceptualizes, and through theological investigation, illuminates the second level which is the ontic, objective rationality of the object of faith; grounding noetic and ontic *ratio* and illuminating both, however, is the *ratio veritatis* which, on the third level, is God's Being, "the divine Word consubstantial with the Father."[29] This "dynamic rationality" is complemented by "dynamic analogy" which makes possible adequate though imperfect statements about God.[30]

Several problems surface with Torrance's assessment of Barth's Anselmian turn. First of all, Jesus Christ as imparter of rational truth is not the Jesus of the Gospels of Matthew, Mark, Luke, or even of John. Furthermore, God as Essential Rationality is hardly a Christian notion. The very presupposition that faith's nature is principally a noetic and rational quest for knowledge is a primary issue at stake in this discussion. Indeed, this thesis proposes that a radically incisive questioning of this ancient presupposition is now required. The foundational notion from Augustine onward that faith's essential quest is for understanding needs to be looked at closely. Presupposing that faith is conceptual, the theologian fails to ask a more important question—to wit, is it not truer to faith to discern that its primary quest is not for intellectual cognition but for accountability which is also understanding? Faith is first of all discipleship, the response of "Here am I, Lord; send me." Thus, faith is at its core not faith seeking understanding, *fides quaerens intellectum*, but faith seeking accountability which understands, *fides quaerens rationem reddere*. The difference is crucial both to theological methodology and to the Christian doctrines which emerge from these positions. With *fides quaerens intellectum*, as Torrance's abstract treatment shows, a church engaged with concrete suffering and pain, and knowing and understanding precisely through that engagement, does not readily come into focus. Without the accountability factor occupying an explicit and primary location in the methodological formula, knowing remains an intellectual exercise detached from concrete data which contribute to the epistemological and hermeneutical endeavor. *Fides quaerens rationem reddere*, faith seeking accountability which understands, on the other hand, locates the church squarely in the midst of human need and historical peril and draws those realities into the event of understanding in the quest not for knowledge so much as for accountable discipleship which knows. The doctrine of the church emerging, then, from a faith-seeking-accountability method offers an understanding of the church's nature and tasks as concerned for all of God's good creation, for justice as well as justification, global peace as well as inner peace, and the hunger of the body as well as the hunger of mind and soul.

It has been a commonplace notion in theology to hold that God's nature is to give to the church a true knowledge of God. This has already been noted in the discussion of Mueller. It is time now to ask, as Barth nascently did in Safenwil, what a true knowledge of God is. Is God the One who as *ratio veritatis* reveals who God is; or is God the Author-izer who realizes who God is? Is God the revealer of true knowledge or the author-izer of genuine accountability?[31] What is at stake here includes, at the least, four things: the doctrines of God, faith, humankind, and church. Is God principally Revealer and Discloser, or Realizer and Transformer? Is faith primarily knowledge and understanding, or is it primarily accountability? Is humanity rational creature who understands God, or accountable creature who, not without understanding, joins in God's work? If men and women are essentially those who know and thus love, then faith seeking understanding may be an adequate notion, but if women and men are most notably those who are divinely claimed and authorized to respond in reasonable accountability to God, neighbors, self, and all of nature in a community of accountable ones, then faith seeking accountability which is understanding is a more adequate notion.

Of crucial importance is a stringent critique of theology's so-called noetic nature. If, as Torrance claims, theology is an "activity of the reason . . . operating within the limits of noetic investigation," dictated by the "necessary relation between the knowledge of faith and the inherent rationality of that which is believed, the very truth and the Being of God himself," then theology is at pains to say how God is not, on that score, sheer Eternal Rationality. It is hard to see how that can be construed as a theological gain. God is finally, on that view, Disclosing Reason. So long as the noetic route is the controlling route, the transforming God of the Bible who acts in a world which experiences God's Realpresence in concrete event remains problematical and a church acting accordingly remains equally so. *Fides quaerens intellectum* understands God as self-disclosing Person; hence, knowledge and understanding are faith's desire and church and theology's purpose is to join God in that disclosure. *Fides quaerens rationem reddere*, on the other hand, perceives God as world-transforming Person; hence, a world of justice and peace is faith's desire and the task of the church and theology is to join God in bringing about that transformation.

Fides quaerens rationem reddere does not exclude intellection but also does not accord to logical intellection alone the monopoly or independence which Torrance suggests. Praxis denies noetic limitations which Torrance insists are fundamental to theology's rationality. Knowing in accountable discipleship is more than a noetic exercise; rather, a reciprocity of intellection and action fosters co-knowing with God in the midst of concrete event and immediate history.

Positive Critiques of the Anselmian Method: George Hunsinger

George Hunsinger has, like Mueller and Torrance, acclaimed Barth's turn to Anselm as the creative move which secured a "conceptually consistent theology" able to ground the *Church Dogmatics*.[32] What Barth had sought since 1915, Hunsinger claims, had been an irreproachably objective conceptualization of "what God is for man."[33] Barth's motivation, Hunsinger stresses, was to escape the liberal decadence of nineteenth century subjectivism. His dissatisfaction with dialectical theology led him to new investigations of the relationship of theology and philosophy and finally to the study of Anselm. With *Anselm: Fides Quaerens Intellectum* Barth then turned from dialectical to analogical theology, "satisfied that he had at last gained a conceptually consistent understanding of 'What God is in himself.'"[34] Hunsinger makes the judgment that with that turn, Barth grounded his socialist interest and political work, his "radical" theology, in Anselmian analogical conceptual theory![35]

Hunsinger explains his conclusion: "This was the study which enabled Barth to overcome theological liberalism, meet the force of Feuerbach's objection and provide a positive basis for the theory and praxis of hope."[36] Resurrection hope, a conceptually consistent deity, and the practical merger of both in socialist struggle, Hunsinger declares, was achieved with the Anselm book and the "key" to theology which Barth affirmed in it. If theology hoped to succeed in overcoming the relativism and anthropocentrism of liberal theology and the subjectivism of faith, Barth had to find an objective basis for conceiving "God as he is in himself" and locating there a "concrete" origin of theological concepts. Barth's focal question, Hunsinger maintains, was "How can theory and praxis be consistently grounded, limited, and oriented in terms of God's sovereignty alone?"[37] Barth's route toward the God than whom nothing greater can be conceived was one which sought understanding, clarification, and meaning. For Barth, in addition, an affirmation basis rather than a dialectical one was being sought because, again it is affirmed, faith itself essentially seeks rational understanding. "Rational understanding is a requirement of faith."[38] Analyzing the Anselm book, Hunsinger enumerates four reasons why this is true. First, faith's object, God, is "a compendium of all rational truth" and hence also the source of theological truth. Thus, faith seeks understanding first of all because of "the rational nature of its object." Second, faith's subject, human beings, are beings of will who rationally choose, and thus faith seeks understanding because of the essential rational nature of its subject. Third, the rational divine object gives to the rational human subject the ability to understand the rational object. Hence, faith seeks understanding "because of the rational relation of the object to the subject." And last, the rational subject apperceives in the rational object its limits in relation to this "compendium of all rational truth."[39] Finally, what theology which is thus rationally made possible arrives at is the understanding of its object's "inner necessity."[40] "Theology," Hunsinger explains in clarification of Anselm and Barth, "is neither a storming of the gates of heaven nor a *sacrificium intellectum*. It does not seek to establish the 'general possibility' of the object, nor does it require a surrender of reason. It starts from an actuality and arrives at an understanding of its rational necessity. . . . Anselm enabled Barth to see that a rational theology was . . . objectively necessary."[41] Subject to no external necessity, the object of faith is subject only to its own inner necessity. Because only God's inner necessity directs faith and theology, theological statements are impossible apart from the divine object's decision to "make its rationality accessible to that of the subject."[42] But because God does choose to do so, analogical statements which are affirmative and nondialectical are made possible under the objective conditions set by the divine object. Theological statements, while true, remain relative and open, allowing progress in theological construction. "On the basis of these conditions, theology proceeds as follows," Hunsinger maintains, "It moves from the actuality to the necessity of its object." The God of the ontological argument necessarily discloses God even as Anselm had described. "God cannot be other than He is; therefore, faith must conceive of him in this particular way. Faith seeks to understand the rationality of God as he actually exists. Understanding can only be derived from God, not God from understanding. God stands over against understanding and cannot in principle be reduced to understanding or to anything else. 'God' is the name of that actuality than which no greater can be conceived. Faith and creation depend on God. God depends on nothing other than himself. It is impossible to conceive of that which exists necessarily, as not existing. With this conclusion, Barth, following Anselm, had achieved the conceptually consistent understanding of God's sovereignty he had sought since 1915."[43]

Hunsinger concludes by returning to his statement that, in the rationally consistent God who discloses Godness to rational minds and makes possible imperfect, but yet adequate, analogical statements, Barth dismantled liberal subjectivism, answered Feuerbach's critique with a concept derived not from anthropos but from "concrete" necessity, and found a basis for the "theory and praxis of resurrection hope."[44] With Anselm, Hunsinger declares, Barth found "unconditional norms" not subject to "the capriciousness of the times" for his social action.[45]

What, then, is to be said for Hunsinger's assessment? It is hard to see how the One than whom nothing greater can be conceived supplies the concreteness which unites theory and praxis. Hunsinger's notion seems to be an idiosyncratic understanding of what "concrete" means. How can the speculative God of rational necessity be considered *concrete!*?

Hunsinger's description of the disclosing God of inner necessity who clarifies through rational understanding is obliquely helpful in that it stresses a tendency in Barth's theology to disclosure rather than, as in his earlier work, transformation. God who is the "compendium of all rational truth" logically is a God concerned with disclosing that truth in rational concept to a humanity which is itself rational will. If one accepts those premises, faith seeking understanding makes perfectly good sense. What is lacking, however, is a convincing argument which establishes the premises satisfactorily.

Though one surely does not want to argue for faith's irrationality, one can hardly ascribe, either, to the notion that the divine-human relation is principally a dissemination of knowledge from divine Rationality to human rationality. Hunsinger maintains that "theological understanding is both a gift and a task. It is a gift to be sought through prayer and a task to be sought through reason."[46] This thesis proposes instead: theological understanding that is accountability which thus understands is a gift of prayer and response to claim, and a task of co-reason in social location with God and the poor with whom God stands in righteousness which is justice and responsibility, and love which is peace and solidarity.

Mueller, Torrance, and Hunsinger have each in their own manner joined Barth in the methodological frame which they assess. Standing in the same place with Barth, then, they read affirmatively both the method chosen through the Anselm study and its theoretical yield. Hence, major problems occasioned for the church by that turn do not appear to be present, in their view. Others, however, have assessed the same event much more negatively.

Negative Critiques of the Anselmian Turn

Colin Gunton's analysis and critique of Barth's Anselmian method is an especially critical one. Noting that at its core theological science is for Anselm a science of the *Credo*, Gunton alleges, "The Credo performs here somewhat the same function that the notion of the superstructure of necessary truth, lying as yet latent in the rational mind, performs for the neoclassical theorist."[47] For Barth, the crucial difference is that no latent deposit of necessary truth is assumed; truth is revealed by God. Still, Gunton insists, starting on the path of ontology, whether one takes the first road with Anselm and the ontological argument, the second with Hartshorne and neoclassical theory, or the third, with Barth and the *analogia fidei*, finally ends in necessity! When that happens, genuine temporality and history are jettisoned.[48] For Barth, as for Anselm, the question of God's Being precedes the question of theological statement. With God's Being coming first, language can follow and conform. Proof, then, *is* the aim of theology, "not in the sense that it is usually understood in philosophical theology, but as something that can perhaps be called intellectual conviction."[49] For Anselm and Barth that conviction is based on noetic content.[50]

Barth's method, Gunton states, is not so different from the neoclassical one which relies on a logically axiomatic system. "By presupposing all the other articles of the creed in order to discuss one of them, the theologian does something very similar to what a geometrician does in constructing a system of axioms."[51] Still, it would be unfair to Barth not to emphasize that theological language is open-ended for him. The God who reveals is absolute in divine freedom to disclose Godness; no *a priori* principles constrain the God of revelation.[52]

It will be instructive to examine how Barth's employment of the analogy of faith is assessed by his critics. The Anselmian investment is a critical component in the formation of the *analogia fidei*.

The Principle of Analogia Fidei

In Volume 2, 1 of the *Church Dogmatics*, Barth writes:

> In His revelation God controls His property, elevating our words to their proper use, giving Himself to be their proper object, and therefore giving them truth. Analogy of truth between Him and us is present in His knowing, which comprehends ours, but not in ours, which does not comprehend His.[53]

Barth explains:

> The activity involved in our knowledge of His creation, to be realized in views, concepts and words, has its truth, hidden from us, in God as its and our Creator. In the first instance, whatever is said by us, was, is and will be said truly in Him. It will be said in Him in a truth which is original, primary, independent and proper truth; by us in a truth which is subsequent, secondary, dependent and improper. It will be said in Him infallibly, by us . . . always in error, and yet in such a way that even in error doubly hidden from ourselves (by our creatureliness and our sin), and therefore in a double sense without any possibility of reclamation, we live by His infallible truth.[54]

Barth's *analogia fidei* has not been lightly assessed pro or con. The following is legion on both sides. Among those who assess it positively are Han Urs von Balthasar, Henri Bouillard, R. E. Hood, Joseph Bettis, F. W. Camfield, J. Y. Lee, George Henry Kuykendall, Jr., Donald Bloesch, Colin Brown, William Hordern, Helmut Gollwitzer, and T. H. L. Parker.[55] According to these thinkers, the Anselmian turn was a felicitous one. In each of these cases the interpreter's own methodological stance which does not appreciably diverge from Barth's informs the evaluation. The *analogia fidei*, in the view of others, however, presents problems.[56] Interestingly enough, these thinkers also critique Barth from a reflective position not unlike Barth's Anselmian one. Analyzing Barth with the same theoretical tools of reflection and conceptualization, they detect weaknesses in his theology but often fail to identify the Anselmian base of those weaknesses.

A case in point is the critique offered by Robert Willis. The use of analogy, Willis argues, tends to denigrate the value of insights from concrete human experience and those disciplines which contribute empirical data for theological and ethical reflection.[57] Ramifications for an adequate doctrine of the church are suggested. Theological language which excludes concrete and empirical data separates the church from reciprocal dialogue with the world outside its walls. A methodological development beyond the criteria of Scripture and tradition alone is needed, Willis suggests, one beyond *sola Scriptura* to a method which faithfully preserves the biblical focus but admits other vital criteria as well.[58] Willis raises an important correlative issue: "Perhaps it is time to explore the possibilities and resources for theological construction that retain a sense of the casual, even *ad hoc,* status of the theological venture itself . . . if theology, like ethics, is in continual process of being formed and reformed under the impact of God's present activity in the world, then this insight might legitimately be reflected in . . . the task theology sets for itself."[59] Still, Willis does not seem to see the significance of the faith seeking understanding methodology which obstructs the kind of open-endedness for which he is calling.

One wonders if Willis' argument for a viable experience criterion does not, in fact, veer in the direction of an Enlightenment plea for human self-constitution and theological autonomy. Willis is joined by Dale Althoff in alleging that Barth's christological center and the practice of drawing analogical statements from it are the primary reason for the loss of the empirical and experiential in his theology. By concentrating all genuine human content in Jesus Christ, they argue, Barth neglects the human and historical and effectually negates human freedom and action.[60] "Barth understands himself as the advocate of God and friend of man. Nevertheless, given the assumptions he makes about the lack of content [i.e.,

genuine human content] apart from Christ in man, it seems inevitable that Barth's advocacy of God and exhortation to believe must
take the turn to polemic."[61] Althoff's concern, too, is that with
Barth's Christology and anthropology, God takes no account of humanity as it is and understands itself to be, and hence makes no
attempt to explain to men and women in terms of their own existence what that existence rightly is.[62] Furthermore, Althoff argues,
a completed eschaton in Jesus Christ leaves "nothing provisional
about the situation of man."[63] Althoff concludes that Barth's thought
is Platonistic, rendering freedom "but an extrinsic confirmation of
God's comprehensively and exhaustively completed act; the meaning of Christian love lies not in any of its own characteristics (essential or not) but solely in that to which it points as its foundation."
What follows, then, is "the criticism that Barth underestimates or
leaves out the suffering of creation and history because he views it as
having already been overcome and displaced by the covenant reconciliation and redemption. The distinct impression left to one is that
human effort and prospects—the stuff of history—are altogether
futile and unnecessary."[64] The reductionism in Althoff's interpretation is apparent, but his analysis is instructive as an example of the
kind of charge to which the *analogia fidei* and Barth's Anselmian
method have lent themselves. Althoff is one of many who read
Barth—and dismiss him—seeing him as irrelevant to a theology for
today.

  Like Althoff, Willis objects to Barth's viewing all of human
culture analogically from the christological perspective. That controlling perspective, Willis charges, prevents Barth's ever turning to
a genuinely phenomenological examination. Willis understands
Barth's commitment to a stance free of sociological or psychological
abstraction, but does not see how this valid concern should obviate
any and all appreciation for what these disciplines might contribute
to an understanding of humanity and history. Barth does mention
these "secular" disciplines, Willis observes, but fails to make significant use of them.[65] Still, Willis acknowledges, "One feels that Barth
has missed opportunities provided by his own theology for a more
sustained engagement with the empirical dimensions of the ethical
context. . . ."[66] The *analogia fidei*, Willis feels, is responsible.

  Willis' and Althoff's objections are familiar, even redundant. It
is at the point of "missed opportunities provided by his [Barth's] own
theology" that they should be engaged, however. In naming
Christology as the root of the problem, both thinkers have missed

the mark: Barth's christological center is not the weakness but the great strength of his theology. Arguments which contend that Barth's viewing humanity from the perspective of Jesus Christ drains humankind of all genuine content, and history of meaning, are tacit arguments for the Enlightenment notion of autonomous human self-constitution. Althoff's claim that Barth's Christology leaves nothing provisional in humanity's situation, and even a void of genuine human content and spirit, is not substantiated. Willis is closer to the truth when he says that Barth's theology offers "missed opportunities" for engaging the ethical demands of a real world. What these thinkers seem not to have considered is that Barth's Christology and his *analogia fidei* are not finally synonymous. That very christological center, this thesis maintains, is the fundamental point where Barth's "missed opportunities" can be reclaimed. The Enlightenment turn implicitly advocated by Althoff and Willis only renders another liberal disclosive theology lacking the strengths of Barth's christological grounding. With the development of a Christology in social location with oppressed humankind and otherkind with Jesus Christ as norm, the meaning of the covenant reconciliation, rather than displacing the "suffering of creation and history," as Althoff alleges, can reclaim and enhance what Althoff and Willis insist has been obliterated. The incarnation, the humanity of the historical Jesus, the cross and resurrection, can all be reclaimed as that which they are in God's Realpresence in history—the authorization of human freedom and human history. Far from being a negation of these, Barth's theology offers the possibility for a genuine reclamation of them. The importance of freedom and ethics in Barth's theology has not been adequately assessed by these critics. Furthermore, there is no realization on their part of a nascent praxis methodology in Barth's theology. The Safenwil method of faith seeking accountability which understands holds potential which they have not seen; that Willis and Althoff fail to see it is the result, at least to some degree, of their own oblique participation in the Anselmian method insofar as it (or a similar method) frames and reflects even for them what is viewed in Barth's theology. Whether standing with Barth (and Anselm) or with Willis and Althoff (and Enlightenment perspectives), a disclosure methodology makes opaque what *fides quaerens rationem reddere*, an accountability methodology, illuminates. Claiming anew the latter, one sees that Barth's *Dogmatics* Christology latently retains the Safenwil insight that Jesus Christ is God's movement for social justice. Far from displacing the "suffering of creation and history," as Willis and Althoff object, Barth's Christology can, from that perspective, be developed as that which meets the very inside of humanity's and nature's travail. With that move, then, the church as the earthly-historical form of the existence of Jesus Christ is, at its core, immersed in the same concerns that Jesus of Nazareth met head on: sickness, hunger, poverty, spiritual usurpation, racial hatred, prejudice, and oppression of the powerless. These themes remain to be developed in succeeding chapters.

Interpretations of Barth's View of History

To be sure, interpretations of Barth's view of history are contradictory and varied.[67] The Anselmian methodology is again at issue. For many of those thinkers who struggle to understand the meaning of history in his theology, Barth's notion of grace lies behind difficulties in bringing God and world together in that comprehensive work. Jersild mentions a "monism of grace," West an "all-embracing grace," Bowden a "theological triumphalism," Casalis an "overwhelming" grace, and Livingston a "swamping" by grace.[68] Shinn, von Balthasar, Bloesch, and Hendry object, as well, to the supremacy of grace in Barth's theology, though with differences of interpretation.[69] Such an emphasis upon grace, these believe, would appear to minimize or deny human history and responsibility.

Analyzing the *Church Dogmatics* 3, 3, G. C. Berkouwer notes Barth's tone of finality in his description of evil's objective elimination by God's grace. The chaos' "apparent" power, or the chaos itself, is mere appearance, which convinces humanity of its efficacy only because of human blindness. Berkouwer challenges, "The question has more than once been asked whether this kind of triumph is indeed the message of the Scriptures. On the one hand, we constantly meet in the Bible the appeal not to fear, to be of good courage and to believe steadfastly in the victory of Jesus Christ. On the other hand, we see that the believer is continually called to resistance and to struggle . . . we are warned against a danger that is very real."[70] The struggle is a joyful one assured of ultimate victory, Berkouwer points out, but a real one nonetheless, and perhaps particularly so for that reason. Furthermore, the battle is a concrete one with concrete forces. Barth's diminution of evil and the demons, Berkouwer argues, vitiates humanity's struggle with existential sin and evil. Wishing to protect the unity of creation and reconciliation, Barth erases important distinctions. "His conception leaves the impression that everything has been done, all the decisions have been taken, so that one can hardly say that the *historical fall* and the *historical reconciliation* are at issue, but only the *revelation* of redemption in history, the *revelation* of the definitive Yes of God's grace."[71] When this conception "becomes the basis of theological thinking," Berkouwer warns, the contradictory nature of sin can be spoken of, but the consequences of sin within history are made problematical.[72] The notion of Christ's relativizing of sin (3, 2) is not intended by Barth as a dismissal of sin's gravity, Berkouwer reminds his readers, and Barth does not intend to say that sin is innocuous; still, "the aprioristic conquest of sin moves over the face of the whole of history," Berkouwer objects.[73] The notion of eternality absorbs creation and reconciliation and, thus, history as well. The human situation in history also is rendered questionable. What is needed, Berkouwer stresses, is not a counter argument which narrows and attenuates grace, but a "larger appreciation" of God's grace. "The criticism that Barth accentuates grace *too much* is a senseless criticism," Berkouwer rightly insists, but an understanding of God's graceful work is needed which is not aprioristic in character and thus an obscuring of God's continued redemptive activity in a genuine history of redemption.[74]

A conquest of evil which takes place not in the eternal council of God, Berkouwer insists, but in the concrete realm of divine-human struggle is possible in a "larger appreciation" of grace. Barth's preference for the *a priori* understanding of sin and grace, however, is related to the notion of God's eternal self-distinction, Berkouwer thinks. In that understanding, sin is that which God is not; apriorily sin is conceived as the rejected evil which in God's eternal self-distinction is judged and canceled. Sin is thus, Berkouwer states, made "understandable" as that which God has rejected as not a part of God. This making sin "understandable" draws sin's sting as much as an *a priori* dealing with it removes sin from the concrete. Berkouwer warns of the risks incurred when the church attempts to "explain" and make "understandable" the reality of sin: "The problem posed by this 'necessary' *a priori* character of the triumph in its relationship to history became the problem of Barth's theology. It will never do to criticize Barth's theology by placing over against it *another* explanation of sin, and of its reality. Whenever sin is 'explained' shadows fall across the path of the

Church and of theology. The way of speculation always leads to confusion."[75] Seeing sin as a "problem" begs for a rational "explanation" which becomes a rationalization; historically, this has been the case from Augustine onward—*sub specie aeternitatis*, sin is a part of God's harmony. So conceived, evil and injustice hardly call for concrete struggle. The triumph of grace of which we need to speak, Berkouwer concludes, is one which "places us in the midst of promise and responsibility, of calling and admonition."[76] When God's victory and redemption are understood as both present and future as well as past, and God's participation itself is understood so, the divine-human struggle with sin and injustice, irresponsibility and war, Berkouwer wants to say, becomes a genuinely present reality.

Berkouwer's critique is powerful, but what he has not seen, apparently, is the relationship between, in his words, the triumph of grace in Barth's theology and the theological method employed, *fides quaerens intellectum*, and its noetic commitment. Faith seeking understanding favors the kind of *a priori* dealing with sin and evil which Berkouwer dismantles. Even as earlier stated, a speculative way dependent on ontology, as Anselm's ontological argument affords theology, finally ends in eternality and necessity. Ergo triumphalism. *Fides quaerens rationem reddere*, the method which Barth employed in Safenwil, on the other hand, understands grace and history in terms that do not subsume the latter in the former. *Fides quaerens rationem reddere*, it is proposed here, is yet retained, if only inchoately and minimally, in the *Church Dogmatics* and if lifted out and developed further can be instrumental in locating faith and theology in the midst of concrete history and the material creation because God is understood to be there first in Realpresence. What has been done in Jesus Christ, faith seeking accountability shows us, is still *being done* and is moving toward a future which yet offers and requires vigorous struggle and victory. The nature of accountability itself is present and immediate engagement, active, forming and reforming, in response to God's own battle with social injustice, the plundering of nature, and the threatened death of God's good creation. *Fides quaerens intellectum* does not explicitly stress that kind of accountability. Noetic limitations such as Torrance insists are necessary to theology's nature are a direct and unfortunate implicate of *fides quaerens intellectum*. With those noetic hedges, however, historical engagement—God's, the church's, and humanity's—is, even as Berkouwer insists, made problematical.

One does not have to charge Barth with Platonism or German Idealism to identify limitations in the "key" which he took from Anselm. *Fides quaerens intellectum* and its noetic commitment appear to be the root problem: the guiding presupposition of faith seeking understanding dictates a theological method committed to noetic, rational reflection and explication not explicitly directed toward historical engagement. The same limitation applies to a hermeneutic; apart from social location with the poor of humankind and the "poor" of nature, the meeting of text and interpreter hazards a sterile engagement which leaves the excluded of God's world still excluded. *Fides quaerens rationem reddere* consciously brings those outcast ones, human and para-human, inside the methodological and hermeneutical spheres. With that inclusive move, theology takes on a different shape.

Surveying the Church Dogmatics: Interpreting with Two Methods in View

As preceding pages have shown, interpreting Barth solely in light of the predominant Anselmian method of reflection on Scripture and Confession obstructs insights which the acknowledgement of a second oblique methodology present with the dominant Anselmian one can bring into focus. Reading Barth in awareness of these two foci helps to explain difficulties in Barth's theology, and also helps to identify potentialities, not formerly appreciated, in a way that does justice to his work. Those potentialities, if not developed fully by Barth himself, can be lifted out and expanded by the scholar who reads with both methodologies in mind. Reading in that way has special importance for understanding and developing further Barth's ecclesiology.

For instance, while it has been objected that the event of the Word of God hardly comes across in the *Church Dogmatics* in human terms as a concrete historical event, listening to Barth with ears attuned for the Safenwil insights, one can hear him declaim that, because that which God does is done in the creaturely sphere of human beings, "there is nothing spiritual which is not also natural or corporeal."[77] This is signified first of all by Jesus' own corporeality, by the verbal nature of Scripture and preaching, by the natural and corporeal in the sacraments, and by the church's essential nature as the body of Christ.[78] Each of these four elements impacts specifically on a doctrine of the church. The incarnational reality affirmed and emphasized in each instance underscores the church's nature as historical, earthly, mundane, and integrally connected to the concrete specifics of human life and struggle. Other chapters of this thesis will seek to develop some of these notions more fully, but suffice it to say here that Barth's theology is redolent with meaning for the concrete situation of human beings and the church's part in that; the historical event has not been excluded. "The Word of God is . . . natural and corporeal, because without that it would not be the Word of God directed to us men as spiritual-natural beings, really coming to us in the way in which we are real."[79] The church, *fides quaerens rationem reddere* helps us to see, also meets men and women "in the way in which we are real," e.g., historically, physically, and socially, as well as spiritually.

Additionally, the knowledge of the Word of God as Barth describes it in *Church Dogmatics* 1, 1 includes fundamentally the element of trust in a way that relativizes the quest for noetic certainty which the Anselmian method tends to foster. For example, Barth explains that it is as the claimed individual that one is known and knows:

> As knowers they are got at by the known object. They exist no longer without it, but with it. So far as they think of it at all they must think of it, with the entire trust with which they venture to think of it at all, as true reality, as true in its existence and nature. Whatever else and however else they may think of it, they must begin by thinking of the actual trueness of its reality. When faced with this trueness they can no longer withdraw into themselves in order from there to affirm, question, or deny it. Its trueness has come home directly to them personally, has become their property. And at the same time they themselves have become the property of its trueness. This event, this verification or proof we call, to distinguish it from mere knowings, knowledge. A knowing becomes knowledge when the man becomes a responsible witness to its content.[80]

Knowledge of the Word of God creates the knower anew. It is, hence, accountable knowledge of which Barth speaks. Barth allows, as well, for intuitive knowledge of God, thus further calling into question the noetic concentration appearing at other points.

> Unquestionably, apart from discursive thought and in every
> variety of combination with it, there is also an intuitive grasp of
> objects . . . why among the possibilities of human existence in
> being determined by this Word, should not the subconscious,
> or intuition, or whatever may be cited here, also have their
> place?[81]

Most importantly, the Safenwil emphasis on discipleship can
be heard in Barth's frequent reiteration that it is for our "self-
determination being determined by the Word of God" that knowledge of the Word of God is given.[82] Barth's integration of ethics into
dogmatics reflects strongly the Safenwil influence. Because the
Word of God is spoken to us, "we ourselves are its realization in our
entire existence."[83] The same is affirmed in *Dogmatics in Outline*.
There, Barth stresses that Christian faith is freedom to hear God's
gracious word *so that* persons may "once for all, exclusively and
entirely, hold to His promise and guidance."[84]

> Faith is not concerned with a special realm, that of religion,
> say, but with real life in its totality, the outward as well as that
> which is spiritual, the brightness as well as the gloom in our
> life. Faith is concerned with our being permitted to rely on
> God as regards ourselves and also as regards what moves us on
> behalf of others, of the whole of humanity; it is concerned with
> the whole of living and the whole of dying.[85]

Barth goes on to say that knowledge of God differs from pure
intellection, sharing more with trust than with noetic certainty.
Faith as knowledge is more than *scientia;* it is more like *sophia* and
sapientia which embrace "the entire existence of man." Wisdom is
linked to practical living and to responsible decision in the public
quarter as well as the private sphere. With that affirmation, Barth
completes a triad of freedoms implicit in faith. Faith is freedom of
trust, freedom of knowledge, and, not separably, freedom of respon-
siblity. Trust and knowledge *for* responsibility is Barth's movement.[86] This responsibility is itself the inner meaning of confession,
Barth wants to say. "Let us be fully on our guard against the idea
that confession is a matter of the faith which should be heard only in
the 'area of the church.' And that all that is to be done is to make the
area visible and perhaps extend it a little into the world. The area of
the Church stands in the world, as outwardly the Church stands in
the village or in a city, beside the school, the cinema and the railway
station. The Church's language cannot aim at being an end in itself.

It must be made clear that the church exists for the sake of the world. . . ."[87] A "worldly, political attitude," Barth maintains, is inseparable from the church's confession itself.[88] Reading these words from the perspective of Barth's early praxis methodology focuses a doctrine of the church in which social engagement and political participation in the quest for justice and peace are understood as the very heart of the church's reality; they are, indeed, its true confession.

Consistent with this interpretation of faith, knowledge, and confession, Barth's ethics again emphasizes that dogmatic knowing is inseparable from the existence of humans in the mundane work and activity of all of life. Human beings claimed by the knowledge of the Word of God are claimed precisely in "the work and action" of their lives.[89] Dogmatics' concern cannot genuinely be one of pure doctrine or of faithful preaching unless it is at the same time a concern with the realities of the Christian life, i.e., with sanctification and thus with ethics. Barth is careful to guard against a common "aberration." While dogmatics is centrally concerned with the existence of human beings, that is true only because God is *first* centrally concerned with the total life of humanity. Ethics does not take its point of departure from the existential situation but rather from the Word of God first addressed to that situation, the Word of God which is itself the origin of the question of human existence before it is the answer. As the Word of God raises the question of human existence, it calls into question human volition and action, challenging it, questioning its validity, and righting it. Thus does human existence acquire theological meaning. Because it is first important to God even before it is important to us, human existence acquires its theological significance through the Word of God—through Jesus Christ. For that reason, theology cannot be separate from ethics. "Dogmatics has no option: it has to be ethics as well. Its dialectics, and its whole attitude necessarily has to be 'existential,' i.e., because it refers to the Word of God, it must also refer to human existence."[90] Again, implications for the church's ethical authorization are set forth: The church is authorized, energized, by God to concern itself with provoking/transforming action in the creation of ethical structures for all. Still, it is not apparent that Barth is expressing any notion of ethical awareness gained through praxis. Indeed, the movement appears to be from reflection on the Word of God *to* the existential, or from theory to application.

To be sure, Barth's theology can be read variously and inconsistently as divorced from human existence and history or, instead, as connected integrally with the struggles and joys of concrete life. One can argue that the tenor of those sections of the *Church Dogmatics* and of *Dogmatics in Outline* quoted immediately above is one of knowledge *for* involvement, or for the concrete and ethical. In other words, the goal of knowledge is not noetic certainty or knowledge for the sake of knowledge, but, indeed, for accountable Christian living. The Anselmian method, it might be contended, also is concerned in the final analysis with discipleship. The problem then takes a new shape.

The significant difference, in that case, highlighted by the divergent methodologies, is *how* knowledge for accountable discipleship is reached, e.g., either on the one hand, with *fides quaerens intellectum*, through reflection on Scripture and Confession, or, on the other hand, with *fides quaerens rationem reddere*, through social location with the poor in action and reflection on Scripture, Confession, and the concrete human situation. The issue becomes particularized, then, at the point of adequacy for accountability. Here is the crisis. Barthian scholarship reveals that Barth's theology rests too easily with the theoretical: the predominant methodology, *fides quaerens intellectum*, seems to be the major causative factor. What that means for ecclesiology needs to be looked at closely. Barth's reflection on Scripture and Creed and the domination of theory and its quest for knowledge tend to exclude those who have no part in that exercise. Faith seeking accountability which then understands, on the other hand, *begins* where faith seeking understanding never reaches; incorporating the poor and their experience as epistemologically ingredient to understanding itself, *fides quaerens rationem reddere* does not seek to understand the plight of an oppressed humanity and a ravaged creation in light of first principles or noetically limited constructions. Indwelling a real world *with* those sufferers, faith seeking accountability which *in* accountability understands, *knows* precisely *because* it is socially located with those to whom it is accountable and with whom it reflects. In the midst of *discipleship,* knowledge happens. For the church, then, social location with the poor of humanity and nature and justice work with God for and with those whom abstract theory tends to exclude are basic to the church's nature, this thesis proposes. The domination of theory over praxis must be revealed for what it is: as the inadvertent obstructor of the very discipleship which faith seeking understands wishes to foster, this time-honored and entrenched methodology preferring theory over praxis is a primary hindrance to the church's faithful actualization of its mission and tasks.

Perhaps it is here that some discussion of the notion of *praxis* itself needs to be made in order to clarify the particular meaning of that term as it is employed in this work. Much obscurity surrounds the usage of the term generally and some effort toward exactitude can only be helpful.

Discursus on Praxis

Some discussion of the notion of praxis is needed. As I employ that term and notion it shares affinities with philosophical ancestors ancient and modern and diverges from them in significant ways. With Aristotle, there is included the idea that praxis involves political life and suggests a distinctive way of being in the world. Unlike the Aristotelian view, however, the notion set forth here does not separate the practical and theoretical and accord to theory a higher place than to practice. With existentialism it is affirmed that our decisiveness shapes our becoming and that changing the world means (in part) changing ourselves. But our action is more than inwardness and more than subjective transformation. Acting is more than choosing in a radical act of freedom. Rather, praxis as it is advanced here, finds both its ground and its goal outside the self. The nothingness of the self and its authentic existence do not exhaust the meaning of praxis. Instead, the pragmatic emphasis on shaping the world comes somewhat closer in certain aspects to praxis as it is here perceived, though pragmatism also fails to comprehend what this thesis intends by that notion. Peirce's emphasis on the social formation of the individual and the community as self-critical principle aligns with the notion of corporate solidarity which I am setting forth, but important differences still exist. Those differences are apparent in Peirce's failure to move in his demand for practicality to concern with immediate political and social issues. Likewise, Dewey's concern to focus on the value of experience not just for its epistemological importance—experience is more than knowing—and his emphasis on the human being as agent are vital ideas. Still, despite his involvement with the educational, social, and political issues of his day, Dewey insisted on theoretical inquiry's abstraction from the immediate context of those issues and, in that regard, his view differs from the one which I am proposing.

Analytic philosophers have seemed to be least concerned with practical agency and action, but they have challenged us to an "appreciation of how deeply [our] language and action is embedded in and conditioned by social practices and institutions."[91] Still, they have left to others questions concerning the dynamics of these practices and institutions. Their concern has not been a praxiological one in the sense of attending to the question of social change, either in the sense of how it occurs or should occur.[92]

It is with Marxist analysis and praxis that the view which I am advancing has most congruity, though important differences pertain here as well. Richard J. Bernstein has pointed out in his book *Praxis and Action: Contemporary Philosophies of Human Activity* that Marx and the Left Hegelians who influenced his thought were concerned "to come to grips with the problems of [their] time" and, in responding and reacting to the Hegelian system informing crucially their work, "felt profoundly that something had gone desperately wrong" with that system.[93] In important aspects it had failed to become the practical philosophy which it had promised to be. The quest for a practical philosophy concerned with concrete activity, thus, motivated their investigations. Hegel's wish to understand *Geist* as Reason concretely actualized in history became for Marx a crucial point of departure. Spirit's essence as action and humanity's essence as action in self-formation informed a fundamental view of humanity for Marx as well as for existentialists. Bernstein goes on to develop an argument that Marx's notion of praxis was theory-shaped by Hegel (despite the inadequacies in that system) even before dealing with the empirical. The French Revolution, the concrete political situation in Prussia in the late 1830's and early 1840's, and the proletariat were all interpreted through Hegelian lenses. Thus, human beings and their products are revealed for what they are, Marx believed, by Hegelian insights. Bernstein writes:

> . . . both Hegel and Marx are challenging this ontological division [between persons and their products]. The object or product produced is *not* something "merely" external to and indifferent to the nature of the producer. It is his activity in an objectified or congealed form. . . . Everything that is of fundamental importance in Marx's outlook depends on grasping this manner of viewing the relation of the objects that a man pro-

> duces and his activity: it is essential for understanding what
> *praxis* means. . . . Echoing the Hegelian claim that the self is
> what it does, Marx maintains that a man is what he does. . . .
> Alienation does not result from the fact that man objectifies
> himself, produces objects—this is man's distinctive character.
> Alienation results when he produces in such a way . . . that his
> products are at once an expression of his labor-power and at the
> same time are not a true expression of his potentialities—what
> Marx, following Feuerbach, called man's 'species-being'. His
> products become hostile to him; they negate and dehumanize
> him.[94]

Hence, for Marx authentic *praxis* is human activity congruent with potential and faithful to "species-being."

Praxis, Marx insisted, is integrally linked to education, consciousness-raising, and criticism of existing institutions and beliefs. On the basis of this intellectual work of understanding and criticism the second moment of praxis is built, e.g., the practical overcoming of those forces which impede species-being. Praxis, for Marx, is a "single, comprehensive and coherent theory of man and his world."[95]

Before continuing with Marx's view of praxis and saying how it does and does not connect with the view which I am proposing, it is important that something of the history of Christian reflection on theory and practice be taken into account. The Alexandrian Fathers Clement and Origen, and others, made it clear that contemplation was superior to action and that the value of practice consisted in its instrumentality for a rational and contemplative union with God. Still, as Lobkowicz points out,[96] there has always been an uneasiness in Christian thought that action is more than mere preparation for the cognitive knowledge of God. It is more than Origen's "stirrup to contemplation." This uneasy realization cannot be escaped in light of the Gospel's consistent goad to love of neighbor which, likened to love of God, manifests in *acts* of love and not mere contemplation. Thus, Christian grappling with θεωρία and πράξιϛ has made the purely theoretical a hard bed in which to lie.

Returning to the Hegelian background of Marx's work, however, we see, even in the work of this man who has changed the way that theory and practice will be viewed in Western thought for all time, difficulties finally not too unlike those of the Christian Fathers who accorded to contemplation a superior status to that of the active life. For Marx as for Hegel, the actualization of Absolute Knowledge in the concrete forms of human life was fundamental. As Lobkowicz observes, for the Left Hegelians who most influenced Marx, namely, Bruno Bauer, Arnold Ruge, and Moses Hess, and for Marx himself, a central preoccupation was the translation of absolute theory into practice.[97] Contemplation still was the first moment. The world was to be changed in accordance with the salvific dictates of Absolute Knowledge. To be sure, Marx's experience with the poor and his own struggle with poverty had informed his perceptions, but the Hegelian confidence in Reason and the maturation of history and humanity remained the philosophical ground and directive of his work. Lobkowicz has argued that Marx's turn to the Proletariat as the material agent of transformation represents a shift in the meaning of praxis in which history rather than Absolute Knowledge became "the true principle of salvation."[98] If this be true, my point remains. Thought's hegemony was a hard one to break for Marx even as it has been for Christian thinkers.

Jon Gunnemann has focused other problems with the Marxist conception of praxis. It is the *revolutionary* aspect that worries Gunnemann. The notion of revolutionary praxis is a problematical one, Gunnemann believes, because it appears to equate liberation and humanization with revolution, even violent revolution. Thus, Gunnemann rejects this kind of particular meaning of revolution and calls for, instead, a "specifically Christian response to revolution."[99] Included is an understanding of Christianity according to its revolutionary content properly conceived. So conceived, revolution cannot be sharply dualistically focused in the mode of the oppressed standing against the oppressors, as it commonly is. What, Gunnemann asks, does such a dualism offer for "after the revolution?" Nor should revolution be simplistically conceptualized as a movement toward greater concretizations of truth teleologically actualized. Most importantly, all kinds of revolutionary change should not be subsumed under the "model of a citizens' rebellion against tyranny," failing as it does to appreciate other modes of creative change.[100]

Instead, Gunnemann proposes a model of revolution which he is in part attempting to develop that "does not entail a progressive view of history in the usual sense of progress and therefore does not tip the balance in favor of a Marxist view of history."[101] In delineating this model, Gunnemann rightly calls for more rigorous language as in the case of liberation theologians' and others' propensity for terming marginalized persons as "dehumanized." Such an emphasis, Gunnemann reminds us, focuses on the weaknesses of oppressed peoples to the detriment of acknowledging and appreciating their unique and very *human* strengths. It is one thing to say that a people are treated in an inhuman way or as less than human; it is quite another to imply with the term "dehumanized" that they have been stripped of their human qualities.

Still, Gunnemann's critique has its own problems. Picking up on Marx's concern to have the common folk claim their indispensable role in history and the value of their story, Gunnemann fails to discern, or if not that, to appropriate important emphases in Marx's insights and thereby acquiesces to a kind of "the hand that rocks the cradle rules the world" myth. [Feminists know immediately that it's the little boys *in* the cradle who rule the world and not the hands doing the rocking.] Gunnemann writes:

> . . . [It] follows from Marx's dialectical analysis that those who have "made" history in the sense of being written about by the historians, those who are recorded as the heroes of history, are only in a superficial sense the makers of history. Granted, they have done the thinking, directed the wars, developed the creative powers of the human mind in art and literature, devised the political and legal systems. But all of this was predicated upon the labor of the classes who were unconsciously the real makers of history.[102]

This touting of the laboring class as the "real makers of history" flirts ominously with a doffing of the hat to these "real" history-makers and considering them duly recognized. Furthermore, what sense does it make to talk of developing humanity's highest creative powers and devising the world's most complex systems of government in a way that implies that these were and are not, after all, the "real stuff" of history-making? No one gains by that kind of conceptual subterfuge.

We can agree with Gunnemann that Marx "still retains Hegel's propensity to subsume too much of the variety of human relationships under a single conceptual scheme."[103] We can hear, too, from Gunnemann that social revolution is more complex and nuanced than generally perceived: "The development and coming together of the various elements needed to produce genuine social innovation is filled with anticipations that first go unnoticed, with false directions and premature proclamations of change, with stubborn resistance—in short, a process in which the revolution and its resolution are only the very last stages."[104] But we cannot agree that those who have been most heavily invested in making a given paradigm work are for that reason the ones most knowledgeable about its deficiencies and most qualified, however reluctant they may be to jump ship with the old paradigm, to devise and institute a competing paradigm. Here, Gunnemann seems to be following too closely Kuhn's model of scientific paradigms and shifts and falling into the pit which Kuhn himself warned against. It is at this point that Gunnemann needs to listen more closely to Marx.

What, then, is the nature of Christian praxis as I propose it in this work? Informed at some point by all the traditions just described, the praxis of faith seeking accountability yet differs and is more. Marx's emphasis upon humanity as agent, his insistence that people are what they do and that the human situation at any given period is not an ontologically fixed one but a historical one of change has been most instructive. This means that poverty and conditions of injustice are not in the order of things but are historically conditioned and can be transformed. Further, praxis as fundamental, guiding human activity rather than mere practice or applied theory is central to Marx's insights.

With Gunnemann and others, however, I, too, reject certain aspects of Marx's conception of praxis. The translation of Absolute Knowledge into concrete history is a focus still concentrated on the superiority of theory and enclosed within the knowledge frame that Marx, it would seem, wished to break. The Hegelian confidence in the maturation of humanity and history is another view that must be rejected. The nature of revolution and change, furthermore, should not be understood simplistically but studied closely in the interest of gaining a more faithful apperception of transformation, its meaning and how it is effected.

One point needs to be focused: praxis is always theory-shaped, even theory-laden, perhaps. However, there is much theory that is advanced without praxis. This work, with that of many others, is in part a call for closer self-examination by Christian thinkers who, whether consciously or not, struggle with questions of theory and practice and how they relate.

What, then, is praxis which seeks to be accountably faithful? Praxis is activity, reflection, critique, concrete solidarity with the oppressed and knowing in accountability, involving all of cognitive and practical life, and, as such, a comprehensive appreciation of humanity and reality and thus a walk of life. It binds Aristotle's θεωάα and πRgráξιζ, contemplation and practice, thereby connecting the Aristotelian bifurcation of the active, politically involved life and the detached life of theoretical reflection. Most importantly, praxis is *not* applied reflection. It is not the translation of absolute theory into practice. Rather, both thought and action take their rise in the context of worship and seek to be accountable to the praxis of the Gospel. This has important implications for a praxis hermeneutic for theology. As Frederick Herzog has stated it:

> . . . the peculiar thing about Messiah Jesus is that for the church the new thought about God did not emerge via pure thought. In Messiah Jesus God acted out a way of being God unheard of before.
>
> Obviously, there was also thinking, hard thinking. But the hard thinking grew out of and was tied to a definite praxis. Jesus' praxis, we need to observe, gave rise to Christian thought. Thinking on his feet, Jesus incarnated God. Thus praxis gives rise to thought.
>
> What we need to understand is that unless we are intimately involved in the same matrix of human life in which Messiah Jesus incarnated God we cannot shape a Christian theology. The Gospel story is not primarily a talk-text, but a praxis-text. God-talk comes in God-walk. Involved in this ministry we begin to understand theology.[105]

The praxis of faith seeking accountability grows out of worship and concrete identification with those ensnared in political, social, and economic structures of oppression. This thought arising from action is self-critical and malleable both giving to and receiving from the active life its content. Most fundamentally, "The Gospel story is the nucleus and basic framework of [this] Christian theology—on the level of praxis. It reflects Christopraxis."[106] Revolution in this context means transformation initiated by God's Spirit and participated in by women and men as co-agents in God's work. Christopraxis is then the hermeneutical "inevitability" of biblical interpretation. Praxis, so understood, is more than action or practice; it is a way of life.

Chapter III will turn to an analysis of Barth's early methodology, one of praxis informing theory, present also in the *Church Dogmatics* but eclipsed by the dominant Anselmian method. Indications may be found there for how knowledge for accountable discipleship and an accountable ecclesiology is gained.

NOTES

/1/   Frederick Herzog has introduced the notion of social location in his seminars at Duke University.

/2/ Karl Barth, *Anselm: Fides Quaerens Intellectum: Anselm's Proof of the Existence of God in the Context of His Theological Scheme* (London: SCM Press LTD, 1960; reprint ed. The Pickwick Press, 1975), p. 11.

/3/ Ibid., p. 18.

/4/ Ibid., pp. 20, 21.

/5/ Ibid., p. 37.

/6/ Ibid., p. 40.

/7/ Ibid., pp. 41, 42.

/8/ Ibid., p. 26.

/9/ Ibid., p. 27.

/10/ Ibid., p. 67.

/11/ Lev Shestov and Etienne Gilson see in Anselm's formula an effort, characteristic of the medievalists, to support faith by reason. Shestov writes in *Athens and Jerusalem* [trans. Bernard Martin (Athens, Ohio: Ohio University Press, 1966), p. 297] that: "Already in St. Augustine it is clearly established that faith is subject to the control of reason, that it almost seeks this control." This struggle is at base, Shestov declares, one between the Greek idea of eternal truth and the Judeo-Christian God who creates all that exists. Gilson likewise writes: "There is no question of maintaining—no one has ever maintained—that faith is a kind of cognition superior to rational cognition. It is quite clear, on the contrary, that belief is a *succedaneum* of ('a simple substitute for') knowledge, and that to substitute science for belief, wherever possible, is always a positive gain for the understanding." See *The Spirit of Medieval Philosophy*, trans. A. H. C. Downes (New York: Charles Scribner's Sons, 1936), p. 35.

/12/ David L. Mueller, *Karl Barth* (Waco, Texas: Word Books, 1972), pp. 37, 38.

/13/ Ibid., p. 38.

/14/ Ibid., p. 39.

/15/ Ibid., p. 40.

/16/ Ibid.

/17/ Ibid., pp. 40, 41.

/18/ Ibid.

/19/ Ibid.

/20/ Ibid., pp. 84, 85.

/21/ Ibid.

/22/ Mueller, *Karl Barth*, pp. 37, 38.

/23/ Thomas F. Torrance, *Karl Barth: An Introduction to His Early Theology, 1910-1931* (London: SCM Press, 1962), p. 182.

/24/ Ibid., pp. 182, 183.

/25/ Ibid.

/26/ Ibid., p. 184.

/27/ Ibid.

/28/ Ibid., p. 185.

/29/ Ibid., p. 187.

/30/ Ibid., p. 189.

/31/ Frederick Herzog has referred to God as Author-izer in his Duke seminars. It is to him that I am indebted for the notion of accountability as it informs this understanding of faith and theological method.

/32/ George Hunsinger, ed. and trans., *Karl Barth and Radical Politics* (Philadelphia: Westminster Press, 1976), p. 218.

/33/ Ibid.

/34/ Ibid., p. 219.

/35/ Ibid.

/36/ Ibid., p. 220.

/37/ Ibid.

/38/ Ibid., p. 220.

/39/ Ibid., pp. 220, 221.

/40/ Ibid.

/41/ Ibid., pp. 221, 222.

/42/ Ibid., p. 222.

/43/ Hunsinger, *Karl Barth and Radical Politics*, pp. 222, 223.

/44/ Ibid., p. 223.

/45/ Ibid., p. 224.

/46/ Ibid., p. 222.

/47/ Colin E. Gunton, *Becoming and Being: The Doctrine of God in Charles Hartshorne and Karl Barth* (Oxford: Oxford University Press, 1978; reprint ed. 1980), p. 119.

/48/ Ibid., p. 166. Also, John Bowden, in *Karl Barth* (London: SCM Press, 1971), makes an interesting observation. In *Romans*, God was "sheer act," Bowden maintains, but with the Anselm move, the emphasis was shifted from God's action to God's being and rationality. On pp. 110, 111, Bowden argues the inadequacy of the *analogia fidei* for any genuine connection to history and political reality.

/49/ Gunton, *Becoming and Being*, p. 121.

/50/ Barth, *Anselm: Fides Quaerens Intellectum*, p. 75. Also, Gunton, *Becoming and Being*, p. 122.

/51/ Gunton, *Becoming and Being*, p. 123. Henri Bouillard states: "The understanding of the faith consists simply in unveiling the intelligible links which connect the various propositions of the Creed," *The Knowledge of God*, trans. Samuel D. Femiano (New York: Herder & Herder, 1968), p. 69.

/52/ Ibid., p. 124.

/53/ Karl Barth, *Church Dogmatics*, Vol. 2, 1: *The Doctrine of God*, ed. G. W. Bromiley and T. F. Torrance and trans. T. H. L. Parker et al. (Edinburgh: T. & T. Clark, 1957; reprint ed., 1964), p. 230.

/54/ Ibid., pp. 228, 229.

/55/ Barth's wish to construct a concrete doctrine of God for a concrete world, von Balthasar maintains, was his reason for turning to analogy. Illumination of Scripture and Confession and the drawing of analogy from God's Word in them "was the guiding consideration for Barth, and this accounts for the purity and beauty of his presentation," von Balthasar acclaims. See *The Theology of Karl Barth*, trans. John Drury (Garden City: Doubleday & Co., 1972), pp. 24, 25. Bouillard defends the theological-philosophical character of Anselm's proof, seeing in it that which rationalizes humankind's adoration of God. Bouillard even suggests that rationality is that which converts to adoration. See *The Knowledge of God*, p. 95. Hood views Barth's Anselmian method as the "watershed" of Barth's theological maturation and, hence, no impediment for an adequate theology and ethics.

See "Karl Barth's Christological Basis for the State and Political Praxis," *Scottish Journal of Theology* 33 (1980):226. Bettis, as well, joins in with a lengthy affirmation of the nature of faith as that which naturally seeks understanding. "Theology in the Public Debate: Barth's Rejection of Natural Theology and the Hermeneutical Problem," *Scottish Journal of Theology* 22 (December 1969):385f. F. W. Camfield also supports the *analogia fidei* in his "Barthian theology" of revelation and the Holy Spirit. See *Revelation and the Holy Spirit: An Essay in Barthian Theology*, with a Foreword by John McConnachie (New York: Charles Scribner's Sons, 1934), pp. 46f. J. Y. Lee considers Barth's substitution of the *analogia fidei* for the *analogia entis* a conquest of faith over reason. "Liberating Christian faith from the fetters of metaphysical speculation," Lee argues, Barth has given to theology a triumphant victory. Jung Young Lee, "Karl Barth's Use of Analogy in His Church Dogmatics," *Scottish Journal of Theology* 22 (June 1969):150. Kuykendall offers no objection to the Anselmian-Barthian methodology of explicating the Creed through reason and the inferences of the *analogia fidei*. See George Henry Kuykendall, Jr., "The Spirit and the Word: An Attempt to Develop a Post-Enlightenment Understanding of the Church" (Ph.D. dissertation, Union Theological Seminary, New York, 1972), pp. 74f. The Evangelical Donald Bloesch writes approvingly, "His [Barth's] theological method, which draws upon Anselm ('faith seeking understanding'), presents a solid alternative to both the rationalism and mysticism that dominate much current theology." See *Jesus is Victor! Karl Barth's Doctrine of Salvation* (Nashville: Abingdon, 1976), p. 14. Colin Brown remarks, "There were two links missing from the early Barth's understanding of revelation. One was a failure to appreciate the part Scripture played in revelation. The other was the doctrine of analogy . . .," and concludes, "it was the orthodox writers of the past, not least Anselm of Canterbury . . . who helped Barth towards a deeper, more biblical understanding of God's revelation of himself." Colin Brown, *Karl Barth and the Christian Message* (Chicago: Inter-Varsity Press, 1967), pp. 21, 22. *Anselm: Fides Quaerens Intellectum*, T. H. L. Parker believes, might well be Barth's supreme gift to theological literature. See *Karl Barth* (Grand Rapids: William B. Eerdmans Publishing Co., 1970), p. 70.

/56/ Tillich believes that Barth engages in self-deception in his rejection of the *analogia entis*. *Systematic Theology*, Vol. 2: *Existence and the Christ* (Chicago: University of Chicago Press, 1957), p. 14. Thielicke objects to "ambiguous, strained, and artificial" analogies inadequate for the derivation of political norms. See Helmut Thielicke, *Theological Ethics*, vol. 2: *Politics*, ed. William H. Lazareth (Philadelphia: Fortress Press, 1969), pp. 578f. Emil Brunner agrees with Thielicke that Barth "evidently does not notice that anything and everything can be derived from the principle of analogy: a monarchy just as much as a republic (Christ the King), the totalitarian state, just as much as a state with civil liberties (Christ the Lord of all; man a servant, indeed a slave of Jesus Christ.)." See Brunner's *Dogmatics*, Vol. 2: *The Christian Doctrine of Creation and Redemption*, trans. Olive Wyon (Philadelphia: Westminster Press, 1952), p. 319. Sebastian Matczak sees in Barth's rejection of natural theology an "existentialist fideism." *Karl Barth on God: The Knowledge of the Divine Existence* (New York: St. Paul Publica-

tions, 1962), p. 327. Emphasis on God's transcendence and resulting methodological implications for immanence and for relevant disciplines like
psychology and sociology which the analogy of faith presents are problems
engaged by several thinkers: for a few of these see Clifford Green, "Liberation Theology? Karl Barth on Women and Men," *Union Seminary Quarterly Review* 29 (Spring and Summer 1974):230; Battista Mondin, *The
Principle of Analogy in Protestant and Catholic Theology* (The Hague:
Martinus Nijhoff, 1968), p. 172; and Gordon Watson, "Karl Barth and St.
Anselm's Theological Programme," *Scottish Journal of Theology* 30 (Febru-
ary 1977):42. The Roman Catholic thinker Jerome Hamer critiques sharply
Barth's rejection of the *analogia entis* and adoption of the *analogia fidei*.
Barth's move, Hamer alleges, amounts practically to a rejection of any
human knowledge of God and the Word of God at all. God requisitions
human language for God's thought, insuring complete correspondence on
God's side but a totally nonexistent correspondence on humanity's side.
"Such, for Barth, is analogy. It leaves man to himself . . . in the *analogia
entis* a very imperfect knowledge of God was possible; in the *analogia fidei*
God knows us, but we do not know God." See Jerome Hamer, *Karl Barth*,
trans. Dominic M. Maruca, S. J. (Westminster, Maryland: Newman Press,
1962), p. 71.

/57/   Robert E. Willis, *The Ethics of Karl Barth* (Leiden: E. J. Brill, 1971),
p. 444. Barth's cultural distancing and refusal to admit much of empirical
significance in the theological task and his aloofness from the social and
political sciences and the contributions which those disciplines might have
added to his work have been widely critiqued. A few of those critiques are
contained in: Dale R. Althoff, "Freedom and Love in the Thought of Karl
Barth" (Ph.D. dissertation, Princeton University, 1975); A. M. Fairweather,
*The Word as Truth: A Critical Examination of the Christian Doctrine of
Revelation in the Writings of Thomas Aquinas and Karl Barth* (London:
Lutterworth Press, 1944); Paul Jersild, "Natural Theology and the Doctrine
of God in Albrecht Ritschl and Karl Barth," *The Lutheran Quarterly* 14
(August 1962). In Reinhold Neibuhr, "Barth's East German Letter," *The
Christian Century* 76 (February 11, 1959); Reinhold Niebuhr, *Essays in
Applied Christianity*, ed. D. B. Robertson (New York: Meridian Books,
1959); Reinhold Niebuhr, "The Quality of Our Lives," *The Christian Cen-
tury* 86 (December 31, 1969); here, Niebuhr's view is modified. George
Casalis mentions Barth's rejection of an adequate experience criterion but
emphasizes what few will deny to Barth, i.e., acknowledgement that Barth's
wish was to preserve theology's freedom from acculturation and to protect
its right to speak from within its own viewpoint of faith. *Portrait of Karl
Barth*, trans. with an Introduction by Robert McAfee Brown (Garden City:
Doubleday & Co., 1963).

/58/   Willis, *The Ethics of Karl Barth*, p. 444.

/59/   Ibid., p. 445.

/60/   Althoff, "Freedom and Love in the Thought of Karl Barth," p. iv;
Also, Willis, *Ethics of Karl Barth*, pp. 385f.

/61/   Althoff, pp. 224, 225.

/62/   Ibid., p. 225.

/63/   Ibid., p. 226.

/64/ Ibid., pp. 229, 230. As Althoff concludes that Barth's theology is overcast by a Platonism which obscures the empirical reality of humanity and history, Jürgen Moltmann's voice has been a major one challenging the Idealism which he sees in Barth's theology. Moltmann is joined by, among others, James Livingston, Stanley Hopper, Colin Gunton, David Mueller, and Robert Jenson. These see in Barth's rationalism a jettisoning of empirical history for a history beyond history. See James C. Livingston, *Modern Christian Thought: From the Enlightenment to Vatican II.* (New York: Macmillan Publishing Co., 1971), p. 340; Stanley Romaine Hopper, "The Modern Diogenes: A Kierkegaardian Crotchet," in *Religion and Culture: Essays in Honor of Paul Tillich*, ed. Walter Leibrecht (New York: Harper & Bros., 1959), p. 106; Mueller, *Karl Barth*, p. 153; Colin E. Gunton, *Becoming and Being: The Doctrine of God in Charles Hartshorne and Karl Barth* (Oxford: Oxford University Press, 1978; reprinted, 1980), pp. 182f; Robert Jenson *God After God: The God of the Past and The God of the Future, Seen in the Work of Karl Barth* (Indianapolis: Bobbs-Merrill Co., 1969), p. 153; and Robert Crawford, "The Theological Method of Karl Barth," *Scottish Journal of Theology* 25 (August 1972):332. In *Theology of Hope* and *Trinity and the Kingdom*, Moltmann argues that German Idealism's absolute, identical subject is the basis for Barth's notion of divine self-revelation. See *Theology of Hope: On the Ground and the Implications of a Christian Eschatology* (New York: Harper & Row, 1967), p. 55 and *The Trinity and The Kingdom: The Doctrine of God* (San Francisco: Harper & Row, 1981), p. 139.

/65/ Willis, *Ethics of Karl Barth*, p. 385.

/66/ Ibid., pp. 384, 385.

/67/ For but a few of these divergent interpretations compare: Richard R. Niebuhr, *Resurrection and Historical Reason: A Study of Theological Method* (New York: Charles Scribner's Sons, 1957), pp. 86f; Eberhard Jüngel, *The Doctrine of the Trinity: God's Being Is In Becoming* (Grand Rapids: William B. Eerdmans Publishing Co., 1976), pp. 39f; Hugh Ross Mackintosh, *Types of Modern Theology: Schleiermacher to Barth* (London: Nisbet and Co., 1937; reprint ed., 1945), pp. 301f; Paul L. Lehmann, "The Concreteness of Theology: Reflections on the Conversation Between Barth and Bonhoeffer," in *Footnotes to a Theology: The Karl Barth Colloquium of 1972;* ed. and with an Introduction by Martin Rumscheidt (Corporation for the Publication of Academic Studies in Religion in Canada, 1974), p. 65; von Balthasar, *Karl Barth*, pp. 164f; Robert E. Hood, "The Thorn of Liberalism in Karl Barth," *Anglican Theological Review* 44 (October 1962):413f.

/68/ Paul Jersild, "Natural Theology and the Doctrine of God in Albrecht Ritschl and Karl Barth," *The Lutheran Quarterly* 14 (August 1962): 256; Charles C. West, *Communism and the Theologians: Study of An Encounter* (London: SCM Press, 1958), pp. 313, 314; John Bowden, *Karl Barth* (London: SMC Press, 1971), p. 106; Georges Casalis, *Portrait of Karl Barth*, trans. with an Introduction by Robert McAfee Brown (Garden City: Doubleday & Co., 1963), p. 30; James C. Livingston, *Modern Christian Thought: From the Enlightenment to Vatican II* (New York: Macmillan Publishing Co., 1971), p. 339.

/69/ Roger L. Shinn, "On Rendering to Caesar and to God," *Worldview* 2

(December 1959):11; von Balthasar, *Karl Barth*, pp. 185f; Donald G. Bloesch, *Jesus is Victor! Karl Barth's Doctrine of Salvation* (Nashville: Abingdon, 1976), pp. 16, 17; George S. Hendry, *The Holy Spirit in Chistian Theology* (Philadelphia: Westminster Press, 1965), pp. 109, 110.

/70/   G. C. Berkouwer, *The Triumph of Grace in the Theology of Karl Barth*, trans. Harry R. Boer (Grand Rapids: William B. Eerdmans Co., 1956), p. 237.

/71/   Ibid., p. 250.

/72/   Ibid., p. 253.

/73/   Ibid.

/74/   Berkouwer, *Triumph of Grace*, p. 380.

/75/   Ibid., p. 382.

/76/   Ibid.

/77/   Karl Barth, *Church Dogmatics*, Vol. 1, 1:151.

/78/   Ibid., pp. 151, 152.

/79/   Ibid.

/80/   Ibid., p. 214.

/81/   Ibid., pp. 232, 233.

/82/   Ibid., pp. 256ff.

/83/   Ibid., pp. 257.

/84/   Karl Barth, *Dogmatics in Outline*, trans. S. T. Thomson (New York: Harper & Row, 1959), p. 15.

/85/   Ibid., p. 21.

/86/   Ibid., pp. 15ff.

/87/   Ibid., p. 32.

/88/   Ibid., p. 33.

/89/   Karl Barth, *Church Dogmatics*, Vol. 1, 2:792.

/90/   Ibid., p. 793.

/91/   Richard J. Bernstein, *Praxis and Action: Contemporary Philosophies of Human Activity* (Philadelphia: University of Pennsylvania Press, 1971), p. 302.

/92/   Ibid., p. 303.

/93/   Ibid., p. xi.

/94/   Ibid., p. 44.

/95/   Ibid., p. 76.

/96/   Nicholas Lobkowicz, *Theory and Practice: History of a Concept from Aristotle to Marx* (Notre Dame: University of Notre Dame Press, 1967), p. 61.

/97/   Ibid., p. 215.

/98/   Ibid., p. 276.

/99/   Jon P. Gunnemann, *The Moral Meaning of Revolution* (New Haven: Yale University Press, 1979), p. 2.

/100/   Ibid., p. 8.

/101/   Ibid., p. 27.

/102/   Ibid., p. 146.

/103/   Ibid., p. 172.

/104/   Ibid., pp. 226, 227.

/105/   Frederick Herzog, *Justice Church: The New Function of the Church in North American Christianity* (Maryknoll: Orbis Books, 1980), p. 3.

/106/   Ibid., p. 4.

CHAPTER III

FIDES QUAERENS RATIONEM REDDERE: THE RADICAL BARTH'S NASCENT PRAXIS METHODOLOGY

While in Chapter II analysis of the dominant Anselmian method of reflection on and explication of Scripture and Confession was made, this chapter will investigate the young Barth's employment of an embryonic praxis methodology socially located both with the working people of his parish and in the context of the church's worship. Influenced by a Marxist-informed notion of praxis, that early interplay of action and reflection linked church and world in Barth's Safenwil ministry, fostering a doctrine of the church integrally concerned with economic and social justice as well as spiritual justification. It will be shown that Barth's early method and insights perdured, though eclipsed by the Anselmian method, in his later work, including the *Church Dogmatics*, relativizing to some degree the theoretical concentration of Barth's academic years and offering alternative insights for development.

Brief attention will be paid to Friedrich-Wilhelm Marquardt's thesis that Barth's theology is based on his socialist commitment, and to the controversy occasioned by that surprising contention. Essays and sermons written by Barth during the Safenwil years will be examined for an understanding of the methodology employed and the theology and ecclesiology developed in that decade. Themes expounded in that period will be traced in Barth's subsequent writings in support of the proposal that, although the Anselmian turn eclipsed the Safenwil beginnings, Barth's theology retains a potential which originated in the early focus. That potential, duly actualized, it is argued, can inform crucially a more adequate doctrine of the church by situating the church and theology immediately in concrete history where accountable engagement with and response to that history become a "hermeneutical inevitability" for theological reflection.[1] The church's immersion in historical reality, then, is not a move to be made after theoretical formulation but along with it, each moment informing critically and indispensably the other, it is proposed.

The Marquardt Thesis

Friedrich-Wilhelm Marquardt advanced a thesis in the early seventies which took most Barthian scholars as much by surprise as it did the theological world at large. Marquardt declared that Karl Barth's theology had originated in, and continued even in Barth's latest works to grow out of, his socialist commitment. The radical pastor of Safenwil had come to theology from solidarity with the proletariat of his parish and the Aargau canton. Seeking the "concept of his praxis," Barth had turned to the Bible and the theological task. It was this orientation, Marquardt insisted, which remained throughout Barth's career the pole star of his work.[2]

Barth's theology originated in the context of the objective economic conditions of the proletariat of Safenwil, Marquardt noted. Researching Barth's early records, sermons, speeches, and papers, Marquardt found that Barth's practical involvement with the economic and political issues confronting Safenwil industrial workers, many of whom were his parishioners, was far more than a subsidiary part of his work as a pastor in the decade between 1911–1921. During those years Barth helped to organize three labor unions, participated in constructing the organization structure for the labor movement in the entire Aargau region, conducted classes in which he informed workers regarding economic and political realities facing them, kept abreast of political developments, especially during the war, and collected data for a critical study of the Sulzer munitions factory and the Bally shoe plant, both of which employed many of his parishioners.

Acknowledging that methodologically Barth had many forebears, each of whom helped to fashion in some way the method which Barth employed in Safenwil, Marquardt named Kant, Hegel, Harnack, Hermann, the Blumhardts, and Kutter. "What they contribute, however, is no more than the elements. The real origin of Barth's theology was his theological existence in Safenwil."[3] What is most significant, Marquardt stressed, is that Barth conceptualized from his experience.[4] Retaining from the nineteenth century an experience criterion, Barth approached the theological endeavor from the inside of the workers' situation as he acted in solidarity with those workers. "For him it was not a matter of interpretation but of transformation."[5] Biblical passages were approached not with "isolated religious views and concepts" but with the poor of Safenwil in mind who were themselves the material of Scriptural exegesis.[6] Marquardt argued that Barth's theological corpus is constructed around a "socially reflected concept of God,"[7] a revolutionary, anarchistic God who is Wholly Other in the sense of the content of revolution which is the new age and the new humanity, but not in the sense of ontological transcendence.[8]

What needs to be established here is one point, namely, that Marquardt called the attention of the theological world to the genesis of Barth's theology in the context of the struggle for social justice in his parish. That small segment of the real world became part of Barth's theological criteria, the content of his scriptural exegesis, and the practical involvement to which theological reflection was joined in a uniting of newspaper and Bible.[9]

Research in Barth's *Gesamtausgabe* confirms Marquardt's insights regarding the social genesis of Barth's early theology. On March 16, 1913, Barth preached to his Safenwil parishioners, "The law and spirit of the new life with Jesus means unconditional fraternity and solidarity, unlimited justice and a lasting willingness to help one another."[10] The sermon of June 1 states: "And if the great and earnest movement of socialism arises to overcome the mighty and free the oppressed, it will only succeed in doing so to the same degree that it is able to teach man to be strong at heart and overcome everything fearful in human nature. Only then will it create the world order it seeks. This means that man must be pure in heart, must know and practice what God expects of him. . . . Without this protection against human nature and closeness to God, socialism is nothing more than empty words and affectation."[11] And on June 22, 1913, Barth identified the work of the Redeemer with the removal of social injustice: "(In reference to the living conditions of the proletariat) One must somehow get over the anger. First we must pull down these worker slums and give the people back their air and light and then we can talk about the peace of God and a good and pure life. That is where the Spirit and Might of the Redeemer must come out against sin and that is where we must say: 'We will no longer accept these conditions that give rise to sin.'"[12]

It is not my concern to argue in support of or against Marquardt the nature and extent of Barth's socialism. Marquardt's thesis does require response, however, to particular points made. It is noteworthy that Barth's early theology drew on left-Hegelian and Marxist insights and the notion of praxis deriving from that intellectual source. Marquardt shows that interpretation of Scripture hinged on the reality of contemporary conditions. What Marquardt has done, *with* Barth, is to show us how exegesis actually happens. Translation is always already interpretation. Any honest and aware translator will acknowledge that fact. The concrete conditions of poverty and economic injustice in Safenwil opened the Scriptures to Barth in ways that had not occurred before his encounter and involvement with those realities. Not general or universal human reality but limited, concrete human experiences were theology's material, Barth saw.

This much Marquardt has played a valuable role in helping us to see. Difficulties arise, however, with Marquardt's contention that Barth's work in the *Church Dogmatics* era and his development there of the doctrine of God proceeded according to the measure or rule of socially reflected conceptualization. *Is* the concept of God in the *Church Dogmatics* a socially reflected one, or has Marquardt extrapolated too much from the early Barth to the later Barth and perhaps principally because he has not assessed perspicuously the dependence on Anselm's method? While it can be argued that Barth's socialism continued to be a motif in his theology, the hegemony which the Anselmian method began to assert after Barth's turn toward the Academy is not recognized, it seems. Marquardt appears to be unaware of the methodological shift which occurred at that time and thus of its consequences for Barth's later theology. The doctrine of God and other doctrines of Barth's *Church Dogmatics* are derived primarily from the Anselmian method of reflection on Scripture and Creed. The praxis methodology of the Safenwil era has faded into the background. It is for this reason that Barth's own students were caught with surprise by Marquardt's jolting thesis.

It will be instructive, it seems, to attend to other scholarly responses to Marquardt's controversial work, in particular those of George Hunsinger and Helmut Gollwitzer. Their responses connect with the analysis of Barth's turn to Anselm as discussed in Chapter II.

Before turning to Gollwitzer's and Hunsinger's expositions, however, it is interesting to note that Barthian studies prior to the seventies (and Marquardt's contribution) took little note of the

Safenwil years and the importance of that era in Barth's development.[13] Apparently none of those studies noted the theological
significance of Barth's involvement with social concerns during that
period. After Marquardt's announcement, however, proponents and
antagonists appeared who either agreed or took issue with Marquardt's contention that Barth's socialist commitment informed crucially, both early and late, his theological efforts.[14] Herbert Hartwell
rejected the contextual genesis even of Barth's socialism, not to
mention his theology. "Barth's socialism was . . . but one of the
fruits of his theological exegesis of the Bible and is determined by
that exegesis. It is but the pragmatic application of that exegesis. In
other words, Barth's thought moved not from praxis to theology, but
from the Word of God, that is, from Jesus Christ, to praxis."[15]
Shelley Baranowski, too, viewed the "conceptual priority" of theology as the foundation of Barth's politics, though Baranowski referred to Barth's later political involvement, not to the Safenwil
experience. "The primacy of theology is apparent in both Barth's use
of socialism and in the intersection of Barth's background with his
political environment."[16] According to Markus Barth, his father
rejected a political focus even before *Der Römerbrief*, as early as
1916. At that time, M. Barth argues, K. Barth turned to biblical
exegesis in a quest for "justice and freedom," turning to a "side
totally other than politics, trade-unions. . . ."[17] Markus Barth does
not seem to regard that quest for justice and freedom as a socialist
quest.

Critical Responses to the Marquardt Thesis: Helmut Gollwitzer

A major voice in agreement with Marquardt, however, has
been that of Helmut Gollwitzer. Arguing in tandem with Marquardt, Gollwitzer mentions Barth's trade union work, his organization of strikes, his speeches delivered in behalf of the Social Democratic party, and his challenges to the factory entrepreneurs of his
community. Agreeing, too, with Marquardt that Barth's socialist
concerns persisted into his later work, Gollwitzer nonetheless sees,
as Marquardt does not seem to, a diminution of that focus in the
Church Dogmatics period. In answer to his own question concerning the reasons for this recession into the background of what
had originally stood out prominently, Gollwitzer proffers two possi-

ble answers, namely, Barth's disenchantment with European socialist parties owing to their participation in the First World War,
and his disappointment with his liberal teachers' support of the war
manifesto of Kaiser Wilhelm II. Those events, Gollwitzer believes,
prompted Barth to search for a more adequate theological base.[18]
Assuming with Barth the need for more rigorous construction,
Gollwitzer asks, "Why did Barth not address his new role and his
new audiences at the same time as an explicitly socialist thinker and
speaker?" Gollwitzer suggests several factors accountable for the
quietism which now marked Barth's socialism, e.g., Barth's need to
devote his time to preparing himself for his academic responsibilities, his early reluctance as a Swiss to interject himself into
German affairs, his disapproval of much that passed for socialism but
which was mere talk of world improvement, and, most importantly,
as already noted, the need for a theological foundation which would
give substance to socialist aims and activity. These, Gollwitzer
claims, turned Barth away from prominent socialist involvement and
toward biblical exegesis.[19]

Gollwitzer believes that Barth's turn toward the academy and
the *analogia fidei* originated in an intention to renew the church and
to reclaim its transformed and transforming nature. "He sought
tendencies that stood opposed, as he did not hesitate to say, to the
church's embourgeoisment. What seemed to many a self-contained
intellectual work, a mere interpretation, was always reinterpretation
for the sake of transformation—of the church as well as the world.
His work was always directed toward a new Christian praxis, and
indeed toward none other than that which he engaged in at Safenwil."[20]

Gollwitzer has seen more clearly than others the meaning of
Barth's socialist involvement for a provoking/transforming church.
His insistence that Barth's turn toward the academy was for a solid
doctrine of the church committed to social concern is helpful for its
focus on the centrality of the dual and complementary concerns of
ecclesiology and method which informed Barth's decision. Although
this thesis argues that the methodological turn made at that time
eclipsed what needs now to be reclaimed and developed anew,
Gollwitzer's insight points in the same general direction, e.g., toward the reclamation of a doctrine of the church which understands
itself as immersed with God in world and history.

Gollwitzer notes that social justice stood to the "decisive

word" as circumference to center or effect to cause in Barth's post-Safenwil theology. In explication, he adduces the *Church Dogmatics* 1, 2. There, Barth's unity of theology and ethics and of Gospel and law appears. "This insight was nothing but a theologically clarified resumption of the unity perceived in Safenwil between the kingdom of God and socialism."[21] Barth's turn toward analogy, Gollwitzer asserts, was the "breakthrough" which he had lacked in Safenwil. The *analogia fidei* made possible the elucidation of the "ineluctable momentum leading from the socialism of God's kingdom to action within the socialist movement. . . ."[22] At another place, Gollwitzer affirms, "That against which and for which God struggles, according to the gospel, is that against which and for which . . . we, too, must struggle. That constitutes the practical shape of the analogy—the *analogia fidei*—on which he was always to insist."[23] Contra Berkouwer, Gollwitzer sees in Barth's reclamation of the Reformation doctrine of grace a revolutionary import which, far from denying humanity's historical role in God's work, is the presupposition and empowerment of that divine-human struggle.[24]

Still, Gollwitzer is bothered by the fact that Barth himself did not make explicit what others are now discovering in his work. Why was not the social justice commitment more obvious? If, as Gollwitzer believes with Marquardt, Barth wanted the entire corpus of his work to be understood as a development and refinement of what had begun in Safenwil, why did Barth himself not make that central fact so obvious as to preclude the eruption of a controversy? Gollwitzer again offers possible answers to his questions. Among those were Barth's rejection of liberalism with which Religious Socialism was connected, his need to devote himself to the "subject matter" of the church, an inadequate understanding of the social presuppositions of state and politics owing to his indifference toward sociological input, an "unavoidable" withdrawal from socialist activity into the academy owing to modern society's division of labor, and an embourgeoisment which Barth's entry into the university occasioned.[25] What Gollwitzer does not account for is why turning to theological elucidation of the subject matter of the church also meant a turning away from practical involvement. He fails, as well, to explain why an emphasis on biblical exegesis required a concomitant departure from social location with those struggling for justice. Even if finding and laying "a solid foundation for Christian thought and action" mandated Barth's new role as a professor of theology, and even if those professorial duties now constituted his "political task," as Gollwitzer claims, those facts still fail to explain fully the methodological shift from explicit social location with the poor to an Anselmian reflection which excepts a criterion of experience. The division of labor explanation does not fully hold; Gollwitzer's own theological work denies that supposition.

Gollwitzer suggests that Barth's turn may have been to witness to the church's central role as the revolutionary agent of socialist society and to develop a theological grounding for that reality. It is in this sense that Barth turned, then, to a church theology. Gollwitzer has sharp criticism, however, for the manner in which Barth's ecclesiology ultimately shaped up. Granting that it is through the miracle of the Holy Spirit that the empirical church becomes the people of God, Gollwitzer charges Barth with failing to say strongly enough that "this trust does not allow us to make things easy, . . . The liberating Word of God is no magic formula which changes everything with one blow. What the Word of God changes consists in the fact that it creates the readiness for change, that it liberates to this readiness."[26]

Barth's final hope, Gollwitzer claims, was in renewed preaching which his theology was developed to support and which would, by the power of the Holy Spirit, renew and invigorate the church and thence the world. Barth contented himself, Gollwitzer alleges, with a "one-sided focus" on the sermon as his hope for freeing both church and society from embourgeoisment. For that reason, Gollwitzer believes that he detects a residue of Idealism in Barth's work. In other words, the power of ideas and right theology constructed on those ideas comprise the possibility of right "praxis."[27]

What Gollwitzer does not seem to attend to is the significance of the Anselmian work for Barth's apparent one-sidedness. His affirmation of Barth's turn toward the *analogia fidei* suggests a lack of critical reflection concerning Barth's methodology centering in *fides quaerens intellectum*. Problematical, as well, is Gollwitzer's use of the term "praxis." For him, as for George Hunsinger, praxis seems to mean practical application, or the practice of the Christian life. The *hermeneutical* significance of social location with the poor is not obviously a part of that definition. Both thinkers' acceptance of the Anselmian turn seems to be at fault. Hence, an understanding of a praxis methodology which consists of active reflection and reflective action in social location with the poor and the church, and accountable to both, is not fully fleshed out, at least in this essay.

Critical Responses to the Marquardt Thesis: George Hunsinger

A particularly able respondent to the Marquardt thesis has been George Hunsinger. It is in that context that Hunsinger's engagement with the Anselm question discussed in Chapter II arose. The subsequent discussion offered here is an enlargement of the one presented earlier. Agreeing that Barth's later theology was decisively influenced by his socialist ideas and activity, Hunsinger takes Marquardt's thesis a step further; it was the impetus of his early socialist views that propelled Barth to a resolution of the theology-ethics hiatus in the adoption of the Anselmian methodology. If Hunsinger is correct in his analysis of how Barth reached the Anselmian solution, major questions revolve around the adequacy of that "solution," even as Chapter II has shown.

Agreeing with Marquardt that Barth's view of God was a transformationist view strongly realist-oriented, Hunsinger demurs with other aspects of Marquardt's doctrine of God, seeing in it a reduction to political function. Still, Hunsinger agrees that Barth's doctrine of God emerged from a socialist context and adduces several early essays as evidence.[28] Believing that he detects in Barth's early thought vestiges of Ritschlian moralism, Hunsinger attests, nonetheless, that "from his earliest essays to his final volumes of dogmatics, [Barth] desired above all else to work out a viable theological solution to the problems of theory and praxis."[29] (Again, praxis, as Hunsinger understands it, seems to be practical or political involvement.) That is what Hunsinger wishes to substantiate; he develops his essay in order to answer *how* Barth related theology and politics. His answer, curiously, is: Anselm.

Acknowledging a dependence on Hans Frei, Hunsinger traces in Barth's early essays a growing discomfort with liberal theology's experiential and historical relativism and with its inadequacy as a theoretical ground for the socialism of God's kingdom. In a question that suggests an understanding of theological method as theory first and application devolving from theory, Hunsinger asks regarding liberalism's relativism and its undermining of universality, "If this [liberal relativism] was the dilemma of modern theology, [as Barth found it] then what theoretical content remained for praxis?"[30] What Barth sought in 1909, 1910, and 1914, Hunsinger declares, was a "theoretical framework" universally valid and adequate to ground the "praxis of God's Kingdom."[31] Indeed, the assumption of pastoral duties, the subsequent involvement in socialist activity in Safenwil, and the relationship which Barth discerned there between church and world necessitated that new framework. A problem emerged for Barth, Hunsinger claims, in reconciling "logically independent" assertions about God's love with affirmations of religious experience in a way that did not make the former derivative from the latter. Barth wished, Hunsinger states, to say that God's independent sovereignty is also a concrete sovereignty which includes a political and external reference, and to say it free of liberal theology and liberal theory.[32] Barth's search for a new conceptual framework was "consummated," Hunsinger declares, with the Anselm book. There, Barth found what he had sought, "a radically new theological relationship between 'theory' and 'praxis' such that the sole foundation of both would be the concrete sovereignty of God. God's sovereignty alone becomes the concrete ground, limit, and orientation of all human thought and action."[33] The God than whom nothing greater can be thought was the Sovereign free of all relativisms. In Jesus Christ, God's sovereignty was made concrete.

What Hunsinger fails to account for is how the need to divest Barth's work of liberal theology's excessive reliance on subjectivism and relativism necessitated, in turn, a rejection of a methodology in social location with the poor. The search for a concept of God not derived from self-understanding alone could have led to *prima Scriptura* with a viable praxis criterion still operant—revelation *and* experience rather than, with Anselm, revelation and reflection on it. It is questionable whether, as Hunsinger claims, a resolution of the theology-ethics hiatus was found in the adoption of the Anselmian method. Frei and Hunsinger see some things but not others. Barth's striving toward a concrete, politically relevant theology and ecclesiology is seen, but apparently not the methodology in social context which relativizes the Anselmian method of reflection on Scripture and Confession and resolves the theology-ethics hiatus through that hermeneutical shift.

Problems attend the Anselmian turn. Does the God of the ontological argument provide an "adequate basis" for "work for a really better world"? If so, how? History shows rather, it seems, that Idealistic notions of God are not conducive to concrete involvement in world. Barth's growing conviction that "God, not the world, is the primary reality" could have led, and did, to a strong dependence on revelation; but why on Anselm as well? It is not self-evident that the Anselmian turn was implicated in that conviction.

A look at Barth's pastoral work in Safenwil and his involvement in the economic and political struggles of his parishioners will be informative for an understanding of the methodology begun there. It appears that the Barthian scholars whom I have researched during this study have not identified fully the importance of Safenwil: the birth of a methodology in social location with the poor in the context of the church's worship has been obscured even for them by the turn to Anselm, it would seem. Most crucially, the implications and potential of what happened in Safenwil for a doctrine of the church concerned with history need now to be received and developed.

The Safenwil Years: Genesis of Fides Quaerens Rationem Reddere

Barth's biographer Eberhard Busch has documented the fervor with which the young pastor engaged his duties in Safenwil. Introduced there to the "real problems of real life,"[34] Barth added to his theological books new studies in economics, the *Swiss Trade Union Journal,* and the *Textile Worker.* The input of economics, a discipline outside theology, was allowed to inform Barth's pastoral work. More than three-fourths of the wage-earners in Safenwil were employed in industrial work; Barth organized those workers and gave them instruction in economic theory and practical application. He lectured to the Workers' Association and studied factory legislation, trade union tactics, and insurance.[35] It was at that time that Barth delivered a speech entitled "Jesus Christ and the Movement for Social Justice." A reading of that speech shows that even as early as 1911 Barth's christological center was established. Socialism *rightly understood* is not, Barth argued, an independent social phenomenon or ideology, but *God's movement* for social justice. Barth employed the metaphor "Jesus Christ is the movement for social justice."[36] This was not a statement of naivete as some have seen it, but an affirmation that true social justice is grounded in Jesus Christ and draws its meaning from that christological center. This was the corrective that Barth offered to the socialist movement burgeoning around him. Though some have read liberal immanentism and reductionism in Barth's metaphor, doing so obscures important meanings intended by Barth then, further developed in *Der Römerbrief* and other early essays, and present even in the *Church Dogmatics.* Rooted in Christ, God's movement for social justice is "self-contained and independent of the behavior of socialists and the tactics of socialist parties." Standing "completely *beyond* the controversy of the day," God's movement for social justice, far from being a "profanation of the eternal," Barth argued, is "the inner connection that exists between what is eternal, permanent, and general in modern social democracy and the eternal Word of God, which is Jesus become flesh."[37] That standing beyond the controversy of the day did not imply a distancing from the concrete struggle but rather its christological grounding in the larger reality of God's justice concern.

God's socialism is both a "movement from below," seen from the human side, and a "movement from above," from God's side. As a movement from below, it is a movement of the poor, the economically oppressed, and finds its counterpart in Jesus' own solidarity with the am h'aretz of Palestine. ". . . It must strike everyone who reads his New Testament without prejudice that . . . He himself [Jesus] came from the lowest social class of the Jewish people at that time. . . . One cannot reach lower down the social scale in the choice of one's associates than Jesus did. And I repeat: That was not a cheap pity from above to below, but the eruption of a volcano from below to above."[38] The movement from below, Barth emphasized further, is a way of life, not a system of ideas. Nor is it a spiritual movement alone. Barth pinpointed what he perceived as the church's cardinal misconception: "Religion beforehand and afterward remains a matter between God and the soul, the soul and God, and only that."[39] Barth had heard this emphasis on God and soul in Harnack's teaching. Stressing, certainly, that Jesus Christ means bringing God to the soul and the soul to God, Barth emphasized as well the social God of solidarity, the one to whom we pray not "my father" but "our Father." This God cares about the whole of life, the external and material as well as the internal and spiritual, the earthly and immanent as well as the heavenly and transcendent. Barth's criticism of a church which has cared for the spiritual and neglected the material is scathing:

> . . . perhaps nowhere else has Christianity fallen farther away from the spirit of her Lord and Master than precisely in this estimation of the relation between spirit and matter, inner and outer, heaven and earth. One might well say that for eighteen hundred years the Christian church, when confronted by social misery, has always referred to the Spirit, to the inner life, to

heaven. . . . She has not said that social misery *ought not to be*
in order then to summon all her power for the sake of this
conviction that *it ought not to be*. . . . She has accepted social
misery as an accomplished fact in order to talk about the Spirit,
to cultivate the inner life, and to prepare candidates for the
kingdom of heaven. That is the great, momentous apostasy of
the Christian church, her apostasy from Christ.[40]

What is significant in this avowal is the presupposition that the
church's concern for social justice is of the very *substance* of its
intended nature and, thus, not an implied task but a fundamental
one. It is only because the church has departed from its intended
nature and failed its quintessential task that it is *apostate from,* or
alienated from, the Christ who identifies with the suffering. The
substance of the church of Jesus Christ is transformation—of the
soul, of the church itself, and of a world of social misery into a world
of justice, Barth argued. The movement for social justice, then,
"does not stand *beside* faith in God the Father in heaven as something added onto it afterward [as implication]; rather, it is inexorably
bound to it [as substance]."[41]

In social location with the poor of Safenwil, Barth saw the
fallacy of a spirit/body dichotomy. There, with those who suffer most
from that fallacy, Barth perceived "not two worlds, but the one
reality of the kingdom of God."[42] "'The Word became flesh (John
1:14), and not the other way around!" Hence, the movement for
social justice is a movement from above to below. As Barth stated it,
". . . it is not that man 'goes to heaven,' but rather that God's
kingdom *comes to us* in matter and on earth."[43] Already here, Barth
issued a warning reminder to Religious Socialism concerning its
need to orient itself first of all in God's justice movement.

In social location with the industrial workers of his parish,
Barth saw the significance of Jesus' own location with the poor of his
day. Because of the primal importance of that location, interpretations of Jesus' life and work which understood him principally as
teacher or pastor whose purpose was to inform people concerning
right belief, Barth argued, had missed Jesus' "essential effec-
tiveness."[44] Before all else, Jesus was a healer, a transformer of life.
Barth suggested that it is to this reality that the church should look
for an understanding of its own mission. Hence, what Frederick
Herzog has termed Christopraxis is that which Barth indicated as
the church's norm.[45] In social location with the disadvantaged and

with Jesus Christ as the church's norm, the church realizes its
communal nature and individual members see that they are communal persons in solidarity with *all* their neighbors.[46]

With the insight that Jesus and church mean social location
with the poor in communal solidarity, Barth saw that the Spirit
means provocation/transformation. Jesus, Barth showed, was and is
concerned with transformation as opposed to disclosure. Working
from the inside out, from changed persons to a changed world, the
Spirit creates new persons *for the purpose of* creating a new world.

Although appreciative of Social Democracy's concern for "the
weak people, those who live in the darkness of society,"[47] Barth was
very much aware, even in those early years, of Social Democracy's
weaknesses. He saw its liberal optimism and its dependence on
human strength and initiative. ". . .The present-day social democracy still has infinitely much to learn from Jesus. It must come to the
insight that we first need men of the future to create the state of the
future, not the reverse."[48] It should not be overlooked that, in
Barth's view, the men of the future are created *so that* the state of the
future will then be created. Individual transformation is not complete in and of itself without the transformation of the whole of social
and communal life. For this transformation to occur, God's act is
primary, not humanity's. Because he saw this fact so clearly, Barth
found much in Social Democracy of which he was critical and with
which he could not align himself. It was "out beyond themselves"
that Barth set himself the task of leading the Social Democrats. On
December 7, 1914, Barth wrote to his friend Eduard Thurneysen:

> Perhaps it will interest you to know what I had to say to the
> Social Democrats in Küngoldingen yesterday. In the discussion
> one man said very pleasantly that what I had described to them
> was indeed the mind of Jesus and his disciples, but did I not
> know of another, easier way for them in view of the imperfec-
> tion of the world and humanity?! A trade-unionist instructed
> me concerning the impossibility of 'waiting' and the necessity
> of the proletarian battle!! Our difficulty in addressing the Social
> Democrats became clear to me once more: either one strength-
> ens them in their party loyalty by providing a religious founda-
> tion and all manner of Christian aims for their political ethos—
> or one tries to lead them out beyond themselves and thereby,
> as I had the impression yesterday, one lays upon them a burden
> which is too heavy for many of them to bear. In spite of
> everything, the latter is the right thing to do if one is going to
> give such lectures at all.[49]

In another letter to Thurneysen on February 5, 1915, Barth referred to the criticisms which he had publicly directed toward the party and reiterated again the "essential orientation" which surpassed all party aims and to which he felt that he could now remain faithful without being swayed by ideological views contradictory to that orientation, as he might have been had he joined the party before that time.[50] Three years later, Barth saw still more clearly the need to avoid Ragaz's excesses and to stress the primacy of God's transforming activity. A more decisive turn toward the New Testament was required, Barth saw. "What have we to set over against the flood of 'right words' which soon will come pouring out triumphantly from the Ragaz people? If only we had been converted to the Bible *earlier* so that we would now have solid ground under our feet!"[51]

Continuing after the 1911 speech to discuss socialism in restaurants, sports halls, and school classrooms, among other places, Barth collected a dossier on the "workers' question" in the winter of 1913–14.[52] That same winter he spoke on "The Gospel and Socialism" and "The New Factory Act." In June and July of 1914, Barth delivered sermons in which he stressed God's centrality in the coming-to-be of a new world. Busch mentions a growing preoccupation in this period with the question of God. A marriage of theology and ethics, Barth was coming to see ever more clearly, depended on God first, authorizing and energizing men and women to join in God's justice work. That authorization was received, furthermore, in social location with those for whom God's justice work is expended— those who have no justice, the forgotten ones whom God does not forget.[53] Influenced by Christoph Blumhardt and disappointed by Ragaz's one-sided activism, "For Barth, the question of according God a place of central importance was becoming more and more fundamental."[54] A doctrine of God and a solution to social injustice which combined the inner and the outer, the spiritual and the material, and healed the theology-ethics hiatus, Barth saw, were not to be found in his liberal heritage, in Religious Socialism, or within the workers' struggle itself.[55] A new theological method had been born. Beginning in the context of the struggle for social justice by the poor within his parish who also filled the pews of his church and worshipped with him, Barth allowed those poor and their suffering to become the social location informing his theological work. Turning to the Scripture *with* those strugglers and reflecting as he acted with them to forge a just society, the young Barth employed a praxis methodology which I have chosen to term *fides quaerens rationem reddere*, faith seeking accountability which then understands. Beginning with the presupposition that "God is," Barth moved to the New Testament and a study of *Romans*.

Safenwil Insights in Process

Like "Jesus Christ and the Movement for Social Justice," *Der Römerbrief*, the *Epistle to the Romans*, was written in social location with the factory wage-earners of Safenwil. Turning to the *Romans* epistle in company with those strugglers, Barth's hermeneutic included a criterion of experience which influenced what he read there. Hence, Barth's exegesis of *Romans* allowed a meeting of interpreter and text which his later methodology and hermeneutic would not. Reflecting *with* the people of his parish in the context of "a real world with real problems," and in accountability to those "small people" with whom he both reflected and acted, Barth saw that the link between theology and ethics and the resolution of the hiatus separating them consist of the suffering poor of this world with whom we stand because God stands there first and authorizes us to join God in that place:

> God is truly a God of the Jews and of the heathen, but not a God of the rich *and* the poor and not a God of the great and the small. He is, without doubt, exclusively a God of the small people. That which is high to men is an outrage to God. He deposes the master from his seat and lifts up the despised. The hungry He fills and the rich He leaves empty. . . . I can indeed be a Jew to the Jews and a Greek to the Greeks, but not a master to the masters. . . . Rather, against all who wish in this world to be great, I must take my stand with the small people with whom God begins.[56]

Indeed, the church's place is on the far left with those ones.[57] It is "the world as such and not some uniquely sacred sphere into which God's kingdom is coming."[58]

In the first edition of *Romans*, Hunsinger believes, Barth was concerned to develop a realistic eschatology of Scripture adequate to sustain his political socialism. Exegetically and conceptually a firm ground was needed for a theology rooted in "the praxis of God." Only then would adequate norms for human action and reflection be found.[59] Barth sought, Hunsinger affirms, the unconditional ground of God's eternal relationship to humanity. He found that objective and irreversible ground in the doctrine of the electing God.[60] In God's free act of grace, God elects concretely in Jesus Christ a new world and a new social reality which is His kingdom. God becomes the Agent of a society wholly different from humanity's structures of oppression and injustice.[61]

A lecture given in 1916 in the Town Church of Aargau entitled "The Righteousness of God" proved to be a forecast of Barth's thought in the 1919 edition of *Romans*. God's prior righteous activity and humanity's listening in conscience to God's voice, Barth emphasized, were necessary prerequisites to human revolution and reform. Even here, Barth referred to God's will as a Wholly Other.[62] Also, in 1916, in "The Strange New World Within the Bible," Barth stressed that the Bible concerns God first and not humanity. "In it the chief consideration is not the doings of man but the doings of God—not the various ways which we may take if we are men of good will, but the power out of which good will must first be created."[63] God's Spirit is the creator of the new earth as well as the new heaven, and thus, the creator, too, of "new politics."[64] It is God's righteousness which is established on earth in the midst of human unrighteousness. The theological ground of social justice action Barth located in God's prior justice action, even in this early essay.

The Tambach lecture in 1919 marked, as Hunsinger and others have noted, a conceptual break with Religious Socialism: "The Christian's Place in Society" contains no reference to an organic eschatology but introduces instead a dialectical one, i.e., God's movement is not a horizontally immanent one, but a vertically inbreaking one in the resurrection of Jesus Christ. To participate in that movement, then, is to move from death to life in God's redemption. Hunsinger traces a development of Barth's dialectical method from the first edition of *Romans* to the second. Intervening between the two is this lecture of 1919. Here, Barth radicalizes the dialectic between all human movements and God's movement, erasing any direct lines from the one to the other. The relationalism or immanent historical process of the first-edition *Romans* has been dissolved.[65]

Robert Willis discusses a use of Hegelian dialectic in the Tambach lecture to affirm the preeminence of God's activity. In the light of God's revelation of the resurrection in Jesus Christ, present moments are merely that in the total movement of God from creation to redemption, the total unfolding of God's kingdom. In transition from death to life, from human injustice to God's justice, individuals and society move within God's total movement in history. On that basis, the human task is both to affirm society and to challenge it, recognizing that God is present there as ground and also as limit; this is the nature of the dialectic. Willis explains that dialectic allows Barth to affirm a continuity between creation and redemption which includes society's structures and movements.[66] Since the thesis consisting of the institutions of established society does not arise from human efforts, neither does the antithesis which denies corrupt structures. Both are located originally in God's creative and redemptive work. Because society is itself first caused by God, humanity's first obligation is to affirm God's presence there; only on the basis of that affirmation can one then move to a denial of that which in society is not of God. "For when we find ourselves in God, we find ourselves committed to the task of affirming him in the world as it is and not in a false transcendent world of dreams. Only out of such an affirmation can come that genuine, radical denial which is manifestly the meaning of our movements of protest."[67] Our joining God's march in history "necessitates," Barth insists, "our advancing from the defense to the attack, from the yes to the no, from a naive acceptance to a criticism of society."[68] As it is God's antithesis in which we join, so too, it will be God's synthesis which will resolve society's unrighteousness. The Christian's place in society, then, is to "follow attentively what is done by God."[69]

Barth's dissatisfaction with the first-edition *Romans* derived largely from the vestiges of Ritschlianism which had understood God's kingdom as an organic process overcoming the world's corruption, Hunsinger states. A full break occurred with the second-edition *Romans*. Hunsinger notes that, "In the 1919 edition of *Romans*, Barth had conceived of God's kingdom as an organic, yet dialectical, process within the world. This conception had implied a relational nexus between God's kingdom and external historical experience. God had been conflated with revolution; Jesus Christ, with eschatology; eschatology, with an immanent historical process."[70] These "relational conflations" needed to be excised, Barth saw, "to provide socialist politics with its proper theological ground."[71] Barth's statement made in a letter to the entrepreneur Hüssy in 1911 regarding the "moral progress of humanity" seems to accord with Hunsinger's thesis.[72]

According to Hunsinger, the second edition of *Romans* was begun in Safenwil in 1920 and completed at Göttingen in 1921.[73]

Eberhard Busch, however, reports that Barth wrote the second-edition *Romans* between the fall of 1920 and the summer of 1921; Barth moved to Göttingen in October of 1921.[74] Marquardt insists that the Wholly Other of the second-edition *Romans* is not the abstract deity of Idealism but the One who is wholly other than humanity's sinfulness, and wholly new in the kingdom which God inaugurates. The language of metaphysical Idealism in the second-edition *Romans* only *seems* to indicate an anti-revolutionary turn, he believes.[75]

Agreeing with Marquardt that Barth's conception of God as Wholly Other was one of primary social meaning rather than metaphysical significance, Hunsinger states, "In the second edition of *Romans*, Barth recast his radical theology as dialectically as possible. His basic intention remained the same: All human thought and action was to be grounded, limited, and oriented solely in terms of God's sovereignty. What changed was the method by which Barth sought to carry out this intention. The change in method was, in part, a direct result of political experience."[76] Now, Barth saw that God's sovereignty was more than the absolute ground of theology and ethics; God was also the limit or "Krisis." Only a dialectical method could express that reality, he believed. Barth's dialectical method functioned in two ways. Positively, God's revolution functioned as ground and orientation of humanity's penultimate revolutions and, negatively, as the elimination of Religious Socialism's immanentism. Humanity now was enjoined to wait upon God's prior activity and to align with that divine work rather than rushing headlong into humanly initiated revolutions scarcely, if at all, oriented in God's prior initiative. The impression of political complacency which many drew from the second-edition *Romans*, Hunsinger argues, was not one intended by Barth, but one which left its indelible mark nonetheless. The weaknesses which Barth later identified in this edition of *Romans*, e.g., the radical transcendence of God and the difficulty with affirming the Incarnation, as well as the philosophical language and assumptions generally, hindered an understanding of the political component in Barth's thought at this period.[77]

Whether Hunsinger is correct to insist with Marquardt that the second edition of *Romans* represents a continued search for a doctrine of God adequate to ground socialist activity, there is, to be sure, a difference between the second-edition *Romans* and the 1911 speech to the Aargau workers. For instance, how is this to be understood: "Our whole concern with the world of time and of things and of men, our continuous business with what the world offers us, is our preoccupation with the fallen Adam."[78] Is it super-history of which Barth speaks when he writes of the "relation between God and man . . . where there is no history to record, because it only occurs, and occurs eternally"?[79] Is it accomplished history of which Barth writes later in that volume: "The action of God is the Cross, the Passion: not the quantity of suffering, large or small, which must be borne with greater or with lesser fortitude and courage, as though the quantity of our pains and sufferings would in itself occasion our participation in the glory of God."[80] What *is* the status and significance of these pains and sufferings and how *does* the "quantity of suffering" connect with the action of God, as Barth views it here? One is reminded of Robert Willis' suggestion that, for Barth, humanity's single ethical act is repentance.[81] Barth states that, "The *works* which a man does in his concrete and visible life are no more identical with his *work* which is righteous before God than are the fetters with which a prisoner is tightly bound . . . with the real limbs of his body. . . . The true ground of boasting before God, however, is repentance."[82]

Still, Barth insists, "Grace means: *thy will be done in earth as it is in heaven.* Consequently, grace, as the existential relation between God and man, is bound to move from the indicative of the divine truth concerning men to the imperative by which the divine reality makes its demand upon them."[83] Quite obviously, Barth sees the indicative of repentance inseparably bound to the imperative of ethical obedience. And here, Barth sounds very much like the Safenwil pastor of earlier days: "God can be known only when men of all ranks are grouped together upon one single step; when those of the highest rank regard 'suffering with the whole social order of their age and bearing its heavy burden' . . . as the noblest achieve-ment of which they are capable; when the rich . . . themselves become poor and the brothers of the poor."[84]

It may well be that theologically and conceptually a bend in the road had been taken with the second-edition *Romans* which would find its destination finally in the Anselm work. It is certain that Barth himself felt a growing discomfiture with the second-edition *Romans* commentary. In the prefaces to the six editions he consistently disavowed his current stance with his former one. For instance, in the preface to the sixth edition, Barth wrote, "The two years and a half which have passed since the publication of the fifth edition of this book have increased the distance separating me from what I had originally written. . . . A great deal of the scaffolding of the book was due to my own particular situation at the time and also to the general situation. This would have to be pulled down. . . . Those who read the book must also bear in mind the quite simple fact that I am now seven years older, and that all our exercise books obviously require correcting."[85] Also, "When I look back at the book, it seems to have been written by another man to meet a situation belonging to a past epoch. . . . They ought not to bind the Professor at Bonn too tightly to the Pastor of Safenwil. . . ."[86]

Fides Quaerens Rationem Reddere in the Later Works

What Barth had learned in the immediate social context of the labor struggle in Safenwil, however, was never obliterated altogether from his theological view. There, Barth had known by name people who were hungry and powerless; he had witnessed human want in the lives of his own friends. Even after his move to Göttingen, Barth wrote to Thurneysen on December 18, 1922:

> The constantly deteriorating condition of the economy here, . . . is sufficient to depress me. . . . Really one asks himself at times whether it would perhaps be more sensible to throw the whole theological business in the corner . . . and transform oneself into a social worker who would bring as many Swiss francs as possible into the country and then disperse them to the different organizations and institutions for distribution. . . . The dollar fell in a few days from 8,000 to almost 5,000 as a result of American hopes. Will it continue? One watches almost breathlessly; but in the meantime the people hunger and freeze notoriously in thousands; tuberculosis and strange hunger sicknesses get the upper hand; students have to quit in the middle of the semester and take up another calling because they have not the means to go on. It is very bad.[87]

Although the movement begun in the second-edition *Romans* was climaxed, perhaps, in *Anselm: Fides Quaerens Intellectum,* the praxis methodology of the Safenwil years continued, at least to some degree, to inform Barth's later work and to offer potential for a church-world relation like that described and practiced in Safenwil. In the thirties and the era of National Socialism, Barth revealed that his concern was for more than the church's institutional and doctrinal integrity alone, and that human freedom was a pivotal concern as well.[88] In 1946, Barth spoke a prophetic word of genuine commitment to the political struggle to fashion a just world for men and women. In the essay "Christian Community and Civil Community," Barth appealed to the church to take the initiative, seeing "that it does not make a habit of coming on the scene too late, of entering the fray only when its opinions no longer involve any particular influence."[89] Stressing the theme of social justice, Barth called again, as at Safenwil, for the church's commitment to "the lower and lowest levels of human society."[90] In Ch. 17 of "Christian Community and Civil Community," Barth identified the marginalized ones, the non-persons of our world, as "always" the church's "primary and particular concern." In that chapter, too, he denounced privilege for the rich and powerful and named social justice the goal toward which any one of several "socialistic possibilities" might be directed. The choice, Barth insisted, should always be made according to the "greatest measure of social justice" guaranteed by it.[91] And in 1956, Barth told Margareta Deschner, "I decided for theology because I felt a need to find a better basis for my [the church's] social action."[92]

The *Church Dogmatics* contains, though at sparse intervals in terms of its vast corpus, eloquent and unimpeachably sincere statements regarding the contextuality and concreteness of God's love and justice and, hence, of humanity's and the church's. Love is particular love for particular persons. It is not extended to a generalized humanity, but to one's "fellow-man who stands to him in a definite historical relationship or context."[93] In Vol. 4, 2, Barth warned that the attempt to universalize love of the neighbor by transposing it to love of humanity itself is not an incremental step but one that vitiates and confuses love.[94]

In Vol. 3, 1, Barth denied universal truth separated from its historical location.[95] In a section of 4, 2 entitled "The Act of Love," Barth insisted that it is because universal love transposed to theoretics is meaningless apart from love conceived in action that such universalized love is not biblical love. The God who loves by acting defines real love. "It is the concrete and not the abstract loving of someone who is concrete and not abstract. In correspondence to the love of God, it is a loving which chooses and differentiates."[96] Differentiating between the poor and the rich, God chooses the outcast and wretched. As in the first edition of *Romans*, Barth described in Vol. 2, 1 a God who takes sides:

. . . it is important to notice that the people to whom God in
his righteousness turns as helper and Savior is everywhere in
the Old Testament the harassed and oppressed people of Israel, which, powerless in itself, has no rights, and is delivered
over to the superior force of its enemies; and in Israel it is
especially the poor, the widows and orphans, the weak and
defenseless. . . . God always takes his stand unconditionally
and passionately on this side and on this side alone, against the
lofty and on behalf of the lowly; against those who already enjoy
right and privilege and on behalf of those who are denied it and
deprived of it. [97]

God in divine righteousness has stood on the side of us in our
impoverished and wretched condition, in our hopeless inability to
secure right for ourselves, and has procured that right for us. That
full intervention on the part of God for us requires that the church
intervene in behalf of those to whom right and privilege have been
denied—as God has acted graciously and justly for us, the church is
to do the same for others. Because God's righteousness has procured
justice for us, a political responsibility is delegated to redeemed
humankind to procure right and justice wherever fellow humans are
oppressed and deprived. To reject that mission, Barth warned, is to
reject divine justification itself. Correspondence to God's own gracious act is the criterion of all humanity's efforts to create a world of
peace and human rights. [98]

And, as in Safenwil, Barth affirmed that God is even now
making things different. The proleptic institution of God's kingdom
in Christ is the sole basis for a just order among people. That "great
alteration of the human situation" in Jesus Christ "can and should
demonstrate . . . that there are other possibilities, not merely in
heaven, but on earth, *not merely one day but already,* than those to
which it thinks it must confine itself in the formation and administra-
tion of its law."[99]

In Vol. 3, 4, Barth stressed the communal life and work of men
and women. Perceiving that justice is either promoted or impeded
in the world of work more than in any other sphere, Barth saw
clearly that genuine work and genuine existence can only be known
in community. Rejecting all polarization of humanity, Barth wrote of
others, "We cannot be men at all unless we live with them . . . are
assisted by and assist them."[100] It is the "humanity of human work"
that is at issue. But that humanity is riddled with crassness and
oppression. Human work can and should take place in co-existence
and co-operation. What is actually experienced, however, is "the

violation and abstraction of one's own needs, wishes and desires, in the ignoring and even the deliberate thwarting and suppressing of those of others."[101] Barth's statements precede a condemnation of the economic exploitation of the many by the few in which the older theologian sounds amazingly like the young Safenwil pastor.[102]

In 1966 Barth challenged the No Other Gospel Movement to concern itself with the problems of the Vietnam War, the proposed arming of the West German army with nuclear weapons, and the issue of anti-Semitism in Germany, as much as with its Confession. Barth admonished those members that, unless their Confession included that concrete application of the Gospel, "for all its correctness, it is a dead, cheap, pharasaical confession which strains out gnats and swallows camels."[103] And in the last year of his life, Barth declared, "The theology in which I decisively tried to draw on the Bible was never a private matter for me, remote from the world and man. Its theme is God for the world, God for men, heaven for earth. This meant that all my theology always had a strong political side, explicit or implicit."[104] Church for the world, church for men and women, church for earth—a political church, explicit and implicit.

Safenwil and Anselm: Assessing the Methodologies Together

Still, Karl Barth has not often been understood, even by those who have concerned themselves most with his work, as a theologian of social action and transformation, and his ecclesiology has not been interpreted as politically relevant, generally. The superordinate Anselmian methodology has shaded the Safenwil focus. Why was the earlier focus obscured? Barth's early dissatisfaction with Religious Socialism's anthropological orientation and resulting differences with Ragaz and Kutter seem clearly to be a factor. Disillusionment with his liberal academic heritage and his former mentors was surely a second element in Barth's growing separation from his earlier stance. Another factor appears to have been a burgeoning vendetta, as Busch suggests, against Tillich, Bultmann, and the Existentialist school.[105] More important than these, however, it is here proposed, was a nexus of events centering in the move from explicit social location with the poor in the context of the church's worship and a focus on accountability, to adoption of the Anselmian methodology. Still, the insights gained in Safenwil remained and at least a tacit location with the poor survived. For the Barth of 1911, there had been less need to understand a conceptually consistent God than *to be accountable* to a biblical God who leads the way. Theory, for him, grew from praxis. The turn to Anselm in 1931, on the other hand, signaled a turn from an embryonic theology in social location with the oppressed to the time-honored theory-above-praxis methodology. Although Barth's work from that point onward was informed more by the Anselmian methodology than by the praxis method, his later work exhibits both influences, nonetheless.

Gollwitzer, Hunsinger, Marquardt, and others acknowledge that Barth's later theology was in some ways shaped by the Safenwil experience with the industrial working class. No one of these thinkers seems to see clearly, however, the full implications of that social location for methodology and hermeneutic and thus for ecclesiology. The importance to interpretation, of explicit social location in the context of oppression, in theology's constructive moment, does not seem to be worked through adequately by these thinkers; otherwise, the Anselmian turn could scarcely be regarded a methodological "breakthrough" enabling Barth to construct an adequate theological framework for social action and a transformed and transforming church. Gerald Butler has seen this more clearly than most. Some aspect of socio-political reality, Butler states, must serve as either hermeneutical norm or focus if a theology is to be regarded a political theology.[106] With the *Anselm: Fides Quaerens Intellectum* of 1931, Barth rejected a socio-political focus. Herein lies the pivotal reason Barth has not been understood as a theologian of social action and transformation, I propose. Barth moved from explicit social location with the poor to a social location within the academy which subordinated his prior methodological position with the oppressed to a secondary level. From that point onward he denied hermeneutical function to the socio-political world; rather, only analogously did Barth draw implications for involvement in that world from his theological reflection.

Things were different in the Safenwil pastorate. A methodology in social location with the poor began there in that concrete location and, through transforming action and involved reflection, Barth sought, in the dual context of struggle and worship, to develop and apply a political hermeneutic of the Gospel to the divine-human work for justice and peace. Church and concrete world were inextricably connected. There faith seeking accountability which understands preceded the faith seeking understanding methodology which gained ascendancy in the *Church Dogmatics* period. Biblical metaphors were crucial. Jesus Christ was God's movement for social justice. Barth himself was the Moses of Safenwil!! Implications for the church were monumental. On September 9, 1917, Barth wrote to Thurneysen, "Here in our midst great decisive events have been exploding: fifty-five women employees in the knitting mill organized themselves last Monday. Now they are threatened with notice of dismissal. In regard to this I talked with the manufacturer this afternoon in his villa, *like Moses with Pharoah*, asking him to let the people go out into the wilderness."[107]

Even with the turn toward Anselm, however, Barth's rejection of his Safenwil experience was not absolute. In that Swiss industrial village, a methodology was begun and employed which perdured, though only inchoately, in the *Church Dogmatics*, and relativized, at least to some degree, I propose, *fides quaerens intellectum*. That praxis methodology stressed the importance of accountability in knowing and the meaning of knowing for accountability. Ramifications for the church's understanding of its nature and tasks yet await development.

Chapter IV will examine Barth's doctrine of the church, attempting to keep in focus both *fides quaerens intellectum* and *fides quaerens rationem reddere*, in the effort to reclaim what is inherent in Barth's theology but not fully developed. I wish to suggest that, with Barth's praxis methodology, his doctrine of the church can be unfolded in ways which crucially and creatively inform that doctrine for today.

NOTES

/1/ Frederick Herzog has proposed in his Duke seminars (in distinction from Hugo Assmann's notion of "epistemological privilege"), the "epistemological inevitability" of the poor. Herzog's notion is that the poor approach the text hermeneutically informed by their suffering in a way that opens the Scriptures to them far differently from the exegete who approaches the interpretative task academically.
/2/ Friedrich-Wilhelm Marquardt, *Theologie und Socialismus: Das Beispiel Karl Barths* (Munchen: Kaiser, 1972).
/3/ Friedrich-Wilhelm Marquardt, "Socialism in the Theology of Karl Barth," in *Karl Barth and Radical Politics*, ed. and trans. George Hunsinger (Philadelphia: Westminster Press, 1976), p. 58.
/4/ Ibid., p. 59.
/5/ Ibid., p. 60.
/6/ Ibid.
/7/ Ibid., p. 68.

/8/ Marquardt, "Socialism in the Theology of Karl Barth," pp. 65f.

/9/ Eberhard Busch notes Barth's early acquaintance with Christian Socialism through the influence of Friedrich Naumann. Barth's father had read Naumann's newspaper *Die Hilfe (Help)* and the young Barth was impressed by its sub-title: "Help for God, help for one's brother, help for the state, help for oneself." Later, Barth became acquainted with Naumann himself but rejected eventually the liberal socialism which Naumann espoused. More influential than Naumann on Barth were two other Religious Socialists, Hermann Kutter and Leonard Ragaz. Both were pastors, Kutter of the Neumunster congregation in Zurich and Ragaz of Basle cathedral. Kutter introduced Barth to a group of Swiss theologians who, Busch notes, "had given a particularly surprising twist 'to the "struggle for the kingdom of God" by endorsing and affirming the eschatology and the hope of the Social Democrat workers' movement, setting it up against the church, theology and Christianity. They saw it as the realization for our time of the faith which Jesus had not found in Israel.'" [Busch quotes *Church Dogmatics* 2, 1, p. 633.] Barth's turn toward the *Romans* exegesis and away from Religious Socialism was a rejection of the theological tenets of that movement as it developed in Switzerland in those early years. He refused to regard socialism as "a preliminary manifestation of the kingdom of God." What he continued to share with the Religious Socialists, however, was a conviction that social concerns are not extraneous to a doctrine of the church which seeks to be faithful to its grounding in Jesus Christ, but instead inseparable from it. See Eberhard Busch, *Karl Barth: His Life from Letters and Autobiographical Texts,* trans. John Bowden (Philadelphia: Fortress Press, 1976), pp. 13, 14, 76–87. For discussion of the socialist movement in Switzerland and Germany during the time of Barth's pastoral work in Safenwil, see Stephen W. Sanders, *The Socialist Movement in Germany,* Fabian Tract No. 169 (London: Fabian Society, February 1913); also, Arthur Shadwell, *The Socialist Movement 1824–1924: Its Origin and Meaning, Progress and Prospects* (London: Philip Allan & Co., 1925). Barth's keen perception of Religious Socialism's weaknesses informs his essay "Past and Future: Friedrich Naumann and Christoph Blumhardt" (from *Neuer Freier Aargauer,* 14 (1919), issues 204 and 205) in James M. Robinson, ed., trans. Keith R. Crim, *The Beginnings of Dialectic Theology,* 2 vols. (Richmond: John Knox Press, 1968), 1:35–45. Ralph P. Crimmann describes Barth's disdain for Religious Socialism's excesses and contends that Barth's was a "critical Religious Socialism" which could not be put into the line of Kutter and Ragaz. See *Karl Barths fruhe Publikationen und ihre Rezeption* (Bern: Peter Lang, 1981), pp. 24–29.

/10/ Karl Barth, *Gesamtausgabe,* I. *Predigten 1913,* herausgegeben von Nelly Barth und Gerhard Sauter (Zurich: Theologischer Verlag, 1976), p. 112.

/11/ Ibid., p. 270.

/12/ Ibid., p. 311.

/13/ Colin Brown mentions in a single sentence the Religious Socialism of Ragaz and Kutter but does not expand. See *Karl Barth and The Christian Message,* p. 18; Jerome Hamer dismisses Barth's socialist involvement as youthful recklessness, pp. 218f., *Karl Barth;* David Mueller comments only briefly on Barth's socialist involvement with no mention of its import for methodology, although he does note the implication for his preaching of Barth's social concern, pp. 18f. of *Karl Barth;* Thomas F. Torrance gives scant attention to this aspect of the Safenwil years though he does mention Barth's awakened social concern and his joining the Social Democrats. See *Karl Barth: An Introduction to His Early Theology, 1910–1931,* pp. 36f. Arnold B. Come passes over the Safenwil years as prolegomena to "getting serious with God." See *An Introduction to Barth's Dogmatics for Preachers* (Philadelphia: Westminster Press, 1963), pp. 29f. R. Birch Hoyle and Wilhelm Pauck each see Barth's Safenwil period as a continuation of his liberal theology. R. Birch Hoyle, *The Teaching of Karl Barth* (London: Student Christian Movement Press, 1930), pp. 27f. Also, Wilhelm Pauck, *Karl Barth: Prophet of a New Christianity?* (New York: Harper and Bros., 1931), pp. 44f.

/14/ See John Deschner, "Karl Barth as Political Activist," *Union Seminary Quarterly Review* 28 (Fall 1972); James Bentley, "Karl Barth as a Christian Socialist," *Theology* 76 (July 1973); Joseph Bettis, "Political Theology and Social Ethics: The Socialist Humanism of Karl Barth," *Scottish Journal of Theology* 27 (August 1974); Gerald A. Butler, "Karl Barth and Political Theology," *Scottish Journal of Theology* 27 (November 1974); Paul L. Lehmann, "Karl Barth, Theologian of Permanent Revolution," *Union Seminary Quarterly Review* 28 (Fall 1972); George Hunsinger, "Karl Barth and Radical Politics: Some Further Considerations," *Studies in Religion* 7 (Spring 1978); Shelley Baranowski, "The Primacy of Theology: Karl Barth and Socialism," *Studies in Religion* 10 (1981); essays by Helmut Gollwitzer, Hermann Diem, Dieter Schellong, and George Hunsinger in *Karl Barth and Radical Politics;* Arthur Cochrane, "The Sermons of 1913 and 1914," in *Karl Barth in Re-View: Posthumous Works Reviewed and Assessed,* ed. H. Martin Rumscheidt (Pittsburgh: Pickwick Press, 1981); Ingrid Jacobsen, ed. *War Barth Sozialist? ein Streitgespräch Um Theologie Und Sozialismus Bei Karl Barth* (Berlin: Verlag Die Spur, 1975); and George Hunsinger, "Karl Barth and Liberation Theology," *The Journal of Religion* 63 (July 1983):247-63.

/15/ Herbert Hartwell, review of *Theologie und Sozialismus, Das Beispiel Karl Barths,* by Friedrich-Wilhelm Marquardt, in *Scottish Journal of Theology* 28 (1975), pp. 70, 71.

/16/ Baranowski, "The Primacy of Theology: Karl Barth and Socialism," p. 454.

/17/ Markus Barth, "Current Discussions on the Political Character of Karl Barth's Theology," in *Footnotes to a Theology: The Karl Barth Colloquium of 1972,* ed. Martin Rumscheidt (The Corporation for the Publication of Academic Studies in Religion in Canada, 1974), p. 78.

/18/ Helmut Gollwitzer, "Kingdom of God and Socialism in the Theology of Karl Barth," in *Karl Barth and Radical Politics,* p. 79.

/19/ Ibid., pp. 80, 81.

/20/ Ibid., p. 82.

/21. Gollwitzer, "Kingdom of God and Socialism in the Theology of Karl Barth," p. 86.

/22/ Ibid.

/23/ Ibid., p. 79.

/24/ Ibid., pp. 92f.

/25/ Gollwitzer, "Kingdom of God and Socialism in the Theology of Karl Barth," pp. 101f.

/26/ Ibid., p. 110.

/27/ Ibid., pp. 111f.

/28/ Hunsinger refers to "Modern Theology and Work for the Kingdom of God," 1909; "The Christian Faith and History," 1912; "Faith in a Personal God," 1914; and "The Problem of Ethics Today," 1912. See *Karl Barth and Radical Politics*, pp. 192ff.

/29/ Ibid., pp. 191, 192.

/30/ Hunsinger, *Karl Barth and Radical Politics*, p. 192.

/31/ Ibid., p. 193.

/32/ Ibid. Hunsinger says of Barth's liberal heritage: "It had no adequate basis to speak about the proper subject matter of theology—the sovereignty of God—and no adequate basis to avoid the force of Feuerbach's objection. It had, moreover, no adequate basis to criticize and counteract the evils of contemporary society, and no adequate basis to hope and work for a really better world, despite the experience of a worse one. By the eve of the First World War, the fault lines of Barth's break with liberalism had become manifest." (p. 199).

/33/ Ibid., p. 204.

/34/ Eberhard Busch, *Karl Barth: His Life from Letters and Auto-biographical Texts*, trans. John Bowden (Philadelphia: Fortress Press, 1976), p. 69.

/35/ Ibid.

/36/ Karl Barth, "Jesus Christ and the Movement for Social Justice," in *Karl Barth and Radical Politics*, p. 19.

/37/ Ibid., p. 21.

/38/ Ibid., pp. 23, 24.

/39/ Ibid., p. 33.

/40/ Barth, "Jesus Christ and The Movement for Social Justice," p. 26.

/41/ Ibid., p. 35.

/42/ Ibid., p. 27.

/43/ Ibid. Barth elaborates: "All those sayings which are often employed against socialism about the unsurpassed significance of the Spirit and its inward testimony are completely right: Jesus knows and recognizes only the kingdom of heaven that is *within* us. But the kingdom must obtain dominion over the external—over actual life—otherwise it does not deserve the name. The kingdom is not of this world, but of God. It is *in* this world, however, for *in* this world God's will is to be done. Humanly considered, the gospel is a movement from below to above. . . . Seen from the divine side, however, it is wholly and completely a movement from above to below. It is not that we go to heaven, but that heaven comes to us."

/44/ Ibid., p. 28.

/45/ Ibid., pp. 27, 36, 37. Barth did not employ the term Christopraxis. Frederick Herzog describes Christopraxis in his volume *Justice Church*, pp. 3, 4. See *Justice Church: The New Function of the Church in North American Christianity* (Maryknoll: Orbis Books, 1980).

/46/ Ibid., pp. 35, 36.

/47/ Ulrich Dannemann, *Theologie und Politik im Denken Karl Barths* (Munich: Christian Kaiser Verlag, 1977), p. 226.

/48/ Barth, "Jesus Christ and the Movement for Social Justice," p. 28.

/49/ Thurneysen-Barth, *Revolutionary Theology in the Making: Barth-Thurneysen Correspondence, 1914–1925*, trans. James D. Smart (Richmond: John Knox Press, 1964), p. 27.

/50/ Ibid., p. 28.

/51/ Ibid., p. 45.

/52/ Busch, *Karl Barth*, pp. 79, 80.

/53/ Again, the notion of social location with the poor apparently was not, for Barth, a consciously explicit one, only a nascent one. Frederick Herzog's work has developed this methodology and given it language which Barth did not. See again *Justice Church*.

/54/ Busch, *Karl Barth*, p. 86.

/55/ Robert T. Osborn describes the importance of indwelling the problem in order to attend *from* it to a solution not immanently inhering in the struggle itself. Utilizing a Polanyian perspective, Osborn writes, "To know the human problem is to indwell bodily the reality of those persons who suffer the problem. However, indwelling as such is not the solution, for in the case of a radical problem one must not only indwell the problem but attend from it to the envisioned solution. . . . Some liberation theologies . . . appear to apotheosize the context, the problem itself, by making it the point of focal attention and the source of its hoped-for solution, as if to say that to be Latin, black or woman in the modern world is not only to suffer the problem of oppression but to possess the liberating powers. Following Polanyi we can designate this kind of positivism, as both a moral and theological 'inversion.' . . . The theological version [appeals to] an immanent divine messianism. In neither case is appeal made to a genuinely higher, more comprehensive reality, one that is eschatologically beyond the marginal limits of the problem, and as such manifests only in the hope born of a personal, faith-held vision." See "Some Problems of Liberation Theology: A Polanyian Perspective," *Journal of the American Academy of Religion* 51 (March 1983):87.

/56/ Karl Barth, *Der Römerbrief*. Unveränderter Nachdruck der ersten Auflage von 1919 (Zürich: Evz-Verlag, 1963), p. 367 (Translation mine).

/57/ Ibid., p. 381. "Dass ihr als Christen mit Monarchie, Kapitalismus, Militarismus, Patriotismus und Freisinn nichts zu tun habt, ist so selbstverständlich, dass ich es gar nicht zu sagen brauche. "Die wir der Sünde gestorben sind, wie sollten wir in ihr weiterleben können?" George Hunsinger notes this emphasis in *Karl Barth and Radical Politics*, p. 207.

/58/ Ibid., p. 328. See also Hunsinger, *Karl Barth and Radical Politics*, p. 207.

/59/ Hunsinger, *Karl Barth and Radical Politics*, pp. 206, 207.

/60/ Ibid. Hans Urs von Balthasar interprets a radical eschatology in the first-edition *Romans*, but one which describes an *apokatastasis* of God's original creation. Seeing in Barth's language the Idealist notion of a dead cosmos springing to life again and uniting with its original source, von

Balthasar regards the conceptual framework of First *Romans* Platonic, Hegelian, and Religious Socialist, but not scriptural. See *Theology of Karl Barth*, p. 48. Busch, too, identifies philosophical deposits in this early commentary and mentions Barth's own later acknowledgement that, "At that time I was still in the process of coming out of the eggshells of the theology of my teachers." What Barth wished to say above all else, however, was that God's revolution stands before, above, and under all humanity's partial revolutions as ground, source and goal. See Busch, *Karl Barth*, pp. 48, 98–101.

/61/   Ibid. [Masculine pronouns for God are retained here in accordance with Hunsinger's expression.]

/62/   Karl Barth, "The Righteousness of God," in *The Word of God and The Word of Man*, trans. and with a Foreword by Douglas Horton (New York: Harper and Bros., 1957), p. 24.

/63/   Karl Barth, "The Strange New World Within the Bible," in *The Word of God and The Word of Man*, p. 39.

/64/   Ibid., pp. 49, 50.

/65/   Hunsinger, *Karl Barth and Radical Politics*, p. 211.

/66/   Willis, *The Ethics of Karl Barth*, p. 17. There, Willis states: "The 'synthesis' to which Barth refers is the unity of all things in God as Creator and Redeemer. The 'thesis' is society; the 'antithesis' is the denial or attack upon societal structures which results from the inevitability of the Kingdom of God, manifested in the resurrection of Christ. Beyond this attack, society is moved, with the whole of creation towards renewal and closure in synthesis."

/67/   Karl Barth, "The Christian's Place in Society," in *The Word of God and the Word of Man*, p. 299.

/68/   Ibid., p. 316.

/69/   Ibid., p. 327.

/70/   Hunsinger, *Karl Barth and Radical Politics*, p. 208.

/71/   Ibid., p. 209.

/72/   Barth, "Jesus Christ and the Movement for Social Justice," p. 43.

/73/   Hunsinger, *Karl Barth and Radical Politics*, p. 216.

/74/   Busch, *Karl Barth*, pp. 118, 125.

/75/   Marquardt, "Socialism in the Theology of Karl Barth," pp. 51f.

/76/   Hunsinger, *Karl Barth and Radical Politics*, p. 211.

/77/   Robert E. Willis argues that the second-edition *Romans* effectually dismantled any possibility for ethical activity by relativizing human values and activities and reducing meaningful ethical action to the one action of repentance. See *The Ethics of Karl Barth*, pp. 52–54.

/78/   Karl Barth, *Epistle to the Romans*, trans. Edwyn C. Hoskyns (London: Oxford University Press, 1950), p. 197.

/79/   Ibid., p. 76.

/80/   Ibid., p. 301.

/81/   Willis, *Ethics of Karl Barth*, pp. 52–54.

/82/   Barth, *Epistle to the Romans*, p. 119.

/83/   Ibid., p. 222.   /84/   Ibid., p. 100.

/85/   Ibid., p. 25.   /86/   Ibid., p. vi.

/87/ Thurneysen-Barth, *Revolutionary Theology*, pp. 118, 119.

/88/ Karl Barth, *The Church and the Political Problem of Our Day* (New York: Charles Scribner's Sons, 1939), pp. 37, 38.

/89/ Karl Barth, "Christian Community and Civil Community," in *Community, State, and Church*, with an Introduction by Will Herberg (Garden City: Doubleday and Co., 1960), pp. 185, 186. Emphasizing the political responsibility of the church and the political nature of the Gospel itself, Barth wrote in Ch. 31: "This gospel . . . is political from the very outset, and if it is preached to real (Christian and non-Christian) men on the basis of a right interpretation of the Scriptures it will necessarily be prophetically political. . . . The Christian Church that is aware of its political responsibility will demand political preaching; and it will interpret it politically even if it contains no direct reference to politics." pp. 184, 185. On p. 175, Barth called for the end of discrimination against persons of other classes and races and of that against women.

/90/ Ibid., p. 173.   /91/ Ibid.

/92/ John Deschner, "Karl Barth as Political Activist," *Union Seminary Quarterly Review* 28 (Fall 1972):55.

/93/ Barth, *Church Dogmatics*, Vol. 4, 2:802.

/94/ Ibid., p. 807.

/95/ Ibid., Vol. 3, 1:60.

/96/ Ibid., Vol. 4, 2:802, 803.   /97/ Ibid., Vol. 2, 1:386.

/98/ Ibid., Vol. 2, 1:387.

/99/ Ibid., Vol. 4, 2:721.   /100/ Ibid., Vol. 3, 4:535.

/101/ Ibid., p. 536.   /102/ Ibid., pp. 541, 542.

/103/ Quoted in Herman Diem, "Karl Barth as Socialist: Controversy Over a New Attempt to Understand Him," in *Karl Barth and Radical Politics*, p. 123.

/104/ Karl Barth, *Final Testimonies*, ed. Eberhard Busch and trans. Geoffrey W. Bromiley (Grand Rapids: William B. Eerdmans Co., 1977), p. 24.

/105/ Busch, *Karl Barth*, pp. 438, 461, 465.

/106/ Gerald A. Butler, "Karl Barth and Political Theology," *Scottish Journal of Theology* 27 (1974):457, 458.

/107/ Thurneysen-Barth, *Revolutionary Theology in the Making*, p. 42.

CHAPTER IV

BARTH'S DOCTRINE OF THE CHURCH

In Chapter II of this study, I have analyzed Barth's Anselmian methodology and significant scholarly assessments of it. The conclusion has been reached that seeking an objective conceptualization of "that which exists necessarily" runs into difficulties in connecting Being and a material world; an ontologism begins to emerge which vitiates that connection. Hence, church and world also fail to connect in ways that prevent charges of revelational positivism and super-history. Faith seeking understanding and its theoretical commitment are not explicitly conducive to historical engagement, I have argued; thus, Barth's early methodology, faith seeking accountability which understands, is needed to correct the theoretical concentration of *fides quaerens intellectum* and its preference for the noetic and abstract.

In Chapter III, I have described Barth's methodology in social location with the poor, employed prior to the turn toward Anselm, and have argued its importance for the reclamation and further development of insights gained in the Safenwil period and their crucial importance to a more adequate understanding and further development of Barth's ecclesiology. The present chapter will seek to identify specific possibilities for understanding Barth's theology in terms of the doctrine of the church, recognizing these as possibilities inherent in the Safenwil experiences and in the *Church Dogmatics*. The Safenwil praxis methodology, *fides quaerens rationem reddere*, or faith seeking accountability which, in accountability, understands, will instruct an analysis of the *Church Dogmatics* and Barth's ecclesiology. It is argued that the historical assertions in Barth's notion of the church as the earthly-historical form of the existence of Jesus Christ can be newly developed through that method, unfolding potential inherent in the *Dogmatics* ecclesiology. The hope is that Barth's theology might be rendered, as D. F. Ford describes it, "more open and comprehensive" regarding "general conclusions" drawn from that theology[1] and, particularly, from Barth's theology of the church. In other words, new conclusions can be drawn from Barth's theology and ecclesiology which have not formerly been clearly apprehended.

Definition and Method in Barth's Ecclesiology

With an Anselmian emphasis on reflection on and explication of Scripture and the church's creeds, Barth developed a theology of the church in which he defined the ecclesia as the Body of Jesus Christ, the earthly-historical form of his existence ("*seiner eigenen irdisch-geschichtlichen Existenzform*"), and, following the Nicene-Constantinopolitan Creed of 381, as the "one holy catholic and apostolic Church."[2] In lectures given in 1935, Barth referred to the Apostles' Creed as "fitted to be the basis of a discussion of the chief problems of Dogmatics not only because it furnishes, as it were, a groundplan of Dogmatics but above all because the meaning, aim and essence of *Dogmatics* and the meaning, aim and essence of the *Credo*, if they are not identical, yet stand in the closest connection. . . ."[3] Barth followed with an argument much like that in *Anselm: Fides Quaerens Intellectum*. He adduced the three levels of reason working in faith and dogmatics in the quest for understanding. On the first level, Barth explained, the Christian recognizes in the Credo "definite cognition won from God's revelation" and answers with, "I believe," *Credo*. This is first-level *ratio*. The articles of faith, those "definite truths," which inspire cognition are ontically the second-level *ratio*. Originating and informing both articles and belief is the Truth which is identical to God, faith's Object, *ratio veritatis*, the third-level *ratio*.[4] Within that frame, then, Barth applied the methodology of *fides quaerens intellectum*, reflection on Scripture and Creed and explication according to those criteria. Seeking knowledge and understanding logically meant that proclamation of knowledge gained and understanding found would be perceived as the church's primary mission. Even as early as 1933, however, critical voices questioned the exclusivity of this orientation.[5] Fears were raised that important aspects of the church's ethical and social tasks were endangered thereby. *Fides quaerens intellectum*, in effect, did not extend far enough; accountability was not explicitly included in the methodological frame.

Church as the Earthly-Historical Form of the Existence of Jesus Christ

Barth strives, in the *Church Dogmatics,* to say that the church *is* accountable. Accountable ultimately to God, this means that it is, for that reason, accountable to the world and to the history within which it dwells. As the earthly-historical form of Jesus Christ's existence, the church is the gathered community of those who have been elected by and in him as his witnesses, and as such, they are a "provisional representation" of the justification accomplished in Jesus Christ for the "whole world of humanity."[6] This founding by the Holy Spirit is a continued founding and refounding which is both divine and human. Thus, the church itself emerges as a historical activity, a specific historical work. The gathering of the Christian community is both God's act and humanity's as the church "is gathered and lets itself be gathered and gathers itself by the living Jesus Christ through the Holy spirit."[7] Holy Spirit and humankind are co-involved in the actualization of the church itself and in its work and mission.

It is at this very point that problems surface in Barth's development of the reality of divine-human act in history. Having adopted the Anselmian methodology and elected to develop his theology of the church according to the articles of faith contained within the Nicene-Constantinopolitan Creed, Barth does not question the Creed nor look outside it for his understandings. Problems regarding how the church can be understood as a genuine historical entity engaged in historical work emerge immediately. Barth constructs an argument in support of the visible historical church which contains ambivalences regarding that aspect of its existence, thus implying that the *real* church, after all, is the invisible church of the spirit. A discomfort with the finite surfaces in the interstices. He writes:

> . . . we emphasize the fact that if the *credo ecclesiam* contains within it a critical caveat in face of its whole earthly and historical form, if it sets it in question, it does not negate it so that there can be no question of an escape into invisibility. On the contrary, if this reservation is taken seriously as such, then we are both challenged and permitted . . . resolutely to take the unavoidable step into visibility. *Credo ecclesiam* thus means that the church can take itself seriously in the world of the earthly and visible, with all humility, but also with all

comfort, at once directed and established by its third dimen-
sion.[8]

Still, although a certain discomfort with the present shape of the
finite is apparent, Barth does wish to affirm the church's historicity.
  It will be helpful to return to Barth's definition of the church.
In addition to the existence of Jesus Christ in the earthly-historical
Body of the Christian community, Jesus Christ lives also in a heavenly-historical form as the Crucified and Risen Lord. Just what a
heavenly-historical existence could be is not clear. Perhaps Barth
wishes to say thereby that Jesus' life is not merely identical with the
church. Still, it is plainly not an above-and-beyond existence which
Barth wishes to emphasize, but the present, earthly, concrete *irdisch-geschichtlichen* form which is the Christian community. *The
historical assertions included in the phrase "the earthly-historical
form of the existence of Jesus Christ" are the focus of this chapter.*
Those historical assertions should not be discounted or overlooked,
as they have often been, but, with the aid of the Safenwil insights,
reclaimed and developed in a manner appropriate to their intent
and potentiality.

Solidarity in Worship and Eucharist

  Significantly, it is in the context of the Eucharist that Barth
develops his theology of the *irdisch-geschichlichen* nature of the
church. Barth comes close in that development to an affirmation of
reoriented human selfhood, the ontological oneness of all humanity
in Jesus' death and resurrection and in their representation in the
Eucharist. Barth argues logically that to proclaim the resurrected
Christ as the Head and Mediator of all persons, as the "last Adam,"
is to enlarge the boundaries of the Body of Christ and the Christian
community. The universal redemption in Jesus Christ is the presupposition of this inclusive Body. "The community itself, sharing the
bread, is only the arrow which points to the unity of the many which
is grounded and—although hidden—actual in the fact that He is the
Mediator and Substitute and Representative of all men."[9] Barth
stresses that, as Body to Jesus Christ's Head, the community must
be open, receptive, defined by his limits and not its own. Barth sees
in the common sharing of the bread a promise of unity for all
persons, one in which "not only Christians but all men are already

comprehended in Jesus Christ."[10] Ephesians 1:23 reflects that great reality, Barth declares. It is the fulness of Him that filleth all in all. Ephesians 1:9 f. contains the same affirmation. What, then, does Barth make of these texts? They suggest to him the unity of humanity represented by the Christian community in its breaking and eating of the one loaf. But what sort of unity does the Eucharist show forth? Is it a unity of selfhood? a unity of purpose? a unity of mission? Though Barth intends to affirm that this unity is comprehensively all of that, differentiation begins to appear with the statement that all which has been said regarding humanity's oneness in the Eucharist and the truth that it represents is a "secondary" christological truth.[11] The importance of theological methodology begins to surface. Working with Anselmian presuppositions, Barth finds it difficult to maintain a socio-historical focus. The taking place in time and space, and in human activity and experience, of God's creation of the earthly-historical Body of Jesus Christ and Jesus' own very explicit identification of himself and the community in Acts 9:4 and Matthew 25:40, 45, Barth can still consider, though of "practical importance for the time of the community in the world," a "very secondary Christological statement." Barth explains: The church and all not yet visibly a part of that community are Christ's Body or will finally be revealed as such when they proclaim Jesus as *Kyrios* (1 Cor. 12:3). It is consensus of assent, assent to proclaimed Kerygma, then, which makes all one. In unity of belief and confession, all persons become one Body of Jesus Christ, the earthly-historical witnesses whose mission is one, viz., to announce the Good News of God's reconciliation of all to God's self. That is their corporateness, their common selfhood.

    Fides quaerens intellectum and its method, e.g., noetic analysis and explication of the Creed and Scripture in the quest for knowledge and understanding, accord little opportunity for examining from a socio-historical focus the nature of the church. Locked into *fides quaerens intellectum* and noetic investigation, Barth finds it hard to open his inquiry to alternative perceptions of what he has seen as "secondary" christological truth. Affirming the historical assertions implied in Barth's definition of the church, we can, however, with the method *fides quaerens rationem reddere* and the insights gained in Safenwil, develop the insight into communal selfhood which Barth had gained in the experience of worship and the Eucharist, and break what emerges as a monopoly of witness and proclamation by emphasizing other equally vital aspects of solidarity in Barth's purview. Thus, accountability can then become a more central and full-bodied notion in Barth's theology of the church, and aid in a reinterpretation of primary and secondary christological truth which heals the dichotomy suggested by those designations.

With Barth's exposition of *credo sanctam ecclesiam*, he offers again what he intends as a sociological view of the church, insofar as the Anselmian methodology lends itself to that possibility. Beginning with the notion of "holy" as designating that which is set apart by God for a special purpose and direction, Barth develops the conception of the ecclesia as a divinely instituted community. In that unique nature the church is differentiated from all other societies. Barth stresses that, unlike a nation, the *sancta ecclesia* is not a natural society; nor does it bear an integral likeness to clubs, unions, and other voluntary groups. Its likeness to economic and cultural unions cannot provide a mode of understanding itself or an indication of its goals. Nor can its methods and standards be those of other societies. Its one pervasive condition for understanding and assessing itself is that of faith. Having made those categorical statements, Barth then affirms that the church is also a human society composed of men and women who inhabit both a divine ecclesia and other human societies somewhat parallel to it. But with that nod to the church's human nature, Barth leaves that topic and returns to a consideration of its divine nature.[12] What began as a sociological treatise has been circumscribed and cut short. In fairness to Barth, we should note that this is one of three sections on ecclesiology, and that Barth's intention in 4, 1 is to focus on the divine basis of the church. Perhaps what is problematical here, however, is Barth's tendency to separate the sections dealing with the divine basis and the human life of the church, inadvertently suggesting, thereby, a separation of that which belongs together.

What Barth *does* say of value in this portion of his ecclesiology is of profound importance indeed. To those who are committed to the cultivation of their own spiritual excellence, he speaks a word of genuine enlightenment, and so, too, to those congregations that foster this individual cultivation of the soul. It is here that Barth's insights can offer a corrective to the Southern Baptist doctrine of soul competency discussed in the first chapter. The Scriptures, Barth points out, emphasize not a relationship, so-called, between Christ and believer, but between Christ and a community. (The "nobler church consciousness" for Baptists, called for by H.

Wheeler Robinson, begins at just this point.)[13] It is not a private relationship between each called or elected man or woman and Christ who calls that is of final significance, Barth shows; indeed, that individual relationship is significant precisely as it is a component of the communal one. "To be awakened to faith and to be added to the community are one and the same thing."[14] "There is only one separation, that of the *communio sanctorum:* the awakening of the faith of individuals, the purpose of which is their gathering into the community. . . ."[15] It is a separation to life and witness within the community to which the Christian is elected. Not to accept that participation and to endeavor to confine one's ministry to an individual pursuit is to cut oneself off from the *communio sanctorum* and perhaps even to forfeit one's part in God's reconciliatory work. Barth warns that the error encountered may even be like that of sinning against the Spirit, as it is to community that the Spirit calls and leads. Barth sees obedience as vital to a right understanding of the individual's role in the community.

It is important to understand that Barth is not discounting the reality and necessity of personal salvation. That, he affirms, is basic to the building of the church. What he is denying is the sufficiency and ultimacy of individual justification apart from God's constitution of the community elected as the Body of Christ.

In 4, 3, the Second Half, Barth denies emphatically again that individuals are called for a solitary and private relationship with God. Individual calling is to a community of called ones whose purpose is found in bringing their several talents and abilities into the one Body for its use and aims; they are a *communio vocatorum* and not "private disciples."[16] "From the very outset Jesus Christ did not envisage individual followers, disciples, and witnesses, but a plurality of such united by Him both with Himself and with one another. To be sure, He was thinking in terms of individuals and not of an anonymous number, collection, conglomeration, or collective. But His purpose in relation to the individual was not just to set him in a kind of unidimensional relationship to Himself. It was to unite both with Himself, and also, if in a very different sense and under very different conditions, with the other individuals whom He has called, and wills to call, and will call."[17] The Baptist theologian David Mueller apparently has read Barth through Baptist lenses, for he maintains that, while Barth does not move directly from God's election in Jesus Christ to that of the individual but stresses the church's mediating and conditioning role, "The election of individuals is the real goal of the election of the community."[18] Mueller's reading does not help to ameliorate the radically individualistic emphasis in Baptist thought.

Barth engages the task of saying in what way the community is a communion. The Latin term *communio* and the Greek term κοινωνια suggest both a complete union and one in which the united members move toward completion through the originating and impelling power of the Holy Spirit and the human response of those energized by the Spirit. Communion, then, is both a divine and a human work in which movement is made from completed union *to* completed union in the incomplete spatio-temporal sphere in which this communion is actualized. The unity that has already been established in Jesus Christ is the source of the unity yet to be completed in the eschaton. God's election calls both the former and the latter into being as well as the intervening unity of those who together move from the original to the final communion.[19]

Barth describes the material content of the *communio sanctorum*. First, it is a fellowship of knowledge and confession. Second, it is a fellowship of gratitude and thanksgiving. Third, a community of penitence leading to conversion. Fourth, of prayer. Fifth, of concern for the world. Sixth, of service to one another. Seventh, of hope and prophecy. Eighth, the community is "Above all, . . . the fellowship of their proclamation of the Gospel, of the Word by which they are gathered and impelled and maintained." Ninth, it is a fellowship of worship.[20] Barth concedes that his is not an exhaustive list, but believes that it includes the essential components of what it materially means for the church to be the *communio sanctorum*. Reiterating the communality of those who are entrusted with the reception and expression of these *sancta*, Barth stresses both that oneness and its nature as event. Again, Barth wishes to keep the church mindful of its concrete historical nature.

Turning in 4, 2 to a description of the community's inner and outer growth, Barth endeavors again to outline what amounts to a social theory for the church's being in the world. Acknowledging that the church expands by human as well as divine efforts, and that it is thus a human institution as well as a divine one, Barth emphasizes, however, the inherent potential for augmentation in quantity and quality of witnesses which the Holy Spirit living within the Body gives to it. Human acts directed towards the upbuilding of the community are not negated by the divine power, but they are not the primary source of the church's expansion either. Further, the *communio sanctorum*'s outward horizontal expansion is so only because it is first an inward, vertical one. That inward spiritual growth requires an outward historical one that the church's purpose might be fulfilled—"It has to attest the Gospel. It has to seek a hearing and understanding for the Gospel's voice. It cannot do this without exerting itself to win new witnesses."[21] Thus the inner and outer expansion are intertwined. "But this cannot become an end in itself. It knows of only one end in itself—the proclamation of the kingdom of God."[22]

Barth essays to express the nature of the church's "effective action in the world around."[23] At the same time, he wishes to explicate the church's history as one of God's preservation. The church's existing in the world, Barth reiterates once again, is for the purpose of witnessing to and conveying the message of God's act in Christ. Immediately, Barth launches into a discourse on the danger which the church faces in its provisional representation of the new humanity in Christ Jesus. That danger is of losing itself in the world; thus Barth's consideration of the church's action in the world is transposed right away into his concern for the preservation of the church's witness.

Preservation of Witness in the German Church Conflict

That same preservation of integrity was Barth's concern in the German church conflict. In *Theological Existence Today,* Barth had enjoined the church to become again the church; only so could it resist assimilation and the perversion and loss of its unique proclamation, and only so could it serve the world. "Of course something has to be done; very much so; but most decidedly nothing other than this, viz., that the church congregations be gathered together again, but aright and anew in fear and great joy, to the Word by means of the Word. All the crying about and over the Church will not deliver the Church. Where the Church is a Church she is already delivered."[24] The church's challenge was to be the church. German National Socialism's threat to the church lay in its assumption of divine status. To accept its promulgation of itself as a "religious institution of salvation," Barth warned, would "plainly signify nothing less than that the Christian Church recognizes herself and her message in this other Church, holds it to be the true Church of Jesus Christ, and thus resolves to be absorbed in it with the utmost expedition. . . ."[25] And in *Trouble and Promise in the Struggle of the Church in Germany*, Barth assessed the threat and temptation introduced to the church in 1933:

> The promise was made to her: if she *now* took the right attitude, if she *now* had the courage to grasp and support the spirit of the new time, then the hour had come at which the great masses, that 80 to 90 percent of the German people which had hitherto stood aloof from the Church, would return to her. . . . Only one *small condition* was attached to this offer, namely this: the Church was to have all this if she were ready in future not merely to proclaim the Christian faith alone and to make that the subject of her message. If she were ready to recognize that what occurred in 1933 was a divine revelation which she had in future to take as seriously as what she had hitherto regarded and announced as the revelation of God in Jesus Christ![26]

Barth contended that a proper holding to and exposition of the Creed was the church's confident answer to history's error. In *Theological Existence Today*, Barth wrote, "Where the Creed is, the One, Holy Church is there present in the fight with error in which she will never lose the day. But, on the other hand, there is always error where there are 'Movements,' and divisions are ever nigh at hand. The Holy Ghost needs no 'movements'; the Devil has probably invented most of them."[27] Correct doctrine, ortho-doxy, was the church's bulwark against its enemies in the German church struggle and later. "Theological existence, in the situation created once more by the 'German Christians' to-day, even more than yesterday, would simply mean 'That we henceforth be no more children tossed to and fro and carried about by every wind of doctrine' (Eph. 4:14)."[28]

In 1938, Barth assessed again what had happened in 1933. The church's proclamation, its confessional integrity, had been threatened. Pressed to dilute its confession with the "revelation," so-called, of National Socialism, the church's doctrinal purity faced relativization and loss.[29] (And when asked to speak to the struggle between East and West and to the conflict of communistic and democratic ideologies, Barth refused to engage that argument on the basis that the church's confession and proclamation were not at issue.[30] Choosing to define his involvement differently, Barth contrasted National Socialism's threat to the confessional integrity of the church with Bolshevism's totalitarianism, seeing in the former an idolatrous temptation not presented by the latter. Arguing that Jesus Christ offers a third way beyond both communism and democracy, Barth refused to involve himself in the East-West conflict according to others' terms. Adopting a controversial position opposing the cold war, Barth involved himself but on a different plane.)

The church's loss of itself evidenced by its loss of a pure sermon and a "pure proclamation," Barth warned the church threatened by National Socialism, derived from the failure to attend to its own regeneration. "If the churches would today bend all their efforts to become once more true to their real mission, and change from well-meaning religious organizations back into real churches—if engaged in this act of repentance and renewal, they would seek, find and probably effectively preach *today*, the right, clear, joyful message pertinent to the anxieties and problems of *today*, including the burdens imposed on the world of fighting the war—that would be the real, sound, prophetic preparation for their mission of tomorrow. . . ."[31] Explicating the Scottish Confession of 1560, Barth had stressed in 1938 the theme of a "sincere and humble proclamation and understanding of the divine Word."[32] Twenty years later, in *The Faith of the Church*, Barth's view was unchanged: "The church . . . must restrict herself to her proper work: the proclamation of the Gospel, the exegesis of the Bible and of the Confession of Faith. Constantly, the Church runs the danger of unduly extending her task. How many ministers busy themselves with a multiplicity of things and take the risk of forsaking the sole thing necessary to the Church!"[33] The insight expressed in 1938 held: "It is by hearing God that the church is built up, lives, grows, works, and glorifies God's name in her own midst and in the world. She is the true church in proportion as she is the listening church."[34]

While such statements argue strongly for (and are the basis of scholarly contentions that Barth's theology is removed from mundane history) the preeminence of word over deed, the context in which the German church conflict statements were made is a significant factor and needs duly to be taken into account. In that context a jealous guarding of the church's proclamation was understandably the primary issue. (Barth's Barmen stance is not unlike his Safenwil stance in its attendance to the concrete historical situation and its significance for the theological event.) A listening church was indeed the true church in that location. However, as Wolfgang Huber has pointed out, the Second Barmen Thesis may have injected into the church's thinking an implicit post-Enlightenment consensus that the world is a sphere autonomous from the church. With that unintended result, the separation not just of ethics within theology but of ethics from theology became the historical distillate with which the church now has to deal. The failure of Barmen to concern itself beyond ecclesiological matters opened the church to an unconscious accommodation to the contemporary trend toward limiting responsibility for specialized fields to those regarded the "exponents of reason," or experts, in those fields, Huber claims. Insufficient reflection on the currents of post-Enlightenment thought affecting the church's view of church-world relations restricted the Barmen Fathers' understanding of what their decisions might portend for the church, Huber argues.[35] [Chapter I showed this same problem in Baptist reflection.]

Fides quaerens intellectum, this thesis proposes, might well have slanted the Barmen insights, making it easy, with its concentration on Creed and Scripture, to stay inside "purely ecclesiastical"[36] struggles. Preoccupying itself with internal theological problems, this methodology lent itself, perhaps, to an insularity which prevented an analysis of the contemporary movement toward autonomy which Barmen might have inadvertently supported. With the move toward autonomy, reason was accorded a primary and independent role which *fides quaerens intellectum* also falls prey to, though unintentionally, since faith remains the first term.

How, then, in light of the threat of assimilation and acculturation, *is* the church a "community for the world"? The *communio sanctorum,* Barth explains, is that fellowship which calls the world to a realization of its true nature. The church alone knows the world as it is addressed by God and joined to God in covenant, and as a part of the world it is the point in which this truth becomes evident. Secondly, the community of Jesus Christ is the fellowship which practices "solidarity with the world," a solidarity that is understood as being "worldly" in it, proclaiming in the midst of humanity God's reconciliation in Jesus Christ. "How can it boast of and rejoice in the Savior of the world and men, or how can it win them—to use another Pauline expression—to know Him and to believe in Him, if it is not prepared first to be human and worldly like them and with them."[37] Thirdly, as the community which knows the world, and is in solidarity with it, the church is obligated to it, made "responsible for it, for its future, for what is to become of it."[38] Barth means, in this injunction to responsibility for the world, responsibility for its confrontation with the Word.

Barth speaks eloquently of the church's rightful location in the midst of humanity's struggles. He writes:

> It [the Church] could perhaps ignore and pass by as non-essential both the world and what takes place in it if it were not that in the world, whether in small things or in great, we are always concerned with the existence, enterprises, and experiences, the acts of commission and omission, the triumphs and defeats, the joys and sorrows, the short life and bitter death of men. It is because this is so, because the call comes to it from the man whom God has elected and loved, that the community of Jesus Christ and the men united in it are bound to the world and everywhere summoned to action in relation to it.[39]

Still, action for Barth seems to be preeminently the action of hearing and preaching. In *The Knowledge of God and the Service of God*, Barth reprimands the church for often having squandered her energy in other pursuits than the primary act of hearing:

> In the church to act means *to hear*, i.e., to hear the Word of God, and through the Word of God revelation and faith. It may be objected that this is too small a task and one that is not enough. But in the whole world there exists no more intense, strenuous or animated action than that which consists in hearing the Word of God—hearing it, as is its due, ever afresh, better, more loyally and efficaciously. Everything besides this is a waste of time here. It is in this act that the content of the church service consists.[40]

It is to Karl Barth's credit that he, more than anyone else, called the church and theology back to its roots in Jesus Christ. Barth said better than all others, perhaps, including Bonhoeffer, that Christianity cannot be known as one of the religions in *a priori* knowledge of what religion is, but only as it is in Jesus Christ. It is at this point, however, that methodology becomes crucial. *Fides quaerens intellectum* shapes what is known in Jesus Christ in a way that obscures important perceptions of what "community for the world" means. Understanding, solidarity, and participation are key terms in Barth's notion of the historical church. Those terms, however, refer in most cases to spiritual redemption. Barth makes it explicit that being the Good Samaritan means caring for the wounded man's estrangement from God.[41] It is that kind of reconciliatory ministry which the church alone of all institutions can offer a broken humanity. Being in the world for the world means, then, reaping the white fields. The historical assertions implicit in the church's "earthly-historical" nature need to come into focus here, as they do at crucial points in the *Church Dogmatics* and other writings. Without losing the previous important focus, *fides quaerens rationem reddere* expands those historical implicates of the church's ministry to caring for the injured man's pain, his thirst and hunger, his abused personhood, and his powerlessness. Most importantly, these concerns are not seen as secondary and incidental, but also with spiritual reconciliation as concerns central to the Gospel; indeed, on the strength of Matthew 25, they are seen as lodged in the very heart of God. God who transforms the world is concerned for the totality of human existence—the hunger and poverty of men and women as well as their spiritual alienation.

Barth's view of community for the world derives from his view of God for the world. That God has loved the world and reconciled it to God's self in Jesus Christ, and thus is for the world, means that the role of the *communio sanctorum* in the divine activity is the proclamation of that reconciliation in Jesus Christ.[42] In the preaching of the divine Word, faith is born in the one addressed and a "genuine and supreme content of knowledge" is imparted. That knowledge which is the content of faith resides in the Creed and waits to be reflected on and proclaimed. Logically, then, the church's business is its Confession. Although Barth acknowledges that Confession takes various forms and includes multiple expressions, he often does not spell that affirmation out in any way that clearly develops his notion beyond confession and proclamation as generally understood. God's being with and for humanity is that which is confessed and proclaimed. But as God is with the church, God is with and for humankind for the purpose of inner redemption for individual and community and the calling of those outside into that circle. Still, "the earthly-historical form of the existence of Jesus Christ" asserts more historical engagement than speech alone; while Barth fails to expound clearly enough that assertion in Vol. 4, 3, 2, it is contained within his definition. Indeed, its ramifications are seen in Barth's description of the co-valency of speech and action in Jesus' and the disciples' ministries.

Solidarity in Deed and Word

There is reason to believe that Barth's early praxis methodology informs his insights at this point. Although Barth stresses the community's nature as proclaimer of the kerygma, he does not ignore the genuine impetus to and emphasis on deeds, not just speech, which the Gospel contains. Indeed, Barth has researched the New Testament closely for an understanding of the relationship between speaking and acting in the lives of Jesus and his disciples. His results are compelling in their suggestion of accountability. The Safenwil method seems to be in evidence.[43] Barth notes that speech and action are so well balanced in Jesus' own life, the paramount example being the life of preaching crowned by the act of death in the crucifixion, that one becomes the opposite side of the other. Speech is the other side of action and action the opposite side of speech for Jesus. The accent is variously placed on one or the other in those texts which report Jesus' ministry. In Luke 4:43f., speech is stressed: "I must preach the good news of the kingdom of God to the other cities also; for I was sent for this purpose. And he was preaching in the synagogues of Judea" (R.S.V.). Acts 10:38, however, mentions first Jesus' deeds: "how he went about doing good and healing all that were oppressed by the devil, for God was with him. And we are witnesses to all that he did . . ." (R.S.V.). Luke 24:17 lays apparent stress on deed in its description of Jesus as "a prophet mighty in deed and word before God and all the people" (R.S.V.). Matthew 9:35 mentions Jesus' teaching and preaching first, but action is also there: "And Jesus went about all the cities and villages, teaching in their synagogues and preaching the gospel of the kingdom, and healing every disease and every infirmity" (R.S.V.). Barth concludes from the scriptural evidence:

> The deed and word or the word and deed of Jesus are twofold in their unity. In both we have His self-declaration, the indication of the kingdom of God drawn near in Him. He gives it both in the form of words and proclamation and instruction and in that of acts of power and aggression and assistance set up as signs in the midst of sinful and suffering humanity and giving distinctive emphasis to the picture as we have it in all four Gospels. For the most part the Word precedes and the act follows. But neither is lacking even where one or the other alone is mentioned or receives prominence.[44]

Barth shows that the disciples, too, combine word and act in integral fashion. Jesus' charge to the twelve in Matthew 10:5f. is to preach, "The kingdom of heaven is at hand." It is also to "heal the sick, raise the dead, cleanse lepers, cast out demons" (R.S.V.). Barth notes that these two commissions are just what they performed when the disciples went out. Luke 9:6 reports: "And they departed

and went through the villages, preaching the gospel and healing
everywhere" (R.S.V.). Mark 6:12,13: "So they went out and
preached that men should repent. And they cast out many demons,
and anointed with oil many that were sick and healed them"
(R.S.V.). Barth decides:

> . . . There can be no doubt that in the light of its origin, of the
> Giver of its task who is also its content, its ministry and witness
> have always to move along these two lines: not merely along
> either the one or the other, but along both; and no less along
> the one than the other, but with equal seriousness and empha-
> sis along both. . . . There is a work of the lips and also of the
> hands.[45]

Although Barth believes that Jesus' instructions to his disciples
clearly established an irreversible sequence of preaching first, followed by action, and goes on to support this view with evidence
from the Pauline epistles, noting that prophecy in the lists of *charis-
mata* always precedes the other gifts, the historical assertions contained in the nature of the church are forcefully evident. Concrete
engagement with pain and want is inseparable from the Word itself,
Barth shows.

Faith Seeking Knowledge

Still, withal, Barth's doctrine of the church remains largely
academic and theoretical. In order to see why, it is important to
understand the vital connection, in Barth's thought, between knowledge and witness as the content of the church's nature and mission.
In his exposition of the Heidelberg Catechism, Barth writes in
answer to question twenty-one:

> *What is true faith?* It is not only a certain knowledge
> [implying that it first *is* that certain knowledge] by which I
> accept as true all that God has revealed to us in his Word, but
> also a wholehearted trust which the Holy Spirit creates in me
> through the gospel, that, not only to others, but to me also God
> has given the forgiveness of sins, everlasting righteousness, and
> salvation, out of sheer grace solely for the sake of Christ's saving
> work . . . those who believe are those to whom it has been
> given to know the truth of God in Jesus Christ, to grasp the
> promise and to place their confidence in it. Faith is not only a
> knowledge [implying again that it is principally a knowledge];

it is also this 'whole-hearted trust'. We are not concerned here
with a particular theory, but with the certainty that redemption
through righteousness is *also for me*, that *also my* sins are
forgiven.[46]

It is significant that the next question concerns the knowledge that is
to be believed, apart from which there is no "wholehearted trust."
"*What, then, must a Christian believe?* All that is promised us in the
gospel, a summary of which is taught us in the articles of the
Apostles' Creed, our universally acknowledged confession of
faith."[47] Barth is explicit:

> Here we are concerned with *doctrine*. The people of God who
> exist for the sake of their commission stand in need of a 'certain
> *knowledge*.' Because we have to do here with the Word of God,
> with the Logos and his proclamation in human words, we need
> this knowledge as the basis of all our speaking. The creed, the
> 'articles of our universally acknowledged confession of faith,'
> contains the standard of knowledge (qq. 19,21) which is com-
> mon to these people wherever they are, without which no one
> belongs to them, without which they cannot fulfill their com-
> mission. In short, the creed contains what is necessary for a
> Christian to believe.[48]

In *The Faith of the Church*, Barth reiterates the centrality of
knowledge. "The catechism, as an exposition of the Revelation, gives
us the object of knowledge."[49] Knowing God is the end for which
men and women were created, as it is in "true and right knowledge"
that humans are enabled to honor God. Trust is the essence of faith
because it is the "condition of all our knowledge of God."[50] The
threefold *ratio* of Anselm: Fides Quaerens Intellectum is apparent.
Turning to the Creed, the second level *ratio*, the trusting believer
finds the "certain knowledge" given by the *ratio veritatis*. "The
substance of this knowledge is the Creed in its entirety. Therefore,
the whole Creed refers to our knowledge of God in Jesus Christ."[51]
As in the *Church Dogmatics*, Barth understands the church's task as
one of proclamation and witness to this knowledge which is the
Creed.[52]

The content of the church's task has vitally to do with knowledge, doctrine, even gnosis. Clearly, *fides quaerens intellectum* is at
the helm. Barth makes it transparent: "Now there can be no doubt
that the content of the task laid upon the community is a matter of
revelation and knowledge and therefore of doctrine and *gnosis*. . . .

Its content is message, *kerygma*, proclamation."[53] It logically follows that humanity, in this view, is first and foremost those who are witnessed to; men and women are addressees. Baptists also view humankind as addressee, hence the great body of missionaries commissioned to address; whatever else they do is provisional to that central aim. For Barth and Baptists (and others) the Great Commission is dissemination of knowledge through witness and address.

However, Barth's allusion to the "earthly-historical form of the existence of Jesus Christ" and *fides quaerens rationem reddere* ask about the inner dynamic of the Great Commission. The historical assertions in Barth's notion of the church indicate that Matthew 28:19, 20 can be acknowledged and appropriated better in the company of other admonitions such as Luke 6:27, 28 and Mark 10:21. Perhaps in a day threatened by nuclear holocaust, faith seeking accountability which understands, which Barth's definition implies, can aid in a new valuing of other words of Jesus: "But I say to you that hear, love your enemies, do good to those who hate you, bless those who curse you, pray for those who abuse you" (Luke 6:27, 28 R.S.V.). In a world where malnutrition and starvation are rampant, Jesus' commission to preach to all nations is joined to his commission to the rich young ruler: ". . . go sell what you have, and give to the poor, and you will have treasure in heaven; and come, follow me" (Mark 10:21 R.S.V.).

Accepting that Jesus' intention was to make disciples, faith seeking accountability and Barth's historical definition of the church ask whether proclamation alone is the mode intended. Is proclaiming the kerygma to addressees what "making disciples" means? Did Jesus, as Barth declares, "constitute the community" by commissioning it to give a message? If so, what is the message and is it by its very nature not mere message but an entire reordering of humanity and world? If this is true, how is all that best conveyed: by preaching, by liturgy, by sacrament, by suffering, by praxis? It is notable that those texts mentioned above, i.e., those dealing with loving God and neighbor, loving our enemies (thus acknowledging them as ourselves), and giving to the poor, combine word and action in a way that expands meaning and does not submerge either in the other. *Fides quaerens rationem reddere*, Barth's Safenwil perspective, sees humanity as addressee differently. Some vital modes of addressing have already been suggested from the Synoptics. Others are also found in the Gospels: feeding, healing, liberating—these, too, are modes of address, even as the Barth of the *Church Dogmatics* is also aware.

Still, Barth emphasizes the preeminence of *knowing*. Not knowing is the origin of humanity's suffering. "The task given to the community is aimed at the human creature which suffers by reason of its ignorance and groans under the burden of its exclusion."[54] Salvation is significantly a cognitive thing, and it is ignorance from which humankind must be freed.[55] The present reality of humanity, Barth writes, is one of ignorance and the Word of God is addressed to that ignorance. Revealing possibilities beyond this present state and leading them forward, God opens to human beings the future, thus "bracketing, transcending and outbidding ignorance and all its consequences."[56] The references to ignorance are copious: "Man's persistence in ignorance and therefore his continuance in misery is indeed the danger under threat of which he stands of himself and to which he would be a hopeless prey if he were only what he is of himself."[57] Faith seeking accountability which then understands challenges the task as the later Barth seems to see it.

One can concede to Barth's theology an understanding of message and the knowing of message which is more than the dealing with concept which knowledge primarily consists of; but even if it is conceded that this knowledge is a knowledge by the whole person, a knowing of heart and affections as well, without the balance offered by a reclamation of the historical assertions already alluded to, Barth's category can still be read primarily as a knowing through recognition, acceptance, and understanding of the spoken and/or written witness, the apostolic message summarized in the Creed. The reasoning goes: at the primal stage, the believer encounters Jesus Christ through the apostolic proclamation. Because that is initial and basic, the task of the church is to herald the scriptural words which are heard, recognized, assented to, and finally heralded in turn. Faith for the community is knowing:

> It [the church] waits for the seeing of that which, receiving the message, it can now believe. . . As it is awakened to faith in the Easter message it hears and *knows* and *understands*. . . . *It knows* it in faith. It does not yet see it—any more than others—but it *knows* it. *It lives in this knowledge of faith. In this knowing of its faith and its life by it,* it is the one holy universal apostolic church, the community of Jesus Christ. In this *knowing* of faith it is stronger than the world and overcomes it.[58] (Emphasis added.)

Fides quaerens intellectum envisions the church's life in its knowing. Chapter V will deal with the problematics of this notion in more detail. At its base lie Barth's doctrine of revelation and difficulties in moving from that starting-point in noetic necessity to engagement with historical reality. *Fides quaerens rationem reddere,* on the other hand, presupposes historical suffering and engagement, and with that interaction, knowing and life.

History, Proclamation, and Witness

It has been noted that Barth's wish, at least in part, was to develop a sociological treatment of the church which established its historical relevance and concreteness. He sought to affirm that what God has perfected in Jesus Christ is to be expressed ever anew in humankind's existential and historical experience. Not wishing to deny the sociological, psychological, and historical pertinence of the church, Barth strove to declare its socio-historical relevance and to help the church to understand itself accordingly. In his commentary on the Heidelberg Catechism, Barth insisted on "the absolute necessity of *the relatedness of the Christian to the world,* the relatedness of the Christian to everything human. . . . Relatedness of the Christian to the world is not optional. . . . Christ rules over *all.* We would be guilty of breaking up the lordship of Christ if we did not will in all seriousness to be Greeks to the Greeks. After all, Christians are also creatures, and therefore they cannot evade the problems of the realm of creation. This realm also is subject to Christ, and we are at home in it also."[59] To be sure, the organizational structure of the church is fashioned, Barth maintained, for the very purpose of implementing that participation. The community's relationship to the surrounding culture and its art, economics, politics, education, morality and social conditions are all part of that in and with which the church has its identity, though indeed, with a maintenance of its own specificity and distinctiveness. As such the church is the *ecclesia visibilis,* the essential complement to the *ecclesia invisibilis.* "The work of the Holy Spirit to which it owes its existence is something which is produced concretely and historically in this world. It is the awakening power of the Word made flesh, of the Son of God, who Himself entered the lowliness of an historical existence in this world, who as very God became and is very man. Like begets like. The Christian faith awakened by Him is a definite human activity and therefore a definite human phenomenon. For all the pecularity of his activity the Christian is an ordinary man with other men. Similarly the Christendom in which there are Christians is a human work and as such a human phenomenon which can be generally observed."[60]

Barth, indeed, castigates a kind of "ecclesiastical Docetism" which abrogates the church's historicality and seeks to keep it separated to an other-worldly existence, an "invisible fellowship of the Spirit and of spirits."[61] He insists that both individually and communally the Christian witness can exist only in time and space and in concrete relationships and activities. No "universum" abstractly conceived can express what the church existentially is through the empowering Word which brings it into being, Barth insists. It is here that Barth's words, while apparently sounding like words affirmative of historical engagement, still tend to reduce to the engagement of witness—verbal, proclaimed, shared message of what God has done for humankind in Jesus Christ. Action appears to be the action of preaching, exposing, explaining, and announcing, primarily. Indeed, it is easy to read Barth in this way; most have. Barth's Safenwil perspective is muted, and though not obliterated, eclipsed, in the *Church Dogmatics*. Still, the inherent dynamic remains and reading Barth without attending to and acknowledging that dynamic is unjust and lacks perception gained in a more rigorous grappling with his ideas.

In Vol. 4, 1, Barth writes:

> In its deepest and most proper tendency it is not churchly, but worldly—the church with open doors and great windows, behind which it does better not to close itself in upon itself again by putting in pious stained-glass windows. It is holy in its openness to the street and even the alley, in its turning to the profanity of all human life—the holiness which, according to Romans 12:5, does not scorn to rejoice with them that do rejoice, and to weep with them that weep.[62]

It is just here that Barth acknowledges *more* than verbal heralding as the church's primary mission. Turning to "the profanity of all human life" is the key. It has been shown that Barth knew existentially what that meant in the Safenwil decade. It is the contention of this study that Barth still knew, and that the potential for a reclamation of that focus permeates the *Church Dogmatics* ecclesiology as well. Barth enjoins the church to turn to the street and the alley and to the weeping ones in the alley, those who are the hungry, naked, bound, ill, and rejected ones; there, something earthly and historical does indeed occur. Turning to the street and alley, the church finds a new meaning for its political and ethical life.

New Meaning for Christian Political Responsibility

In the late fifties Barth published in *The Faith of the Church*, under a section entitled "The Specific Work of the Church," this declaration:

> Many tasks are needed in the world: the building of a better society, of a better economy, of a more perfected monetary system. It is quite natural that men would like to live in a better organized society than this one whose remains we see around at present. . . . However, it is out of the Church's line to seek to improve human society and to make plans and projects for this purpose. The work of the Church is more modest: to call men, to recall to them that God reigns and is present, clearly to tell that man does not live by his own strength, but by the grace of God. It belongs to other human undertakings—equally submitted to God even though they yet ignore it—to build a better society . . . The Church . . . must restrict herself to her proper work: the proclamation of the Gospel, the exegesis of the Bible and of the Confession of Faith. Constantly, the Church runs the danger of unduly extending her task. How many ministers busy themselves with a multiplicity of things, and take the risk of forsaking the sole thing necessary to the Church![63]

Because the state is also of the order of reconciliation, the church need not and should not assume its tasks, Barth admonished. Still, the church is not absolved from a concern for and involvement in "the service of setting up and preserving human right and human justice."[64] Indeed, Barth insisted, "from the faith and life of the Christian Church, there is a way leading directly to co-operation in the external, worldly and extremely relative but nonetheless divinely willed and commanded work of a just state. . . ."[65] How, then, is that co-operation understood and for what is it instituted?

Barth explains that the church's center is, although the state does not recognize it so, the state's center as well. The "dual benefaction of Church and State"[66] is of the order of God's covenant, the order of reconciliation, whose center is God's act of justice and justification in Jesus Christ. Barth protests that the church must not attempt to force this view upon the state but that the primary need is that the church keep it clearly in mind.[67] Robert Willis' study of church and state in Barth's theology is helpful.[68] As "a genuine and specific order of the covenant" (Bundesordnung),[69] the state is "given continuance and meaning only as an aspect of the 'kingly rule' of Christ over the world."[70] Church and state are seen as parallel structures, each commissioned with special tasks and goals. The state's responsibility is specifically that of providing an ordered sphere amenable to the collective life and open to the preaching of the Gospel. Barth's understanding of the state, based on Romans 13:6, as God-ordained means that the church will render obedience to the state, pray for it, and conduct its own work in responsibility to it. Opposition to and judgment of the state and its practices can and will sometimes occur, but even this critical challenge will be an expression of the church's commitment to the state's well-being.

The concurrent responsibilities of church and state will be expressions of the redemption of humanity itself secured in the reconciliation by God through Jesus Christ. Thus, both will, in their particular spheres, be "agents of reconciliation," for both are "called into existence at the point of man's justification."[71] The church's primary task will consist of witness and service in the light of the event of reconciliation and the state's will consist of providing a context in which a just and free individual and corporate life can be maintained. Willis notes crucially that such a just order "insures the one thing needed by the Church for its particular activity of proclamation: freedom."[72]

In the context of Barth's social and political ethics, the *analogia fidei* expresses this relationship between church and state. In the 1938 essay "Church and State," Barth argues that the New Testament describes the new order in the new age as a political order in which the church sees the hope of a heavenly state. Analogously, then, the earthly state finds its possibility and legitimation in that true state. Barth writes, ". . . the State, as such, belongs originally and ultimately to Jesus Christ . . . in its dignity, its function, and its purpose, it should serve the Person and the Word of Jesus Christ and therefore the justification of the sinner."[73]

Arguing that the Christian community and the civil community share a common origin and center in Jesus Christ, Barth declares that the state's true function is that of analogue to the

Kingdom of God preached by the church. Exercising its "analogical capacities," the state as allegory reflects indirectly the heavenly state.[74] The political responsibility of the church is to inform the state in its understanding of itself as this allegory. Barth states in "The Christian Community and the Civil Community": "If the Church takes up its share of political responsibility . . . The distinctions, judgments, and choices which it makes in the political sphere are always intended to foster the illumination of the State's connexion with the order of divine salvation and grace and to discourage all the attempts to hide this connexion. Among the political possibilities open at any particular moment it will choose those which most suggest a correspondence to, an analogy and a reflection of, the context of its own faith and gospel."[75] Fostering the "illumination of the State's connexion with . . . divine salvation and grace" is done by the church's modelling the "real State." Gathered consciously around their common center of Jesus Christ, the church provides "the model and prototype of the real State."[76]

Willis rightly notes that Thielicke's and Brunner's objections that the *analogia fidei* allows any kind of analogy to be drawn, overlook the fact that Barth places analogy within the greater frame of God's reconciliation in Jesus Christ. As the elected covenant partner of God, the church can legitimately draw only those analogies which foster genuine fellowship and communality among persons.[77] Still, it can be argued that Barth's Anselmian method tends to control the way in which Barth derives his analogies. Theoretically drawn, those analogies often lack praxiological content and remain abstract.

Barth's understanding of church and state holds valuable seeds which, with the historical assertions inherent in his doctrine of the church and, with *fides quaerens rationem reddere*, need to be cultivated. His notion that the state's center is Jesus Christ can move in polar directions—toward acquiescence to the *status quo* or toward motivation for activity in cooperation with God's activity. Barth declares that the church is to "give positive expression to its own understanding of itself . . . decisively in the contours of its life and activity within the sphere of the state."[78] This is the church as earthly and historical. Understanding itself as acting subject with God as Acting Subject, the church can, not despite the state, but within that very sphere, work for justification and justice, a "cosmic reconciliation" of the whole of creation.[79] So doing, this thesis holds, the church expresses its nature as the earthly-historical form of the

existence of Jesus Christ. In social location with the poor of humanity and para-humanity, the church perceives a political responsibility which is otherwise obscured. It had been so for Barth in
Safenwil. Understanding the church as the *irdisch-geschichliche*
body of Jesus Christ who is himself God's movement for social
justice has power to break the Anselmian frame.

Christian Social Action and Cosmic Reconciliation

Working with the state and within the state for a cosmic
reconciliation of the whole of creation, the church perceives a larger
meaning for its diaconate than the giving of alms. Barth points out
that diaconate means generally the rendering of service including all
the church's activity, "the whole breadth and depth of its action,"
not, as it is commonly understood, a specific, compartmentalized
service. In those parts of the New Testament outside Acts, Barth
notes, διακωνια refers to the "relationship of service in which . . .
the apostles stand, but also all other Chrsitians, and Jesus Christ
Himself at their head (Rom. 15:8)." Thus the history of the term
itself, Barth states, indicates a wider service than that which diaconate generally has meant. Nonetheless, *fides quaerens intellectum* at
points leads Barth toward a merging of diaconate and proclamation
which finally subordinates the former to the latter by understanding
the church's general service, its true diaconate, "the whole breadth
and depth of its action," as proclamation of God's reconciliation of
humanity in the election of Jesus Christ. *Fides quaerens rationem
reddere* and the historical assertions contained in Barth's definition
of the church, however, emphasize implications in the history of the
diaconate which suggest that the general rendering of service which
includes all the church's activity is more than mere verbal proclamation and that "the things done in diaconate" cannot be subsumed
under heralding alone. If the primary quest is for accountability, the
latter conclusion is reached.

Barth oscillates from the affirmation that diaconate comprises a
major understanding of what the church means to the notion that
diaconate can never be more than "drops in a bucket."[80] *Die
Kirchliche Dogmatik* states literally that acts of social concern such
as those emphasized in the parable of the Last Judgment (Mt.
25:31ff.) are *"offenkundig immer nur um Tropfen auf einen heisen
Stein"* (obviously always only a drop in the bucket).[81] Barth acclaims

the formally small place that the diaconate holds in the total ministry of the church, believing that its customary individual focus encourages a selflessness which public acts tend to vitiate, and, hence, that it is a purer and more indispensable form of witness. Indispensable though it might be, however, Barth does say that the diaconate is and "can never be more" than "drops in a bucket." Why? The parable of the Good Samaritan, to which Barth refers, was given in reply to a query as to who the neighbor is whom one is to love as oneself; this kind of loving, Jesus reminded, is, with love of God, *the fullness of the Gospel*. Why, then, Barth might be asked, can such love never be more than a drop in the bucket? Is that what this parable and other parables have conveyed? Has the church's shifting of these acts from their original meaning of rendering service broadly, to a narrowly focused diaconate, restricted and eclipsed Jesus' meaning and intention? The Gospels appear to weigh the Good Samaritan's act quite heavily in a way that the church has substantially failed to do. If what Barth wishes to emphasize is that, compared to Christ's saving work, the church's social ministry is less central than Christ's total service, then some clarity is reached, perhaps. Still, if that is Barth's concern, he might have expressed it with less ambiguity and in a way which preserved Christ's centrality without denigrating the full importance of the church's social action.

Barth argues for keeping the diaconate small, humble, a quiet and unobtrusive aspect of the church's total ministry. The rationale seems to be that small acts are purer, nearer the gospel injunction "to go and do likewise," while public, large-scale actions are apt to be tainted by hubris. Materially, Barth wants to say and does say movingly that the diaconate stands with the poor and locates the church in the midst of human need:

> But the material point has to be considered that in diaconate the community explicitly accepts solidarity with the least of the little ones . . . with those who are in obscurity and are not seen, with those who are pushed to the margin and perhaps the very outer margin of the life of human society, with fellow-creatures who temporarily at least, and perhaps permanently, are useless and insignificant and perhaps even burdensome and destructive. In the diaconate these men are recognized to be brothers of Jesus Christ according to the significant tenor of the parable of the Last Judgment (Mt. 25:31f.), and therefore the community confesses Jesus Christ Himself as finally the hungry, thirsty, naked, homeless, sick, imprisoned man, and the royal man as such. In the diaconate the community makes

claim its witness to Him as the Samaritan service to the man who has fallen among thieves—a service fulfilled in company with Him as the true Neighbour of this lost man. In the diaconate it goes and does likewise (Lk. 10:29f.). And woe to it if it does not, if its witness is not service in this elementary sense! For if not, even though its proclamation of Christ is otherwise ever so powerful, it stands hopelessly on the left hand among the goats. If not, even though its zeal in other respects is ever so ardent, it is on the steep slope which leads to eternal punishment. Without this active solidarity with the least of little ones, without this concrete witness to Jesus the Crucified, who as such is the Neighbour of the lost, its witness may be ever so pure and full at other points, but it is all futile.[82]

Does the church, *fides quaerens rationem reddere* asks, accept and establish solidarity with these marginal ones, then, only on the scale suggested by a formally small diaconate? Barth exegetes Matthew 25:31ff. as an identification of Jesus Christ with the hungry and naked, but does not, at this point, draw certain important conclusions from that fact. He does warn that a failure to serve in the social location of the poor is tantamount to aligning oneself with the goats. The church's witness, in fact, is sterile, Barth warns, however full its proclamation might otherwise be, if that failure occurs.

That Barth grapples seriously with problems of theory and practice for the Christian diaconate is amply documented in 4, 3, Second Half. Here, I feel, his Safenwil insights inform his perspective and relativize an otherwise Anselmian focus. Wishing to emphasize the diaconate's importance, Barth is uneasy that all the church's *words* are finally hollow without obedience to this "second direction" given by Jesus to the disciples. One questions, thus, all the more the weight of the *Church Dogmatics* toward the side of preaching and proclamation. Nonetheless, although Barth's rich insights were constricted by his later method and his understanding of faith and theology as *fides quaerens intellectum*, the church today, enabled by *fides quaerens rationem reddere*, can still unfold the potential in Barth's doctrine of the church. Crucially valuable is his notion of God's "cosmic reconciliation," e.g., of the "totality of human existence." All that Barth has said about diaconate as no more than a drop in the bucket has finally to be contradicted by his own insights:

> . . .here *in the diaconate* it [the church] has the opportunity to reveal at least in sign *the cosmic character of the reconciliation* accomplished in Jesus Christ, of the kingdom, of love for God

and one's neighbor and therefore of the content of the witness
which it has to give to men in its preaching, evangelization,
cure of souls and missionary work. It has this opportunity at the
point where it *intervenes for man more specifically in his
physical and material existence and therefore for the whole
man*. For here it escapes the misconception that in its message
its final concern is only with words, thoughts, ideas, feelings
and moral injunctions. To be sure, even here it will not act
without granting the Word as well to the least of the little ones,
without calling them urgently and explicitly to God who, as He
is the primary and proper Preacher, Teacher, Evangelist, Pastor and Theologian, is also the primary and proper Deacon.
Nevertheless, its distinctive action here is to hold out a helping
hand, indicatively and in part at least *causing the good deed
which corresponds to the good Word to be tasted and felt, and
thus enabling the good Word to be understood in the fullness of
its truth* . . . Specifically in the diaconate the community . . .
can be obedient to the second and easily overlooked element in
the direction for service given by Jesus to His disciples, thus
*serving the whole truth which otherwise is divided and re-
duced to a purely intellectual word and sentimental form, so
that it is no longer the truth of Jesus Christ at all*.[83] (Emphasis
added.)

This is crucial. The reflective social action which correlates the good
deed and the good word *and thus creates understanding*, which is
apprehension of truth in its fullness, is precisely what *fides quaerens
rationem reddere* is about. It should not be overlooked that Barth is
saying here that understanding occurs precisely *in* that union of
deed and word. Faith which seeks to be accountable in deed makes
full the truth of its word. Barth has enunciated inchoately again, as
he did earlier in Safenwil, just this praxis methodology in his call for
obedience to the "easily overlooked" second direction of Jesus to his
disciples.

As Chapter III showed, the older Barth's inchoate understanding of faith seeking accountability derived from an earlier period of
his work, the Safenwil decade 1911-1921. It was then that Barth
recognized and first reminded the church that human suffering is
rooted in social evil as well as individual disorders. At Safenwil first
and later in Basle, Barth insisted that the church has the responsibility to confront social injustice with the Gospel and its denuncia-
tion of that evil. Social, economic, and political problems, Barth
wanted to say, will be acknowledged as the church's responsibility,
too, at least insofar as the ecclesial community as a human institution within the larger totality of society has acquiesced in unjust

structures and failed to challenge their domination. Indeed, Barth insisted, failing its political responsibility, the *communio sanctorum* becomes one of "dumb dogs serving the powers-that-be" if it does not "tackle *at their social roots* the evils by which they are confronted in detail."[84] (Emphasis added.) So far from separating itself from the concerns of the state should the church be, Barth maintained, that it should provide men who will be ready to assist the state in its necessary work.[85] Most emphatically, the diaconate was far more than "drops in a bucket" to Barth.

Again, Barth stated: "In this situation there is need for the *open word of Christian social criticism in order that a new place be found for Christian action and a new meaning given to it*."[86] (Emphasis added.) This is vitally to the point! A *new place for Christian social action* implies more than just the diaconate commonly conceived; a *new meaning for Christian social action* calls for a true reclamation of and development of Jesus' imperative to social ministry. Re-appropriating a previous methodology and understanding of faith and theology, and of the church and its nature and tasks, Barth expressed again insights gleaned in the Safenwil pastorate. In a 1925 essay bridging the Safenwil era and the turn to Anselm and *fides quaerens intellectum*, Barth had written: ". . . it [theology] is conditioned in its basic assumptions by human misery."[87] In the context of worship and embracing a definition of the church redolent of historical responsibility for human misery, Barth gave to theology and the church a doctrine of the church which holds potential not yet claimed.

This chapter has enumerated several of those areas of potential ripe for development with reclamation of Barth's early praxis methodology. They include: (1) a corporate Body of Christ truly comprehensive in unity, not just in verbal witness, but in the manifold expressions of solidarity which a larger understanding of the diaconate, for instance, gives to the church as the earthly-historical form of the existence of Jesus Christ, (2) a closer word-deed union which recognizes the co-inherence of word and action in Christ's ministry and, hence, in the church's as well, (3) the centrality of worship and the Eucharist for the church's life and its understanding of its tasks, (4) the church's responsibility to work precisely within the sphere of the state in expressing its own understanding of itself, (5) the development of a new and more adequate meaning for Christian social action and a new priority assigned, one which sees diaconate in the original general terms of Christian ministry broadly expressed and not relegated to a small subsection of the church's function, and (6) a new appropriation of Paul's insight of *cosmic reconciliation* and a more profound apprehension of what that means, e.g., intervening in the "physical and material existence" of human beings and thus in the whole of human reality and experience. Also included is the healing of the para-human creation and a new regard for its value.

If Barth himself did not develop these most important insights in ways that render his ecclesiology fully adequate to the needs of our world today, it is suggested that an applying of the Safenwil insights to those of the *Church Dogmatics* can yield that more adequate ecclesiology still. Fundamental to that successful construction, however, will be a reclamation of the praxis orientation begun in Safenwil and a re-ordering of methodological priorities which retain an emphasis on Scripture but reject its noetic exclusivity, allowing the suffering of a real world to function hermeneutically in the reading of Scripture.

Chapter V will pursue further directions for reclaiming Barth's praxis methodology by approaching his work from the focus of the doctrine of the church as opposed to approaching it from the focus of revelation. Situating the church immediately in the context of mundane reality, Barth's theology can be developed beyond abstract ecclesiological statements about, to praxiological engagement with, social justice concerns. In the meeting, then, of word and deed, as Barth suggests, the full truth of the church's nature and tasks can be seen.

NOTES

/1/   D. F. Ford, "Barth's Interpretation of the Bible," in *Karl Barth: Studies of His Theological Method*, ed. S. W. Sykes (Oxford: Clarendon Press, 1979), pp. 86, 87.
/2/   Barth, *Church Dogmatics*, Vol. 4, 1:643.
/3/   Karl Barth, *Credo: A Presentation of the Chief Problems of Dogmatics with Reference to the Apostles' Creed*, trans. J. Strathearn McNab (New York: Charles Scribner's Sons, 1936), p. 1.
/4/   Ibid., pp. 2, 3.
/5/   Adolf Keller, *Karl Barth and Christian Unity: The Influence of the Barthian Movement Upon the Churches of the World*, trans. Werner Petersmann and Manfred Manrodt, with an Introduction by Luther A. Weigle (New York: Macmillan Co., 1933), pp. 252, 254.
/6/   Barth, *Church Dogmatics*, Vol. 4, 1:643.
/7/   Ibid., p. 650.
/8/   Ibid., pp. 659, 660.

/9/ Ibid., p. 665.
/10/ Ibid.
/11/ Ibid., pp. 666, 667.
/12/ Ibid., pp. 685, 686.
/13/ See Chapter I, p. 10.
/14/ Barth, *Church Dogmatics*, Vol. 4, 1:687.
/15/ Ibid., p. 688.
/16/ Barth, *Church Dogmatics*, Vol. 4, 3, 2:682,683.
/17/ Ibid., pp. 681, 682.
/18/ Mueller, *Karl Barth*, p. 108.
/19/ Barth, *Church Dogmatics*, vol. 4, 2:641, 642.
/20/ Ibid., p. 643.
/21/ Ibid., p. 646.
/22/ Ibid., pp. 646, 647.
/23/ Ibid., pp. 660f.
/24/ Karl Barth, *Theological Existence Today: A Plea for Theological Freedom*, trans. R. Birch Hoyle (London: Hodder and Stoughton, 1933), p. 77. Eberhard Busch describes the history of the early thirties and the threat to the church imposed by German National Socialism at that time. The events leading to the "Barmen Declaration increasingly concentrated administrative power in the hands of the "German Christians," the ecclesiastical vehicle of the National Socialist party. On September 6, 1933, the Church Law concerning the Legal Status of Ministers and Church Officials which excluded non-Aryans and their spouses from employment in the service of the church was imposed. On September 27 Ludwig Müller assumed leadership as Reich Bishop of the Evangelical Church. Against this movement, Martin Niemöller called together the Pastors' Emergency League which led to the organization of the Confessing Church. The Confessing Church concerned itself with opposing the notion that any legitimate authority besides the Scriptures obtained for the message and ecclesiology of the church. Busch observes that the concern of the Barmen Fathers and Barth was the rejection of all natural theology, this latest manifestation of which was an especially pernicious one. "Barmen designated Jesus Christ, as he is witnessed to us in Holy Scripture, the one Word of God whom we have to trust and obey in life and in death. It rejected as false teaching the doctrine that there could be a different source of church proclamation from this one Word of God and . . . stated that to recognize the truth and to repudiate the error was 'the indispensable theological foundation of the German Evangelical Church.' This was a discovery, the significance of which went far above the heads of the poor German Christians and far beyond the immediate situation of the church in Germany. If it was taken seriously, it meant a purification of the church not only from the *new* natural theology which was specifically under discussion, but from all natural theology. . ." (p. 247). Busch notes that Barth later expressed regret for not having made the Jewish question a more central concern, although he did not believe that anything he might have said would have been acceptable at that time. See Busch, *Karl Barth: His Life from Letters and Autobiographical Texts*, pp. 228–248. Daniel Cornu's volume also contains incisive essays treating Barth's political and ecclesiological concerns during

the Barmen period and beyond. See Daniel Cornu, *Karl Barth und die Politik Widerspruch und Freiheit* (Wuppertal: Aussaat Verlag, 1969).

/25/   Karl Barth, *The Church and the Political Problem of Our Day* (New York: Charles Scribner's Sons, 1939), p. 44.

/26/   Karl Barth, *Trouble and Promise in the Struggle of the Church in Germany,* trans. P. V. M. Benecke (Oxford: Clarendon Press, 1938), pp. 4f.

/27/   Barth, *Theological Existence Today,* p. 78.

/28/   Ibid., p. 80.

/29/   Barth, *Trouble and Promise in the Struggle of the Church in Germany,* pp. 4f.

/30/   Karl Barth, *How to Serve God in a Marxist Land,* with an Introduction by Robert McAfee Brown (New York: Association Press, 1959), p. 73.

/31/   Karl Barth, *The Church and the War,* trans. Antonia H. Froendt with an Introduction by Samuel McCrea Cavert (New York: Macmillan Co., 1944), p. 37.

/32/   Barth, *Knowledge of God and Service of God,* pp. 209, 210. Barth states: "Some form of activity or other is not enough, even though it be very well meant and in other connections doubtless thoroughly useful and laudable. The church is neither a charitable institution, nor an institution for the general betterment of the world and man. . . . The church in modern times has frequently overlooked that and let herself be driven into activity in all these directions, and owing to this she has forgotten and neglected her own proper activity and the reason why she allowed this to happen is simply that she had already forgotten and neglected her own proper action, and wanted, by busily wasting her time, to preserve at least the appearance of active existence in these other activities—a hopeless undertaking. By this means it is indeed not possible to preserve more than the appearance. The content of the church service corresponds to revelation and faith and does not consist in a busy waste of time."

/33/   Karl Barth, *The Faith of the Church: A Commentary on the Apostles' Creed According to Calvin's Catechism,* ed. Jean-Louis Leuba and trans. Gabriel Vahanian (New York: Meridian Books, 1958), p. 148.

/34/   Barth, *Knowledge of God and Service of God,* p. 210.

/35/   Wolfgang Huber, "The Barmen Theological Declaration and the Two Kingdom Doctrine," *Lutheran World* 24 (1977):30–44.

/36/   Ibid., p. 33.

/37/   Barth, *Church Dogmatics,* vol. 4, 3, 2:775.

/38/   Ibid., p. 776.

/39/   Ibid., p. 777.

/40/   Karl Barth, *The Knowledge of God and the Service of God According to the Teaching of the Reformation,* trans. J. L. M. Haire and Ian Henderson (London: Hodder and Stoughton, 1938; reprint ed., 1955), p. 210.

/41/   Barth, *Church Dogmatics,* vol. 4, 3, 2:778.

/42/   Ibid., p. 786.

/43/   While it might be argued that Barth's inclusion of ethics as a focus of the doctrine of God suggests that his Anselmian method of reflection on Scripture and Creed suffices for the construction of an accountable theology, examination of the *Church Dogmatics* Volumes 2, 2 and 3, 4 indicates that problems inhere in the ethics which can be traced to the faith seeking understanding method itself. Barth's notion of grace can, without the Safen-wil perspective, lean toward triumphalism even as the discussions of Berkouwer and others in Chapter II suggested. In *Church Dogmatics* 2, 2, Barth writes:

> "Our contention is, however, that the dogmatics of the Christian Church, and basically the Christian doctrine of God, is ethics. This doctrine is, therefore, the answer to the ethical question, the su-premely critical question concerning the good in and over every so-called good in human actions and modes of action.
>
> It is the *answer*—this must be our starting-point. But we must be more exact and say that it is the attestation, the 'tradition,' the repeti-tion of the answer. For the answer is not theology, or the doctrine of God, but their object—the revelation and work of the electing grace of God. But this, the grace of God, *is* the answer to the ethical problem. For it sanctifies man. It claims him for God. It puts him under God's command. It gives predetermination to his self-determination so that he obeys God's command. . . . The sanctification of man, the fact that he is claimed by God, the fulfillment of his predetermination in his self-determination to obedience, the judgment of God on man and His command to him in its actual concrete fulfillment—they all take place here in Jesus Christ. The good is done here . . . beyond all that merely pretends to be called good. . . ." (pp. 515–17)

Barth stresses the ethical good already fulfilled in Jesus Christ. Immanent in the conception of God the Commander is the notion of an obedient humanity represented in Jesus Christ. The grace and command of God obviate the possibility of a general moral enquiry. A tone of finality colors the following: "For the question of good and evil has been decided once and for all in the decree of God, by the cross and the resurrection of Jesus Christ. . . . It [theological ethics] can only be as receptive and open as possible to this revealed foundation of all things, as true and complete as possible in its attestation of it. . . . Even as ethics, theology is wholly and utterly the knowledge and representation of the Word and works of God. . . ." (2, 2:536–38) God's election of humanity in Jesus Christ is also, Barth states, humanity's sanctification and establishment of the divine law. Barth's ethics can be, and has been, read as a finalization of God's Word and work which leaves to humanity only the act of repentance. His conception of Jesus Christ as the one Subject of ethical action suggests to some an exclusion of human beings as subjects also; Barth refers to human beings as "predicates." As predicates of Jesus Christ, men and women participate in the righteousness of Jesus. Passages like the following tend to promote for some that kind of reading: "In Him the obedience demanded of us men has already been rendered. In Him the realisation of the good corresponding to divine election has already taken place—and so completely that we, for our part, have actually nothing to add, but have only to endorse this event by our action. The ethical problem of church dogmatics can consist only in the question whether and to what extent human action is a glorification of the grace of Jesus Christ." (2, 2:540)

Clearly, at least to this reader, Barth does not intend to leave human-ity's action extraneous to the sanctification of human life but, rather, intends to ground it in human freedom given to us in Jesus Christ. The following comes through as God's enablement which transforms human weakness into effective action: "[The Law] is valid because, in becoming man in Jesus Christ, God has claimed for Himself our human freedom. It is valid because, once God has Himself become man for us in Jesus Christ, there is no longer any excuse for our human weakness." (2, 2:565).

The fact that Barth's ethics lends itself to interpretations which question the genuineness of human ethical action requires explanation. Again, it appears that the theoretical commitment of *fides quaerens intellectum* is at issue. *Fides quaerens rationem reddere* escapes the conceptual bind which the former methodology does not. Located in the concrete context of ethical decision-making, faith seeking accountability which understands emphasizes the freedom in Christ Jesus *for* ethical engagement which Barth wishes to stress.

/44/ Ibid., p. 862.

/45/ Ibid., p. 863.

/46/ Karl Barth, *The Heidelberg Catechism for Today*, trans. Shirley C. Guthrie, Jr. (Richmond: John Knox Press, 1964; 1st published 1948), pp. 53, 54.

/47/ Ibid., p. 54.

/48/ Ibid. Barth's perception of theology as a quest for "certain knowledge" is the subject of numerous studies of Barth's doctrine of revelation. See Philip C. Almond, "Karl Barth and Anthropocentric Theology," *Scottich Journal of Theology* 31 (October 1978); Robert Brown, "On God's Ontic and Noetic Absoluteness: A Critique of Barth," *Scottish Journal of Theology* 33 (December 1980); R. Birch Hoyle, *The Teaching of Karl Barth* (London: Student Christian Movement Press, 1930); David McKenzie, "Barth's *Anselm* and the Object of Theological Knowledge," *Foundations* 21 (July–September 1978); Charles Edward Raynal, *Karl Barth's Conception of the Perfections of God* (Ann Arbor: Xerox University Microfilms, 1978); Klaas Runia, *Karl Barth's Doctrine of Holy Scripture* (Grand Rapids: William B. Eerdmans, 1962); Steven P. Stahl, "The Concept of Revelation in the Theology of Karl Barth," *The Saint Luke's Journal of Theology* 23 (March 1980); Gordon Watson, "Karl Barth and St. Anselm's Theological Programme," *Scottish Journal of Theology* 30 (February 1977); Gustaf Wingren, *Theology in Conflict: Nygren, Barth, Bultmann*, trans. Eric H. Wahlstrom (Philadelphia: Muhlenberg Press, 1958).

/49/ Barth, *Faith of the Church*, p. 30.

/50/ Ibid., p. 35.

/51/ Ibid., p. 40.

/52/ Ibid., pp. 144, 145.

/53/ Barth, *Church Dogmatics*, Vol. 4, 3, 2:802.

/54/ Ibid., p. 809.

/55/ R. D. Williams discusses this presupposition and its significance for Barth's theology in "Barth on the Triune God," in *Karl Barth: Studies of His Theological Method*, ed. S. W. Sykes (Oxford: Clarendon Press, 1979).

/56/ Barth, *Church Dogmatics*, Vol. 4, 3, 2:809.

/57/ Ibid., p. 810.

/58/ Barth, *Church Dogmatics*, Vol. 4, 1:726, 727.

/59/   Barth, *Heidelberg Catechism*, p. 83.

/60/   Barth, *Church Dogmatics*, Vol. 4, 1:652.

/61/   Ibid., p. 653.

/62/   Ibid., p. 725.

/63/   Barth, *The Faith of the Church*, pp. 146ff.

/64/   Barth, *The Church and the Political Problem of Our Day*, p. 75.

/65/   Ibid., p. 76.

/66/   Barth, *The Church and the War*, p. 30.

/67/   Barth, *Church Dogmatics*, Vol. 4, 2:687.

/68/   Willis, *The Ethics of Karl Barth*, pp. 392ff.

/69/   Barth, *Church Dogmatics*, Vol. 3, 4:342.

/70/   Willis, *The Ethics of Karl Barth*, p. 392.

/71/   Ibid., pp. 394, 395.

/72.   Ibid., p. 395. Willis refers also to *Kingdom of God and Service of God*, p. 226.

/73/   Karl Barth, "Church and State," in *Community, State, and Church*, p. 118.

/74/   Karl Barth, "The Christian Community and the Civil Community," in *Community, State, and Church*, p. 169.

/75/   Ibid., p. 170.

/76/   Ibid., p. 186.

/77/   It is true that Barth's political ethics affirms a kind of "hands-off" stance which allows the church to take a "wait-and-see" attitude toward political changes, even toward new forms of government. Hence, Barth's refusal to become embroiled in the East-West controversy. So long as dogma was not an issue, Barth could sit lightly with various kinds of political systems. This had not been the case earlier in the German church conflict. When it became emphatically clear that doctrine *was* the issue, Barth refused to give ground. "In the course of this trouble the Church in Germany has been allowed to make a discovery; the discovery, in fact, of the majesty of the foundation on which the Church stands, of the *majesty of the Word of God*, as the bread on which she may nourish herself, as the fountain from which she may drink, as the might that is strong when men in the Church are weak." [*Trouble and Promise in the Struggle of the Church in Germany*, p. 20.] In 1944 Barth's view remained the same. [See *The Church and the War*, p. 37.] The church's faithfulness to its doctrinal integrity insured, Barth believed, its proper ethical engagement with social and political issues. The Barmen Confession of 1934 reflected that conviction. Barth's handling of the East-West issue re-affirmed that conviction. In 1934 and two decades later, Barth's central concern remained a doctrinal one. It is proposed that his predominant method in both instances was *fides quaerens intellectum*. Committed to reflection on Scripture and Creed and zealous for confessional purity, Barth held a church-to-church view which tended to except concerns that the Safenwil method might have retained, perhaps, had it directed Barth's work more explicitly.

/78/   Barth, *Church Dogmatics*, vol. 4, 2:689.

/79/   Barth refers to the "cosmic reconciliation" of the whole of life and creation on p. 891 of 4, 3, 2.

/80/   Ibid., pp. 890–892. ". . . the things done in diaconate, e.g., caring for the sick, the feeble, and the mentally confused and threatened, looking after orphans, helping prisoners, finding new homes for refugees, stretching out a hand to stranded and shattered fellow-men of all kinds, *can obviously never be more than drops in a bucket* and are usually done in concealment, so that by their very nature no great glory can attach to them, and they can be undertaken and executed only as pure, selfless and unassuming service which might well be hampered or even totally spoiled by even occasional attempts of domination. In this respect the community has a unique chance unequivocally to accomplish and manifest its witness as a ministry of witness. This is what makes the diaconate formally so important and indispensable as a basic form of witness." (Emphasis added.) p. 891.

/81/   Karl Barth, *Die Kirchliche Dogmatik*, Vol. 4, 3, 2:1021.
/82/   Barth, *Church Dogmatics*, Vol. 4, 3, 2:892.
/83/   Ibid., pp. 891, 892.
/84/   Ibid., p. 893.
/85/   Ibid.
/86/   Ibid., p. 892.
/87/   Karl Barth, "Church and Theology," in *Theology and Church: Shorter Writings 1920–1928*, trans. Louise Pettibone Smith, with an Introduction by T. F. Torrance (London: SCM Press, 1962), p. 299.

CHAPTER V

UNITING CHURCH AND WORLD: BARTH'S DOCTRINE OF THE CHURCH AND ITS INDICATIONS FOR A PRAXIOLOGICAL APPROACH TO CHURCH AND THEOLOGY

The questions and issues with which this thesis has dealt arose in the context of concern for and reflection on the tragic Atlanta murders of 1979–81. How the church (and the Southern Baptist Convention particularly) saw and expressed its ministry in relation to the poverty, racial hatred, and oppression which formed the social matrix of those tragic events became for me a primary question. Remembering Barth's engagement with social issues during his early pastorate in Safenwil, I began to inquire how the church might understand itself and its purpose as related to such concerns and what those factors are which inhibit its doing so. Theological method, it seemed, was a crucial and primary factor, in regard to both facilitation and inhibition. Barth's early and late methods became the focus of research as I sought to identify directions for today's church and theology. Barth's early methodology in social location with the disadvantaged people of Safenwil and the major shift occurring in 1931 with the Anselm book, I concluded, were significant for an understanding of Barth's ecclesiology and for the further development of an ecclesiology for today.

Chapter II has shown that the dominant methodology in the *Church Dogmatics* is that of the Anselmian theory-over-praxis method. There are interludes, however (sparse comparative to the corpus as a whole), which suggest another methodology. Those interludes indicate that the earlier Safenwil method, if reclaimed and permitted to correct and reshape the Anselmian one, can yield an ecclesiology which unites church and world in a way that is faithful to Barth's christological insight and focus. *Fides quaerens intellectum,* it has been argued, hampers the getting of the doctrine of the church out of the theoretical and into the historical. Because of its exclusive commitment to noetic investigation and its dependence on reflection on Scripture and Creed, the Anselmian method has difficulties in extricating itself from theoretical abstraction and relating church and world in concrete specifics. *Fides quaerens rationem reddere,* on the other hand, begins at the outset with the natural and historical to which the church is accountable, including it, even, in the hermeneutical matrix.

Chapter III has analyzed the beginning of *fides quaerens rationem reddere* in the concrete stuff of human history where the church is situated immediately in the real world. Approaching the scriptural text or the Creed in company with the poor whose questions arise in the context of their experienced suffering, faith seeking accountability which understands is a methodology which begins where God is incarnated, e.g., in the pain and struggle of divinity/humanity for justice and peace. *Fides quaerens intellectum,* faith seeking understanding, makes no effort to locate its hermeneutic in the context of human suffering. Rather, insights are developed from reflection on Scripture and Creed, and these are, in turn, analogously *applied to* situations of oppression and peril. A crucial question arises concerning the adequacy, even the *legitimacy,* of this method of applying the Gospel *to* historical reality. The Gospel itself emerged from the very concrete context in which Jesus of Nazareth encountered nontheoretical problems like leprosy, prejudice, demon possession, hemorrhage, spiritual aridity, poverty, social rejection, and powerlessness in the lives of actual people. Socially located with the poor of whom he was one, Jesus Christ related to his Father as One who *identifies* with—establishes his identity with—the hungry, sick, rejected, and bound. "Then shall the King say . . . For I was an hungred, and ye gave me meat: I was thirsty and ye gave me drink: I was a stranger, and ye took me in: Naked, and ye clothed me: I was sick, and ye visited me: I was in prison, and ye came unto me" (Matthew 25:34-36, KJV). The kerygma was born on the road, in the dust, with the people for whom Jesus had been claimed by God as preacher, liberator, healer, builder-of-justice. *There,* in the midst of what Frederick Herzog calls "God-walk," Jesus understood his Father, the suffering world around him, and the nature of his Father's claim upon him. No abstract Gospel was applied to the crises of Jesus' fellow strugglers; their suffering itself, and God's, participated in the shaping of the Gospel which engaged their need.

Faith seeking accountability and thus knowing forged a kerygma intimately—integrally—connected to those for whom it was good news.

Chapter IV has identified both potential and obstruction to the actualization of potential in Barth's *Church Dogmatics* ecclesiology. The Anselmian method of faith seeking understanding and its theoretical commitment, I have argued, are principally at fault concerning Barth's failure to develop a doctrine of the church adequate to his own definition of the church as the earthly-historical form of the existence of Jesus Christ.

The focus of this chapter is to draw together insights set forth in these earlier chapters and to assess their contribution to a theology of the church for today. The search for a more faithful and thus adequate ecclesiology is informed by the following presuppositions:

(1) The God of the Bible and of the Christian faith is a world-transforming God who acts in history more to realize than to reveal. Thus, the view of God as world-transforming Person is more faithful to the biblical witness than God as self-disclosing Person.

(2) *Fides quaerens intellectum* focuses on God's self-disclosure to the detriment of God's world-transformation. A correlative implication of this methodology for church and theology is that the mission of the church is to make God known more than to join God in the transformation of unjust structures.

(3) *Fides quaerens rationem reddere* presupposes that God acts to claim disciples for the transformation of a world blighted by sin and unrighteousness into a world of peace and justice. Correlative implications for church and theology impinge on issues of ministry and purpose, and theological method and hermeneutic. The church's mission is seen as one of accountable engagement with God in the construction of a just and peaceful world. Theology facilitates the church's discipleship by locating its reflection with the poor (those without justice and peace) in a reciprocity of active and reflective involvement.

(4) Choice of methodology is crucial to the formation of a doctrine of the church. *Fides quaerens rationem reddere* fosters an ecclesiology which is faithful to God's world-transforming activity and purpose by situating the church in the immediate context of historical movement and process. Karl Barth's doctrine of the church can be read anew from the focus of *fides quaerens rationem reddere*—faith seeking accountability which understands. Insights inherent in Barth's work deriving from the employment of such a

methodology in the Safenwil decade can be developed in order to claim for the church a more profound appreciation of worship, diaconia, and the reconciliation of all spheres of life in Christ Jesus.

This concluding chapter will further advance the argument with the thesis that (5) approaching Barth's theology from the focus of the doctrine of the church itself rather than, as is usual, from the focus of revelation, is consistent with those presuppositions just enumerated. A doctrine of God which acknowledges God as the world-transforming One, who claims both covenant partner and covenant community more for accountable discipleship in justice action than for correct thinking, stresses the accountable community's embodiment of Christ rather than its knowledge of Christ. Beginning with Jesus Christ, as Barth's christological commitment wishes to do, is facilitated by beginning with the earthly-historical form of Jesus' existence—the church which is his Body. However much the theologian's intention (Barth's or others') might be to keep faith seeking understanding, *fides quaerens intellectum*, christologically grounded and oriented, that methodology tends toward locating theological reflection with Being in revelation. *Fides quaerens rationem reddere*, however, begins with Jesus Christ *in the church* as his Body. Although Barth's theology is *church* dogmatics, the issue seems to be the location of the church. With *fides quaerens intellectum*, church dogmatics tends to remain theoretical and academic. With *fides quaerens rationem reddere*, however, the church itself has its locus with the poor to whom it is accountable. The ecclesiologies which emerge through the two methodologies differ significantly. What this means practically will become clear as we analyze this subject further. In engaging in such analysis, our concern is more than remaining faithful to Barth; it is a concern to appreciate Barth's genius as the catalyst for further development of what in Safenwil was perhaps only nascent.

It will be instructive to examine what beginning with the doctrine of revelation yields for Barth's theology.

Beginning with the Doctrine of Revelation

As shown in Chapter II, those who have studied Karl Barth's theology have generally employed a methodology not unlike the one adopted with the Anselm turn and have approached Barth's thought from the angle of faith seeking understanding, as well. For these, it has been natural to read Barth's theology from the focus of the doctrine of revelation.[1] The quest of *fides quaerens intellectum* for knowledge and that method's preoccupation with the knowability of God tend to orient in revelation for the purpose of receiving in faith and understanding, through rational reflection, God's self-disclosure.

Barthian scholars who affirm Barth's revelational approach with him stress several foci within the larger frame of revelation. These include: the hiddenness of God and God's veiling and unveiling in Jesus Christ, the concreteness (as they perceive it) of revelation, and the importance of knowledge for faith and theology.

1. God's hiddenness and concrete revelation

Eberhard Jüngel and Herbert Hartwell are among those who have studied the doctrine of God's hiddenness and the way it becomes integral to an understanding of God as self-disclosing Person in Barth's theology. Barth focuses on the divine hiddenness and self-disclosure in Jesus Christ in 1, 1 of the *Church Dogmatics*. Both Jüngel and Hartwell argue the importance of the *deus absconditus* to the notion of revelation, seeing in it, indeed, the grounding of theology itself.[2]

The notions of God's hiddenness and the concrete revelation in Jesus Christ are correlative notions—the hidden God is concretely veiled and unveiled, hidden and revealed, in Jesus Christ. Barth states in 1, 1 of the *Church Dogmatics* that this revelation is a "concrete revelation given to concrete men."[3] Because it is an event in the lives of human beings, it is an historical event. This reality also allows us to think of God's being as concrete event. For Barth, the being of God is concrete as historical occurrence and as the fellowship with humanity which ensues from the concrete self-giving of God in history. Additionally, the doctrine of *perichoresis* emphasizes that God's concreteness in Jesus Christ is shared by the other Persons of the Trinity.[4] Given to particular individuals at specific times through Word and sacrament, God's truth is not a general concept nor an abstract verity. The Christian revelation is rational, concrete, and particular.[5]

Jüngel and Hartwell are joined by numerous scholars eager to explicate Barth's notion of the concreteness of revelation. Various angles on that notion are taken. Generally, however, arguments fall into one of two categories. Either they are constructed to show that eternity and time converge in Barth's theology, making revelation

concrete and historical, or they labor to specify *how* revelation is a
concrete occurrence.

Those in the first group include E. L. Allen who argues that
eternity's breaking into time and maintaining a changeless, incor-
ruptible existence alongside the historical realm of contingency and
decay exhibits a timelessness in time in which Christ becomes
contemporaneous with successive generations of humanity.[6] Questions regarding the meaning of "concrete" in theological usage are
raised with efforts such as Peter Monsma's contention that the
historical event *(geschichtliches Ereignis)*, though a part of history, is
not historical in the ordinary sense. Though an occurrence involving
concrete persons, revelation's essence is not historical; furthermore,
it differs in that it does not require extension or completion. Jesus
Christ revealed or unveiled God in history at a definite place and
time and thus in a genuinely historical event on a continuum with
other spatio-temporal occurrences. Still, historical event and Christian truth are clearly distinguished.[7]

Seeking to explicate more fully the physical-historical nature of
revelation and how concrete revelation is a supportable notion is the
concern of Barthian analysts like Christopher Morse. Morse mentions Barth's Safenwil metaphor—Jesus Christ is God's movement
for social justice—and sees beginning there a "movement of formation" continuing in the *Church Dogmatics* which conceived God's
Word as dynamically taking form in the human context. Although
spiritual event, it is not thereby abstracted from the physical. God's
physicality inheres in the spirituality of Jesus Christ as Word of God,
and in the full context of Barth's thought, God's revelation is physical
and historical. As sacrament, as historical fact in the original event,
as incarnation in word and event in a fallen creation, and finally in
the eschatological vindication of the divine will in the culmination of
God's movement in history, Barth's actualism is not detached but
specific. God's revelation is a concrete Person speaking to concrete
persons in the context of their earthly lives.[8]

Linked to other occurrences in the chain of world events, the
concrete revelation in Jesus of Nazareth is not enclosed in God but
happens in the world in which people live. A living person, Jesus
Christ, this concrete revelation is neither abstract nor impersonal;
Jesus Christ is God's speaking in history through a human life.
Finally, the historical nature of God's revelation is concrete in its
goal-directedness, i.e., the consummation of God's Kingdom.[9]

Barth's actualism/concreteness is the active, moving history of Jesus Christ which is always present.[10]

Paul Lehmann stresses the concreteness of revelation in Barth's work and his own, seeing the basis in God's action in the world in which God's being is revealed. Lehmann is concerned to identify the concreteness which he deems inseparable from the integrity of theology itself. Lehmann takes issue with Frederick Herzog's assertion that theology needs to begin with the poor. Seeing the event of God's revelation in Jesus Christ as inclusive of the liberation of the poor, Lehmann suggests instead the completeness of that divine action and its efficaciousness for the healing of the plight of the oppressed. He writes:

> The mystery of presence and pressure upon "the world of time and space and things, our world,"—under which and by which the *marginales* are *being* liberated and *to be* liberated for the human-ness which is their righteousness and their destiny,— *transcends,* in its sovereign majesty and purpose (its *incomprehensibile* and its *incognito*), the unrighteousness and suffering and sin in the world, and *condescends* in the miracle of Christmas, to be involved in that world, *concretissime: vere deus, vere homo.* That happening—then, and now—is the center and occasion of a *Magnificat*—again *concretissime*— both in song and in the basic sense and structure of things. . . . If, and in so far as, theology today must begin with the wretched of the earth, it is because "a new order has already begun." To begin here in theology is precisely to risk "the bold endeavor to speak about the way in which Jesus Christ takes form in our world."[11]

It is clear that Lehmann wishes to avoid the error made by those who fail to centralize God's act in Jesus Christ and espouse instead a kind of immanent historical messianism. His contention, however, that the oppressed are thereby already *being liberated,* while true in its affirmation that Christ is the power of that liberation and, hence, undergirds and moves ahead of all human efforts, tends still to discount the provoking/transforming work of the church in co-action with God in the physical and material spheres.

It is apparent that the efforts of Allen, Morse, Lehmann, and others with them, to establish the concreteness of revelation in Barth's theology succeed in establishing that God's self-disclosure occurs in a concrete original event, in a person, that of Jesus of Nazareth, and for the reconciliation and enlightenment of living persons in an actual world. What has not been done, however, and has not been tried, is an effort to say how that revelation affects materially and physically (socially, politically, economically), not just spiritually, the lived existences of the real people to whom truth is disclosed. Making God known takes precedence over other considerations. Concreteness abstractly analyzed and described is the yield. *Fides quaerens intellectum* lends itself to this kind of analysis and description, reposing in academic and theoretical statements and foregoing the move to praxiological engagement.

2. Knowledge and the Self-Disclosing God

Fides quaerens intellectum begins with revelation and a concern for how faithful men and women know God. Those who approach theological reflection from this angle concern themselves with the integrity and purity of revelation as regards that "how," the method of humanity's knowing. The whole *analogia entis/analogia fidei* argument is a preoccupation with how human beings know. So, too, the Barth-Brunner natural theology debate. The faith/philosophy debate is of the same order. Even the issue of actualism/essentialism is at base one of revelation—how God is known by human beings.

> *Human knowing,* in so far as man is its subject, never attains in any way to God. If it does, it is only in so far as God himself is its direct subject . . . God is known only by God.[12]

God is known by humans only in faith. Receiving in faith God's illumination, the pious and loving believer is enabled to participate in God's own knowledge because God discloses that knowledge through self-revelation. Hence, "Theology is the becoming incarnate of divine knowledge."[13] Anselm's *fides quaerens intellectum* which, as O'Grady states, advances this notion, presupposes that God is preeminently self-disclosing Person. To be sure, if God *is* preeminently One who discloses divinity to rational humanity, theology *is* knowledge in faith. The principal task of individuals and of the church, then, is to receive that knowledge and then to join God in further disclosure to those who do not yet know.

God's knowability is the subject of numerous studies of Barth.[14] Colin Brown sees Barth's major significance in his bringing to the front those questions concerning how we know and how Jesus Christ relates to that knowing. Theology's fundamental questions, Brown claims, are those which Barth has challenged the church to think about: "How do we know God? How does man stand with God? . . . What part does Christ play in revelation? What is the nature of religious truth? Is the Bible our only source of knowledge about God?"[15] David McKenzie asserts that the Anselm study answered Barth's central epistemological question—that which asks how there can be knowledge of a God who is wholly other.[16] Whether or not McKenzie is right to say that Barth's notion of God was, at the time of the Anselm turn, that of a Wholly Other, God's unavailability to reason apart from faith is a notion which Barth maintained to the end.

Hans Küng focuses on the cognitive nature of faith itself, a primary Anselmian datum. Interpreting Barth's thought in 4, 1 and 1, 1, Küng writes: "As the fundamental act of the Christian life, it is a cognitive process which simply takes cognizance of the already completed being and work of Jesus Christ—faith is a *knowing* . . . This taking cognizance entails, however, a passing on of knowledge. Thus acknowledging and knowing are simultaneously a *making-known*."[17] Agreeing that faith is trust, Küng disclaims that faith as trust can be understood rightly except as acceptance of the Christian kerygma. Knowing that God has acted in Christ to disclose the divine Person is faithful trust.[18]

Whether Barth's readers have understood his doctrine of revelation correctly or not is significant to this discussion only inasmuch as the thesis proposed here is maintained or disclaimed by their interpretations. These readers' analyses support my proposal that Barth's doctrine of revelation, informed by Anselm and *fides quaerens intellectum,* tends to point his theology in abstract, theoretical directions which both begin and end somewhere other than the material realm of historical event. If so many have understood Barth in ways described in preceding pages, this tendency in his method and theology can hardly be ignored. Still, as I have argued in previous chapters, there are other possibilities for reading Barth from a quite different focus. Before returning to his Safenwil methodology, however, it will be instructive to attend to arguments of other scholars who have critiqued negatively Barth's doctrine of revelation as approach for theology and what they perceive as Barth's orientation in the notion of humanity as knower of God.

Critiques of Barth's Doctrine of Revelation as Approach for Theology

Arguing in much the same vein as G. C. Berkouwer, Gustav Wingren objects that Barth's theology contains no viable doctrine of sin; hence, there is no evil against which God opposes the divine will and purpose. For Barth, Wingren believes, there are only two realities—God and humanity. Wingren attributes this "caricature" to Barth's liberal heritage and continued grounding in his nineteenth century intellectual matrix. As with Schleiermacher, Barth's theology, Wingren holds, is developed within a particular, controlling framework—the knowledge structure.[19] This knowledge structure emphasizes the knowing subject and the known Object. Wingren suggests that a new frame, a new structure, is needed: not God known by human beings, but God making human beings righteous. "Man's predicament is not that he lacks knowledge, but that he is guilty."[20] For this reason, "The fundamental mistake in the system cannot be removed within the old structure. The removal of the foundational mistake would mean the destruction of his [Barth's] theology. It is his own methodological approach to the historical material that prevents a correct understanding of it."[21]

Wingren charges Barth with an anthropocentrism of his own, a centering of humanity's knowledge which becomes the "axis" around which Barth's entire theology turns. His doctrine of revelation is the structural frame which lends itself to an obscuring of the Gospel's emphasis on justification, Wingren insists:

> When the idea of revelation becomes the governing point of view, man's realization of [understanding of] the revelation becomes in fact the dominant point of view. . . . But anyone who poses the question, "Where is all this revealed to us?" places man's knowledge in the foreground . . . the fundamental sin is false thinking and . . . faith becomes correct thinking.[22]

With knowledge of God at the center, sin is ignorance which needs illumination; God is self-disclosing One who unveils the divine nature; and "God's character as the living and active God becomes obscured and his coming is interpreted as 'revelation' in a sense foreign to the New Testament."[23] Wingren suggests that there is, then, no real engagement with sin/injustice by the God of noetic necessity, only a dealing with ignorance.

While much of Wingren's analysis fails to do justice to important emphases in Barth's theology which indicate that Barth's concern is for more than humanity's knowledge of God—justification is very much at the center of Barth's work—Wingren's critique is helpful for lifting out the *tendency* which *fides quaerens intellectum* gives to theology with revelation as the focus. With revelation at the helm, knowledge is considered faith's paramount question. While faith seeking understanding—in Anselm and Barth—does not intend to eliminate God's action and humanity's trusting, loving activity *with* God, the fact that Barth's theology can be read as Wingren has read it supports the contention of this thesis that faith seeking understanding as a methodology, a theological frame, tends to obscure important foci of the Gospel and distort or obstruct the apprehension of those crucial elements.

Issue might be taken with Wingren as to whether the knowledge structure which he regards as a liberal focus does not have much older roots. He might be asked whether that structure and its primary datum, the understanding self, are not originally important to patristic and medieval as well as modern theology. However, Wingren's proposal that a new frame needs to replace the knowledge frame is very much to the point. Barth's methodological approach, he declares, is itself Barth's "fundamental mistake." What Wingren is not aware of in Barth's work, however, is the embryonic Safenwil methodology which does, indeed, have the power to break the knowledge frame's hegemony. This methodology centers not a new knowledge, but salvation and authorization through God's Spirit to join God's redemptive and transforming work. In that new frame which locates theology with the poor in the context of the church's worship, Barth's christological focus shows that the meaning of Jesus Christ is more that of justifying and authorizing for discipleship than making God known. The full content and significance of God's becoming human is then preserved within that accountable frame— a frame not of knowledge but of accountable discipleship.

Focusing on the doctrine of the church, this thesis asserts, might more adequately encourage an accountable discipleship frame than focusing on the doctrine of revelation. More will be said about this in concluding pages of this chapter. Suffice it to say for the time being that inclusion of Barth's Safenwil insights has potential for breaking the knowledge frame *through ecclesiology*. Wingren calls for a realization that "divine activity reaches its highest intensity in an incarnation characterized by humiliation."[24] God's social location with the poor, the lowest of the human family, in Jesus' own location with the poor of Palestine and in Jesus' location with the poor of today's world, is that incarnation characterized by humiliation. A church socially located in the same place embodies that core reality.

R. D. Williams' and Ronald Gregor Smith's critiques of Barth's starting-point in revelation agree substantially with Wingren's.[25] One can detect exaggerations in Williams' and Smith's analyses of Barth without losing the point relative to the thesis advanced in this paper: Barth can be interpreted—there is a tendency toward reading his thought—in ontological categories which are abstract, theoretical, and dislocated from the heart of history and the existential faith and life of men and women. *Fides quaerens intellectum*, faith seeking understanding, and Barth's interpretation of what that means through his study of Anselm, lie at the base of that predisposing tendency in his work. Integrally connected as presupposition to the method itself is the doctrine of revelation which holds that God is self-disclosing Person who gives to humanity knowledge.[26]

Beginning with the Doctrine of the Church

If Barth's doctrine of revelation is a problematical starting-point for understanding church and world together, as the foregoing analysis has suggested, ecclesiology itself, this thesis proposes, can offer a corrective. Barth's primary intention, despite what his doctrine of revelation might suggest otherwise, at least to those who read him the way that Wingren, Williams, Smith, and Roberts have done, is consistently a christological one. Barth wishes to *begin* with Jesus Christ. Beginning with the earthly-historical form of the existence of Jesus Christ, the church, if it is itself located with the poor, is beginning with Jesus in a way that situates theology immediately in the historical context. In social location with the poor of humanity and para-humanity in the context of the church's worship itself, theology establishes a focus which includes humanity and nature at the outset.

A church located with the poor feeds upon and is enriched by metaphor and its provocative/transformative power. *Fides quaerens rationem reddere* deals in metaphor. That methodology takes seriously the metaphorical assertion—the church is the earthly-historical form of the existence of Jesus Christ. Developing Barth's ecclesial metaphor in conjunction with his christological one can situate the church immediately in the pain and struggle of divinity/human-ity for justice, love, and peace. (1) "Jesus Christ is God's movement for social justice" and (2) "the church is the earthly-historical form of the existence of Jesus Christ," can merge to give to the church a new vision of itself as God's covenant community for social justice. Join-ing those two crucial metaphors, this thesis proposes, can forge a "master image" of profound transformative power.

Ray L. Hart observes that fruitful master images both "profuse themselves in time" and "profuse time from themselves."[27] They create new time for the actualization of new meanings. That new time is often the only "real time" which some have known. *Fides quaerens rationem reddere* recognizes that much of the human family and virtually all of nature have possessed no time of their own. Accountability creates time for them in which they, too, are included and enabled to thrive in mutuality with all others. Images of accountability, entering into historical causality, hence, are time-bearers for those who have known no time. In Safenwil, Barth employed such time-bearing images and opened to the workers in the Hüssy factories and Hochuli knitting mills new time for *human* life. The image of Jesus Christ as God's movement for social justice entering "actual lived time" created for those women and men "their first 'real time' in which to live."[28]

Hart emphasizes that master images met by the "answering imagination" evoke new meanings. Fundamental, as well, are the "antecedent complexes" of event and image which "stand under" new permutations and apprehensions. Those offer a limit or a self-critical principle for the evaluation of new interpretations.[29] While they are not controlling, they are instructive and comprise a rich and indispensable part of the effective history of event and image in its original and traditional manifestations.

Southern Baptists, too, have recognized the fundamental im-portance of image and its union with event in the religious imagina-tion. James McClendon, asking if he is thereby an "alienated, left-wing Southern Baptist," shows the critical role of image and meta-phor in Christian thought.[30] McClendon proposes that such images as Martin Luther King's use of Egypt, Moses, and the Promised Land, *"are of the very substance of religion; . . .* these sacred images are not . . . peripheral to faith; . . . while not the only constituent of religion, [they] are of central importance in it."[31] Identifying the oppressive situation of the black Southern people whom he inspired and led as analogous to that of the Israelites in

Egypt, King fused analogy and metaphor in an imaginative synthesis which fired the hearts of those who marched with their Moses to the Promised Land. Given "real time," perhaps for the first time, those Israelites knew Martin Luther King, Jr. as a Moses. "I've been on the mountaintop. . . . He's allowed me to go up to the mountain. And I've looked over, and I've seen the promised land."[32]

The interplay of biblical image and historical event were revelatory for Martin Luther King, Jr. and the civil rights marchers and activists who followed his leadership. And the interplay of image and event shaped an understanding of the nature of the church as well, even as it did in the early Christian decades. This is crucial: *where* images encounter event and the events themselves are not accidental elements. Where were the images encountered? In the Old Testament certainly. Also in the New Testament. But, and this is important, the biblical images offered truth-telling meaning *in* the lived experience of the black men and women of the South. Separated from the oppressed experience of those who struggle for liberation, images of Moses, Egyptian Pharaohs, and a Promised Land tend to languish in sterility. But *in* the concrete context of the civil rights struggle, those images became alive with transformative metaphorical power. Scripture, tradition, *and* the people's experience, a dynamic interplay of biblical image and concrete history, forged in the American South new images and new meanings for old images—in that sense, *people's images* emerged from the creative ferment. It had been so primally with Jesus. Himself one of the poor of Palestine and applying "certain dominant images" to Himself, Jesus was the "presence of the kingdom; . . . he was somehow Israel . . . he was the bearer of the role of suffering servant given by Isaiah and by Jewish tradition to Israel; and in the Supper he was the broken loaf, the wine poured out in sacrifice."[33] Infusing those images with new meaning in the interplay of Scripture, tradition, and the concrete events of his own specific work and life and the people's experience which he inhabited *with* them, Jesus transformed those images into people's images pregnant with justice, peace, and accountable love. *Fides quaerens rationem reddere* seeks to continue that justice-building, peace-making, and accountable loving in the church, the earthly-historical form of Jesus' existence, as it opens itself to the reception of people's images through the Spirit given originally in the action and thought of Jesus.

As McClendon is careful to point out regarding his biographical theology, a methodology in social location, *fides quaerens rationem reddere*, does not repudiate or dismiss the value of propositional statements and theological conceptualization. To be sure, these are indispensable. What should be stressed, however, is that concept and proposition need to be connected intimately with lived experience. Too often the historical has been bypassed in favor of the superhistorical. People's metaphors keep that vital connection alive.

Ian Barbour helps us to move in the direction of understanding the central importance of people's metaphors. Though Barbour does not deal explicitly with the question of *whose* lived experience is vital to the fleshing-out of metaphors, he does recognize the importance of the interpreter's subjective involvement. If, however, as Barbour affirms, the reader is "encouraged to draw from various dimensions of his [her] own experience,"[34] then what cannot fail to be asked as sincerely is the question of *which* experience. Surely it is not true that one experience is as evocative of truth as another. McClendon offers some light with his notion of metaphor-in-community. People's metaphors are always metaphors-in-community. Accountability is a nonsensical notion apart from community, and *Fides quaerens rationem reddere* is a methodology-in-community. What still has not been fully addressed, however, is *which* community. Here, the early Barth's experience is instructive. Barth's Safenwil adventure as a pastor situated him in the particular community of the poor and made him aware of the importance of that "inevitable" location. Christopraxis (locating with the poor *because* Christ is first located there) focused for Barth *which* experience and *which* community were truth-bearers.[35]

Importance of Social Location for Beginning with Ecclesiology

I have advanced the thesis that theological method is crucially and inseparably bound to a perception of faith. Further, an adequate doctrine of the church will depend fundamentally on those prior decisions and commitments. If faith is understood and experienced as claim and accountability, the response of "Here am I, Lord, send me," the implications for theological method are congruent. Faith which seeks accountability and in accountability understands, *fides quaerens rationem reddere*, assumes that faithfulness to the received tradition and intelligibility to today's women and men require acting and thinking with those who have not commonly been involved in the formulation of theological positions.

In Safenwil, Barth located himself with the poor and grounded his social location theologically by adopting as his norm Jesus' own location with the poor of Palestine. In that hermeneutical location and sharing the prejudgments of those with whom he worked, worshipped, and reflected, Barth understood and experienced faith as accountability to God and to those *with* whom God had already located Jesus Christ. Today, theologians are again understanding the significance of God's original location of Jesus Christ with the poor and of their own social positioning for hermeneutic and engagement with the text. Frederick Herzog writes: "We are realizing that without direct encounter with the exploited in our theological method at the beginning, we ultimately stay withdrawn in our own group or class, buttressed in a fortress of sheer self-interest."[36]

The crucial value of social location and its meaning for theological reflection was perceived, again as with the young Barth, nascently if not explicitly, by Martin Luther King, Jr. in the late fifties in this country. Some attention has already been given to King's methodology in social location with the poor. Further examination of how that notion functioned in King's thought and action can elucidate what I am proposing regarding the integral importance of social location to the theological endeavor.[37] In *Stride Toward Freedom*, King, more privileged as a Black than some, tells of working two summers as a youth in a factory which oppressed both poor Blacks and poor Whites. "Here I saw economic injustice firsthand . . . Through these early experiences I grew up deeply conscious of the varieties of injustice in our society."[38] At Crozer Theological Seminary, King developed the theological basis for "the social concern which had already grown up in me as a result of my early experiences."[39] In the privileged epistemological location of the poor,[40] King saw that righteousness means justice. Hence, he declared, "Not every minister can be a prophet, but some must be prepared for the ordeals of this high calling and be willing to suffer courageously for *righteousness*."[41] (Emphasis added.) Whatever else righteousness is, it cannot be less than justice, King saw.

Most significantly, in the concrete social location of Southern injustice/unrighteousness, King developed a doctrine of the nature of the church as social righteousness.

[The church] has too often blessed a status quo that needed to
be blasted, and reassured a social order that needed to be
reformed. So the church must acknowledge its guilt, its weak
and vacillating witness, its all too frequent failure to obey the
call to servanthood. Today the judgment of God is upon the
church for its failure to be true to its mission [viz., social
righteousness].[42]

King was antedated by Barth in Safenwil. There, it will be
recalled, Barth named the church's failure to actualize its justice
commission the central apostasy of its history. Only with an understanding that the church is primally and essentially accountable for
social righteousness can the failure to struggle against injustice be
deemed the church's preeminent apostasy. And only in social location with those who suffer from that apostasy were Barth and King
enabled to make that judgment.

A second crucial insight not widely held even by those who
accept the church's responsibility for social justice is the priority and
centrality of *God's* struggle for social righteousness and *God's placing* of those who labor for justice in the hermeneutical position of
the poor. Influenced by Reinhold Niebuhr, but identifying a significant weakness in Niebuhr's theology, Martin Luther King decided at
Boston University that Niebuhr had not allowed sufficiently for
God's grace in his pessimistic stress on the corruption of human
nature. This, too, was Barth's difference from Niebuhr. "His pessi-
mism concerning human nature was not balanced by an optimism
concerning divine nature. He was so involved in diagnosing man's
sickness of sin that he overlooked the cure of grace."[43] Conversely,
at Boston University School of Theology, King developed "a passion
for social justice that stemmed, not from a superficial optimism, but
from a deep faith in the possibilities of human beings *when* they
allowed themselves to become *co-workers with God*."[44] (Emphasis
added.) And on the day that King first preached at Dexter Avenue
Baptist Church, he reminded himself, "Keep Martin Luther King in
the background and God in the foreground and everything will be all
right. Remember you are a channel of the gospel and not the
source."[45] Because King knew that God went ahead and called him
to join God's own justice march, he could envision his peculiar role
as that of Moses.

So, too, Barth in Safenwil. As Moses of the Exodus was not the
liberator but the chosen agent of God's liberation, Barth and King

understood clearly their own agential roles as co-workers with God. Employing a nascent methodology of *fides quaerens rationem reddere*, Barth approached the theological task in social location with the poor and as co-worker with God. Recognizing his responsibility for exercising a self-critical principle that would keep his theology faithful to the scriptural witness and tradition, and aware of the liberal excesses of Ragaz and Kutter and Social Democracy's humanistic predilections, Barth sought to emphasize God's centrality in the struggle for social justice. His turn toward *Romans* marked a quest for surer scriptural footing and a self-critical norm to guide his action and reflection.

Most striking of all Barth's insights in the Safenwil experience was his "metaphorical adventure"—Jesus Christ is God's movement for social justice. As Chapter III disclosed, the young Barth's insight has been either overlooked, dismissed as youthful impetuosity, or critiqued as liberal naivete. What has not been considered heretofore is the metaphorical power lodged in that image. Its power, furthermore, this thesis proposes, resides in its character as a people's metaphor. Barth did not devise that image in the aseptic environs of an academic study. Indeed, he did not devise it. It sprang from the experience of the people themselves, and Barth gave to it theological rationalization. Jesus Christ was not Social Democracy, Barth remonstrated, but Jesus Christ *was God's movement for social justice*. With that powerful and power-breaking image, justice became particularized, concretized, in Jesus Christ.[46] Christ as God's movement for social justice has the power to inject into history a biblical root metaphor opening up avenues for a new organizing paradigm. Justice and accountability can "roll back to a timeless problematic" apart from their transformation from symbol to metaphor by particularization with the specific. As racial prowess did not mean black power until Stokely Carmichael focused it so,[47] justice does not mean accountability to God and the poor of humanity and para-humanity until it is given metaphorical concreteness in the way which Barth offered at Safenwil, viz., Jesus Christ is God's movement for social justice. With that transforming root metaphor and a realization of its own importance as the earthly-historical manifestation of Jesus Christ, and keeping in mind always that Jesus Christ is Subject, the church can reclaim *all* its mission. The logic can't be missed. If Jesus Christ is God's movement for social justice, the church as his Body is *God's covenant community for social justice. Fides quaerens rationem reddere* leads ineluctably to that affirmation.

Conclusion

Seeing in Barth's doctrine of the church a correlative focus to his christological one, Robert T. Osborn wrote in 1971: "[Barth's] *Dogmatics* might still have a positive role to play in contemporary theology. And that role may be, above all else, that of helping theology to understand the place of the church in the divine strategy." That place in the divine strategy as regards ethics is as follows: "God does not call the Christian directly into the world as such, to engage it as it understands itself, but rather into the church, and through the church into the world as God knows it. The church is the body of Christ in his absence, the place and time where his presence is manifest. . . . The church is the biblical alternative to a religious interpretation of Christianity; it is the cruciform in which Christ lets the world be, but not be alone."[48]

Stuart McLean is another who has seen the potential in Barth's doctrine of the church for a more genuine church-world engagement. Noting that the *Church Dogmatics* 1, 1 and Barth's treatment of the Word of God seem to reduce the church's function to reflection on and proclamation of the Bible, McLean states that a closer reading of Barth's theology in subsequent volumes renders a more profound conception of the church's tasks and nature. Acknowledging Jesus Christ as the Word of God, a more faithful understanding is contained in the root metaphor "covenant" which embodies the action and relationship which Jesus Christ as God's Word conveys. The metaphor of covenant, McLean believes, has not been seen as the centrally important metaphor which it is. Covenant refers immediately to the church, the covenantal community which is Christ's fleshly existence on earth; relationship with culture, McLean suggests, through the *"logos* made flesh" is opened up thereby. McLean hopes, with his analysis, to "counter the tendency of some of Barth's critics and adherents to narrowly understand his discussion of the Word of God in terms of Scripture and Jesus Christ, and thus find him separating the church and scripture from the world and culture."[49] McLean insists that understanding Jesus Christ in terms of the word made flesh joins church to world and

society, requiring Bible study and preaching "to tread the *logos*
catwalk Barth gives us to more fully relate the gospel to culture."[50]
McLean sees the covenantal community, the church, as affording a
neglected but crucial way of understanding Barth's theology of the
Word of God.

Robert Osborn has more recently expanded his 1971 insight
regarding the "place of the church in the divine strategy" and how
Barth's theology might aid contemporary theology in appropriating
an understanding of that place. Analyzing Barth's essay "The Christian Community and the Civil Community," Osborn finds that
Barth's political ethics focuses not immediately on Christology but
on the new humanity in Jesus Christ and thus on the preliminary
representation of that new humanity in the church. The church as
"model and source of models" for ethical/political responsibility
relates the Word of God to the "concrete, historical, and political
situation."[51] Empowered by the Holy Spirit to be this provisional
manifestation of the new humanity in Jesus Christ, "The Christian's
first though not ultimate responsibility in and through the Holy
Spirit is thus his political responsibility for this provisional *polis*—
the church. His final and ultimate responsibility is for the civil
community, to help it discern, with the model that is the church,
those tokens of its own promise and future."[52] In the church God
provides, not principles and middle axioms of ethical responsibility,
but a "living model" which affirms a living covenantal relationship
between God and humanity. Osborn emphasizes the foundational
thesis underlying his analysis—"the issue is finally whether God is a
living God or not, or if he is a living God, whether he is a factor in
the ethical situation. . . ."[53]

While it appears that Barth was indeed concerned to relate the
church politically to the world, much still remains to be asked. Was
Barth's dialogue finally a church-to-church dialogue? Was his concern primarily to explain his position to other theologians rather
than to facilitate directly and concretely the church in its struggle for
accountability? Was Barth's encounter still an intellectual one with
fellow theologians? Does Barth articulate concretely how the church
functions in being the church? Does his church-to-church/theology
dialogue fail to become a church-to-world communication? Answering to the church, has Barth stopped short, finally, of answering to
the world? As this study has shown, Barth has been read predomi-
nantly in ways that leave his theology academic and theoretical and
his ecclesiology, as well, separated from concrete involvement in

world and history. This issue may concern the tasks and limits of theology: perhaps we must concede to Barth that one cannot do all things.

Except during the Barmen period and the German church struggle, however, the later Barth does not appear to have been struggling with the life of the church in the world. Although he included ethics in his dogmatics, the Anselmian method led to a preoccupation with epistemology and how one knows. Despite his concern in the ethics with issues of war, economic exploitation of the poor, and the just State, Barth's *method* remained that of Anselm's. It is this methodology which, as preceding pages have shown, intrudes upon the substance of a theology which never intended to reduce to knowledge alone. Those who find problems with Barth's christological center have not identified the methodological problem which made it difficult for Barth to execute the theology which he constructed. Still employing an Enlightenment style deriving from his liberal education which focused knowledge, Barth's further employment of the Anselmian methodology vitiated his more essential theology. It is for this reason that it is important to reclaim Barth's early method and allow it to execute what the Anselmian one cannot. Barth's theology should not be reduced to the tendencies toward abstraction for which he has been so often criticized. Viewing this eminent theologian's work from the perspective of his earlier praxis methodology helps to correct those tendencies and develops emphases which *fides quaerens intellectum* has obscured.

The burden of this thesis has been the proposition that Barth's methodology drawn from his study of Anselm and its dependence on knowledge have been the primary inhibitors of a church-world engagement which is not abstract and academic. The doctrine of God which underlies that methodology fails to define the concreteness of revelation in categories which include the full scope of historical event and time as men and women experience them. Congruently, the church has understood its primary tasks as those of reflection, study, and preaching, more than engagement with temporal issues of discrete social injustice.

A correlative proposition which I have advanced concerns an alternative approach to Barth's theology offered by the method which he employed in his Safenwil pastorate. Socially located with the poor of his parish and canton in the context of worship, the "radical" Barth understood faith's quest as one for accountability and, hence, knowledge in accountability. There, his reflection arose in a church located with the poor which was itself the perspective from which faith and theology were understood. I have suggested that reading Barth's ecclesiology from that focus can reclaim and develop insights inherent in Barth's work in ways which instruct the church today in its relationship to the world to which and in which it is given by God.

As Chapter IV suggested, with *fides quaerens rationem reddere*—faith seeking accountability which understands—concrete indications for the church's understanding of its nature and tasks can be apprehended which are not theoretically detached from the world where its questions arise and its accountability is directed. Issues of poverty, racial hatred, and oppression such as those which formed the social matrix of the Atlanta murders of 1979–81 and evoked this study are seen, then, as the church's pressing responsibility.

The concrete Atlanta situation provoked in me a theological quest for a doctrine of the church adequate to the realities of prejudice, want, and human oppression manifested in that context. A quietistic church, and a quietistic Southern Baptist Convention, had not been challenged by the dominant theologies of our time to assess the church's nature in the light of today's injustices, I decided. My purpose was not to identify a solution for the Atlanta crisis but to ask, with my church, questions important to its faithful existence as the Body of Christ in the midst of the responsibilities of this day.

Because Karl Barth's theology of the Word of God has been, perhaps, as influential as any modern theology on Baptist thought, I decided to examine his method and ecclesiology for suggestions regarding the way that Barth has been read by Baptists (and others) and for possibilities for reading him anew. The Safenwil study disclosed the alternative possibility of reading Barth from the perspective of faith seeking accountability, a praxis methodology engaged with concrete human and para-human misery. Further study of Barth, particularly of the Anselm book and its influence on Barth's later methodology, and of the *Church Dogmatics*, revealed that, while Barth's theology after the Safenwil decade was dominated by *fides quaerens intellectum*, his embryonic praxis methodology continued, at least in some measure, to inform his work and can yet be developed in ways which yield a doctrine of the church adequate to Barth's notion of the ecclesia as the earthly-historical form of the existence of Jesus Christ.

As the earthly-historical form of the existence of Jesus Christ, *seiner eigenen irdish-geschichtlichen Existenzform,* the church is also God's movement for social justice. Empowered by that master image, the church can forge with a world-transforming God a paradigm of justice suitable to the demands of this age. Engaging a finite world and concrete history, the church becomes anew God's provoking/transforming covenant partner in the quest for accountable peace, love, and justice which knows.

Southern Baptist leaders have cited the need for a new theology of the church and a new theological base for social action which affirms its integrality to the church's nature and mission. Presupposing God's own initial activity and the ecclesia's correlative action, an ecclesiology is needed, these see, which reshapes Baptist individualism, correcting Enlightenment excesses and permitting a corporate solidarity which protects the personal nature of faith but does not militate against a "nobler church-consciousness."[54] This study of Barth's methodology and ecclesiology has, I believe, identified possibilities for that new church vision. Reclaiming the historical assertions in Barth's doctrine of the church and developing the radical Barth's early insights with the methodology which I have characterized as *fides quaerens rationem reddere,* faith seeking accountability, can centralize in a new way "the involvement of the Risen One in history."[55] This is, to use Frederick Herzog's words in *Justice Church,* the antidote to "the present powerlessness of the church."[56]

Fundamental to the reclamation of an historical Gospel intimately connected to the mammoth problems which we face today are a methodology and hermeneutic which include social concern and concern for the natural creation as part of the hermeneutical premises themselves. Without that crucial starting-point, social and environmental issues will not "pervade the entire dogmatic work."[57] For a nobler church consciousness, it is imperative that the "entire dogmatic work" be informed by the sufferings of humanity and parahumanity (nature) into which the Risen One has come. *Fides quaerens rationem reddere* offers a methodology and hermeneutic adequate to that challenge.

NOTES

/1/   Only a few are: Geoffrey W. Bromiley, *An Introduction to the Theology of Karl Barth* (Grand Rapids: William B. Eerdmans Publishing Co., 1979);

Fred H. Klooster, *The Significance of Barth's Theology: An Appraisal With Special Reference to Election and Reconciliation* (Grand Rapids: Baker Book House, 1961); Joe Robert Jones, *Karl Barth and Informative Revelation: A Conceptual Analysis* (Ann Arbor, Mich.: University Microfilms, 1970); Klaas Runia, *Karl Barth's Doctrine of Holy Scripture* (Grand Rapids: William B. Eerdmans, 1962); and Theodore W. Jennings, Jr., *Introduction to Theology: An Invitation to Reflection Upon the Christian Mythos* (Philadelphia: Fortress Press, 1976).

/2/   See Eberhard Jüngel, *The Doctrine of the Trinity: God's Being Is in Becoming* (Grand Rapids: William B. Eerdmans Publishing Co., 1976), pp. 6–18; and Herbert Hartwell, *The Theology of Karl Barth: An Introduction* (Philadelphia: Westminster Press, 1964), pp. 64, 65. See also George W. Stroup, III, *Revelation and the Word of God: the Hermeneutics of the Christian Story* (Ann Arbor, Mich.: University Microfilms, 1974), p. 10.

/3/   Karl Barth, *Church Dogmatics*, Vol. 1, 1:325.

/4/   Jüngel, *The Doctrine of the Trinity*, pp. 30–32.

/5/   Hartwell, *Theology of Karl Barth*, p. 68.

/6/   E. L. Allen, *The Sovereignty of God and the Word of God* (New York: Philosophical Library, 1951), p. 33.

/7/   Peter Halman Monsma, *Karl Barth's Idea of Revelation* (Somerville, N.J.: Somerset Press, 1937), pp. 148, 149.

/8/   Christopher Morse, "Raising God's Eyebrows: Some Further Thoughts on the Concept of the *Analogia Fidei*," *Union Seminary Quarterly Review* 37 (Fall-Winter 1981–82):45–7.

/9/   Dale Norman Snyder, *Karl Barth's Struggle with Anthropocentric Theology* (Boekhandel Wattez-'s-Gravenhage, 1966), pp. 217–220.

/10/   Colm O'Grady, *The Church in Catholic Theology: Dialogue with Karl Barth* (London: Geoffrey Chapman, 1969), p. 14.

/11/   Paul L. Lehmann, "The Concreteness of Theology: Reflections on the Conversation Between Barth and Bonhoeffer," in *Footnotes To a Theology: The Karl Barth Colloquium of 1972*, ed. Martin Rumscheidt (Corporation for the Publication of Academic Studies in Religion in Canada, 1974); see pp. 56–62.

/12/   O'Grady, *The Church in Catholic Theology: Dialogue with Karl Barth*, p. 8.

/13/   Ibid., p. 9.

/14/   Footnote 1 lists a few of those.

/15/   Colin Brown, *Karl Barth and the Christian Message* (Chicago: Inter-Varsity Press, 1967), pp. 152, 153.

/16/   David McKenzie, "Barth's *Anselm* and the Object of Theological Knowledge," *Foundations* 21 (July–September 1978):274.

/17/   Hans Küng, *Justification: The Doctrine of Karl Barth and a Catholic Reflection* (Philadelphia: Westminster Press, 1981), pp. 84, 85.

/18/   Ibid., pp. 252–255.

/19/   See Gustav Wingren, *Theology in Conflict: Nygren, Barth, Bultmann*, trans. Eric H. Wahlstrom (Philadelphia: Muhlenberg Press, 1958), p. 25. Although Barth has, in reaction to Schleiermacher, turned this structure upside down—"he has moved the ascent within liberal theology from 'man' to 'God'"—the basic problem remains; he has not been able to break up the structure of the problem." Although God is back in the center rather than religious humanity, knowledge still defines the structure. It is true that Barth "rearranges freely" within what remains a liberal framework, but knowledge rather than evil is the central concern with Barth, as with his predecessors, Wingren believes.

/20/   Ibid., p. 32.

/21/   Ibid., p. 27.

/22/   Ibid., pp. 35–37.

/23/   Ibid., p. 38.

/24/   Ibid., p. 31.

/25/   See R. D. Williams, "Barth on the Triune God," in *Karl Barth: Studies of His Theological Method,* ed. S. W. Sykes (Oxford: Clarendon Press, 1979), pp. 147–193. See also Ronald Gregor Smith, *The Doctrine of God* (Philadelphia: Westminster Press, 1970), pp. 90, 91.

/26/   R. H. Roberts analyzes the problem, as he sees it, of identifying Greek and biblical categories and an involution and convolution of being and time in Barth's theology. Charging that Barth's notion of revelation is one whose structure "remains enclosed within its own temporal envelope," Roberts believes that Barth's actualism merges the categories of ontology and temporality, resulting finally in an "implosion into timelessness" of that which he, at the same instant, wishes to establish as historical. Approaching Barth's theology from the focus of revelation, he concludes, tends to create an "ontological exclusiveness" which risks a "total disjunction and alienation of his theology from natural reality" (p. 145). What shocks and disturbs most about this tendency in Barth's theology, Roberts suggests, is the contribution of orthodox Christian theological categories to this kind of construction. Although he does not name Anselm specifically again (he has previously), Roberts alludes to him and other Church Fathers who synthesized Greek and Christian categories, transposing the acting, transforming God of the Bible into the self-related Being of Greek rationalism. One is made aware that Christianity's traditional categories lend themselves, and have lent themselves, congenially to such interpretation and usage. One questions all the more the adequacy and continued viability of the sort of noetic commitment which *fides quaerens initellectum* encourages, even requires. As a creation of the faithful intellect, theology thus constructed runs into problems connecting with lived experience. Roberts has not accounted adequately, however, for Barth's contention that Jesus Christ creates time *for* human life. Perhaps the superordinate Anselmian preoccupation with knowledge in the *Church Dogmatics* has contributed to this failure on Roberts' part to consider an important emphasis in Barth's theology. See R. H. Roberts, "Karl Barth's Doctrine of Time: Its Nature and Implications," in *Karl Barth: Studies of His Theological Method,* ed. S. W. Sykes (Oxford: Clarendon Press, 1979), pp. 88–146.

/27/   Ray L. Hart, *Unfinished Man and the Imagination: Toward an Ontology and a Rhetoric of Revelation* (New York: Herder and Herder, 1968), pp. 302, 303. Hart gives an example from the Black Power Movement: "'Black power' was an aside from the lips of Stokely Carmichael until it entered into historical causality. As the phrase inserted itself into the occurrence of events and became an inescapable 'category' through which they had to be understood, it was inserted into actual lived time; and simultaneously it afforded to some persons their first 'real time' in which to live. Neither Exile nor 'black power,' so long as each functions as a master image, rolls back to a timeless problematic of 'alienation' or 'racial prowess.'"

/28/   See Hart's quote above.

/29/   Ibid., p. 308.

/30/   James William McClendon, Jr., *Biography as Theology: How Life Stories can Remake Today's Theology* (Nashville: Abingdon, 1974), pp. 90f.

/31/   Ibid., p. 93.

/32/   McClendon, *Biography as Theology*, pp. 84, 85. McClendon quotes William Robert Miller, *Martin Luther King, Jr.: His Life, Martyrdom, and Meaning for the World* (New York: Weybright and Talley, 1968), pp. 287–88.

/33/   Ibid., p. 94.

/34/   Ian Barbour, *Myths, Models, and Paradigms: A Comparative Study in Science and Religion* (New York: Harper & Row, 1974), p. 14.

/35/   Other studies dealing with the significance of metaphor and imagination in the construction of models and paradigms important for a just world include: Sallie McFague, *Metaphorical Theology: Models of God in Religious Language* (Philadelphia: Fortress Press, 1982); Jeremy Rifkin with Ted Howard, *The Emerging Order: God in the Age of Scarcity* (New York: G. P. Putnam's Sons, 1979); and Gibson Winter, *Liberating Creation: Foundations of Religious Social Ethics* (New York: Crossroad, 1981).

/36/   Herzog, *Justice Church*, p. 107. Abraham Heschel comes close to saying that the hermeneut must be socially located where the prophets are, if they are to be understood rather than merely explained. See Abraham J. Heshel, *The Prophets* (New York: Harper and Row, 1962), p. xiii.

/37/   Frederick Herzog, in seminars at Duke University, has repeatedly stressed the importance of social location for theological reflection.

/38/   Martin Luther King, Jr., *Stride Toward Freedom: The Montgomery Story* (New York: Harper & Bros., 1958), p. 90.

/39/   Ibid.

/40/   Hugo Assmann, *Practical Theology of Liberation* (London: Search Press, 1975), p. 35. In his classes at Duke, Frederick Herzog has stressed, rather, the hermeneutical "inevitability" of the poor.

/41/   King, *Stride Toward Freedom*, p. 210. King also wrote of the American slaveholders of the nineteenth century: "Their rationalizations clothed obvious wrongs in the beautiful garments of righteousness." See *Strength To Love* (New York: Harper & Bros., 1963), p. 30. In that same book, King merges justice and righteousness again: "God's unwillingness to deal with evil with an overbearing immediacy does not mean that he is doing nothing. We weak and finite human beings are not alone in our quest for the triumph of righteousness." See p. 65.

/42/   Ibid., p. 96. Frederick Herzog affirms the centrality of the church's mission as social righteousness. In *Justice Church*, he writes: "*Church is Justice Covenant*. The church is people called in covenant to join God's struggle for the new age of justice." See p. 145.

/43/   King, *Stride Toward Freedom*, p. 100.

/44/   Ibid.

/45/   Ibid., p. 17.

/46/   Frederick Herzog offers just such a concretized metaphor in *Justice Church:* Jesus Christ is "embodiment of God's Justice." See p. 145.

/47/   See footnote 27.

/48/   Robert T. Osborn, "Positivism and Promise in the Theology of Karl Barth," *Interpretation* 25 (July 1971):302.

/49/   Stuart D. McLean, *Humanity in the Thought of Karl Barth* (Edinburgh: T. & T. Clark, 1981), p. 59.

/50/   Ibid.

/51/   Robert T. Osborn, "A 'Personalistic' Appraisal of Barth's Political Ethics," *Studies in Religion* 12 (Summer 1983):318.

/52/   Ibid.

/53/   Ibid., p. 324.

/54/   See Chapter I, footnote 59.

/55/   Herzog, *Justice Church*, p. 24.

/56/   Ibid., p. 25.

/57/   Ibid., p. 61.

SELECTED BIBLIOGRAPHY

Alldredge, E. P. *Southern Baptists Working Together*. Nashville: Sunday School Board of the Southern Baptist Convention, 1925.

Allen, E. L. *The Sovereignty of God and the Word of God*. New York: Philosophical Library, 1951.

Almond, Philip C. "Karl Barth and Anthropocentric Theology." *Scottish Journal of Theology* 31 (October 1978):435–47.

Althoff, Dale R. *Freedom and Love in the Thought of Karl Barth*. Ann Arbor, Mich.: Xerox University Microfilms, 1977.

Annual of the Southern Baptist Convention. Nashville: Executive Committee, Southern Baptist Convention, 1963, 1966, 1967, 1968, 1970, 1971, 1979, 1982.

Anselm. *Saint Anselm: Basic Writings*. Translated by S. N. Deane. Introduction by Charles Hartshorne. La Salle: Open Court, 1962; 2nd ed., 1979.

Assmann, Hugo. *Practical Theology of Liberation*. London: Search Press, 1975.

Bailey, Kenneth K. *Southern White Protestantism in the Twentieth Century*. New York: Harper & Row, 1964.

Balthasar, Hans Urs von. *The Theology of Karl Barth*. Translated by John Drury. Garden City: Doubleday & Co., 1972.

Baranowski, Shelley. "The Primacy of Theology: Karl Barth and Socialism." *Studies in Religion* 10 (1981):451–61.

Barbour, Ian. *Myths, Models, and Paradigms: A Comparative Study in Science and Religion*. New York: Harper & Row, 1974.

Barth, Karl. *Against the Stream: Shorter Post-War Writings 1946–52*. London: SCM Press, 1954.

———. *Anselm: Fides Quaerens Intellectum: Anselm's Proof of the Existence of God in the Context of His Theological Scheme*. London: SCM Press, 1960; reprint ed., Pickwick Press, 1975.

———. "Biblical Questions, Insights, and Vistas." In *The Word of God and the Word of Man*, pp. 51–96. Translated by Douglas Horton. New York: Harper, 1957.

————. "Christian Community and Civil Community." In *Community State, and Church*, pp. 149–89. Introduction by Will Herberg. Garden City: Doubleday & Co., 1960.

————. "The Christian Community in the Midst of Political Change." In *Against the Stream: Shorter Post-War Writings 1946–52*, pp. 53–124. London: SCM Press, 1954.

————. "The Christian's Place in Society." in *The Word of God and the Word of Man*, pp. 272–319. Translated by Douglas Horton. New York: Harper, 1957.

————. *The Church and the Churches*. London: James Clark & Co., 1936.

————. "Church and Culture." In *Theology and Church: Shorter Writings 1920–1928*, pp. 334–54. Translated by Louise Pettibone Smith. Introduction by T. F. Torrance. London: SCM Press, 1962.

————. *Church Dogmatics*. Edited by G. W. Bromiley and T. F. Torrance. Vol. 1: *The Doctrine of the Word of God*. Vol. 2: *The Doctrine of God*. Vol. 3: *The Doctrine of Creation*. Vol. 4: *The Doctrine of Reconciliation*. Edinburgh: T. & T. Clark, 1936–1969.

————. *The Church and the Political Problem of Our Day*. New York: Charles Scribner's Sons, 1939.

————. "Church and Theology." In *Theology and Church: Shorter Writings 1920–1928*, pp. 286–306. Translated by Louise Pettibone Smith. Introduction by T. F. Torrance. London: SCM Press, 1962.

————. *The Church and the War*. Translated by Antonio H. Froendt. Introduction by Samuel McCrea Cavert. New York: Macmillan Co., 1944.

————. *Community, State, and Church*. Introduction by Will Herberg. Garden City, N.J.: Doubleday & Co., 1960.

————. "The Concept of the Church." In *Theology and Church: Shorter Writings 1920–1928*, pp. 272–85. Translated by Louise Pettibone Smith. Introduction by T. F. Torrance. London: SCM Press, 1962.

————. *Credo: A Presentation of the Chief Problems of Dogmatics with Reference to the Apostles' Creed*. Translated by J. Strathearn McNab. New York: Charles Scribner's Sons, 1936.

————. *The Faith of the Church: A Commentary on the Apostles' Creed according to Calvin's Catechism*. Edited by Jean-Louise Leuba. Translated by Gabriel Vahanian. New York: Meridian Books, 1958.

————. *Dogmatics in Outline*. Translated by S. T. Thomson. New York: Harper & Row, 1959.

————. *Evangelical Theology: An Introduction*. Translated by Grover Foley. Grand Rapids: William B. Eerdmans Co., 1963.

————. *Final Testimonies*. Edited by Eberhard Busch. Translated by Geoffrey W. Bromiley. Grand Rapids: William B. Eerdmans Co., 1977.

————, *Gesamtausgabe*. I. Predigten 1913. Herausgegeben von Nelly Barth und Gerhard Sauter. Zürich: Theologischer Verlag, 1976.

————. *The Heidelberg Catechism for Today*. Translated by Shirley C. Guthrie, J. Richmond: John Knox Press, 1948; reprint ed., 1964.

————. "Jesus Christ and The Movement for Social Justice." In *Karl Barth and Radical Politics*, pp. 19–45. Edited and translated by George Hunsinger. Philadelphia: Westminster Press, 1976.

————. *Die Kirchliche Dogmatik*. Vol. 1: *Die Lehre vom Wort Gottes*. Vol. 2: *Die Lehre von Gott*. Vol. 3: *Die Lehre von der Schöpfung*. Vol. 4: *Die Lehre von der Versöhnung*. Zürich: Evangelischer Verlag, 1932–1959.

————. *The Knowledge of God and the Service of God According to the Teaching of the Reformation*. Translated by J. L. M. Haire and Ian Henderson. London: Hodder and Stoughton, 1938; reprint ed., 1955.

————. "Letter to a Pastor in the German Democratic Republic." In *How To Serve God in a Marxist Land*, pp. 45–80. Introduction by Robert McAfee Brown. New York: Association Press, 1959.

————. *The Only Way: How Can the Germans Be Cured?* Translated by Martin K. Neufeld and Ronald Gregor Smith. New York: Philosophical Library, 1947.

————. "Past and Future: Friedrich Naumann and Christoph Blumhardt." In *The Beginning of Dialectic Theology*, pp. 35–45. Edited by James M. Robinson. Translated by Keith R. Crim. Richmond: John Knox Press, 1968.

————. "Poverty." In *Against the Stream: Shorter Post-War Writings 1946–52*, pp. 243–46. London: SCM Press, 1954.

————. "The Problem of Ethics Today." In *The Word of God and the Word of Man*, pp. 136–82. Translated by Douglas Horton. New York: Harper, 1957.

————. *Protestant Theology in the Nineteenth Century: Its Background and History*. Valley Forge: Judson Press, 1973.

————. "The Righteousness of God." In *The Word of God and the*

Word of Man, pp. 9–27. Translated by Douglas Horton. New York: Harper, 1957.

―――. *Der Römerbrief.* Unveränderter Nachdruck der ersten Auflage von 1919. Zürich: Evz-Verlag, 1963.

―――. "The Strange New World Within the Bible." In *The Word of God and the Word of Man*, pp. 28–50. Translated by Douglas Horton. New York: Harper, 1957.

―――. "A Theological Dialogue." *Theology Today* 19 (July 1962):171–77.

―――. *Theological Existence Today: A Plea for Theological Freedom.* Translated by R. Birch Hoyle. London: Hodder and Stoughton, 1933.

―――. *Theology and Church: Shorter Writings 1920–1928.* Translated by Louise Pettibone Smith. Introduction by T. F. Torrance. London: SCM Press, 1962.

―――. *Trouble and Promise in the Struggle of the Church in Germany.* Translated by P. V. M. Benecke. Oxford: Clarendon Press, 1938.

―――. *The Word of God and the Word of Man.* Translated by Douglas Horton. New York: Harper, 1957.

Barth, Karl and Hamel, Johannes. *How To Serve God in a Marxist Land.* Introduction by Robert McAfee Brown. New York: Association Press, 1959.

Barth, Markus. "Current Discussions on the Political Character of Karl Barth's Theology." In *Footnotes to a Theology: The Karl Barth Colloquium of 1972*, pp. 77–94. Edited and Introduction by Martin Rumscheidt. The Corporation for the Publication of Academic Studies in Religion in Canada, 1974.

Bellah, Robert N. *The Broken Covenant: American Civil Religion in Time of Trial.* New York: Seabury Press, 1975.

Bentley, James. "Karl Barth as a Christian Socialist." *Theology* 76 (July 1973):349–56.

Berkouwer, G. C. *The Triumph of Grace in the Theology of Karl Barth.* Translated by Harry R. Boer. Grand Rapids: William B. Eerdmans Co., 1956.

Bernstein, Richard J. *Praxis and Action: Contemporary Philosophies of Human Activity.* Philadelphia: University of Pennsylvania Press, 1971.

Bettis, Joseph. "Political Theology and Social Ethics: The Socialist Humanism of Karl Barth." *Scottish Journal of Theology* 27 (August 1974):287–305. Also, In *Karl Barth and Radical Politics*, pp.

159–79. Edited and translated by George Hunsinger. Philadelphia: Westminster Press, 1976.

⸻. "Theology in the Public Debate: Barth's Rejection of Natural Theology and the Hermeneutical Problem." *Scottish Journal of Theology* 22 (December 1969):385–403.

Black, Max. *Models and Metaphors: Studies in Language and Philosophy.* Ithaca: Cornell University Press, 1962.

Blevins, Kent B. "Southern Baptist Attitudes Toward the Vietnam War in the Years 1965–1970." *Foundations* 23 (July–September 1980):231–44.

Bloesch, Donald G. *Jesus Is Victor! Karl Barth's Doctrine of Salvation.* Nashville: Abingdon Press, 1976.

Bouillard, Henri. *Karl Barth.* Deuxieme Partie: *Parole De Dieu Et Existence Humaine.* Paris: Aubier Editions Montaigne, 1957.

⸻. *The Knowledge of God.* Translated by Samuel D. Femiano. New York: Herder & Herder, 1968.

Bowden, John. *Karl Barth.* London: SCM Press, 1971.

Bromiley, Geoffrey W. *An Introduction to the Theology of Karl Barth.* Grand Rapids; William B. Eerdmans Co., 1979.

Brown, Colin. *Karl Barth and the Christian Message.* Chicago: Inter-Varsity Press, 1967.

Brown, Robert. "On God's Ontic and Neotic Absoluteness: A Critique of Barth." *Scottish Journal of Theology* 33 (December 1980):533–49.

Brown, Robert McAfee. "Introduction Essay." *How to Serve God in a Marxist Land,* by Karl Barth and Johannes Hamel. New York: Association Press, 1959.

Brunner, Emil. "An Open Letter to Karl Barth." In *Against the Stream: Shorter Post-War Writings: 1946–52,* pp. 106–13. London: SCM Press, 1954.

⸻. *Dogmatics.* Vol. 2: *The Christian Doctrine of Creation and Redemption.* Translated by Olive Wyon. Philadelphia: Westminster Press, 1952.

Buchler, Justus. *The Concept of Method.* New York: Columbia University Press, 1961.

Busch, Eberhard. Introduction to *Karl Barth in Re-View: Posthumous Works Reviewed and Assessed.* Edited by H. Martin Rumscheidt. Introduction by Eberhard Busch. Afterword by Hans Frei. Pittsburgh: Pickwick Press, 1981.

⸻. *Karl Barth: His Life from Letters and Autobiographical*

Texts. Translated by John Bowden. Philadelphia: Fortress Press, 1976.

Butler, Gerald A. "Karl Barth and Political Theology." *Scottish Journal of Theology* 27 (November 1974):441–58.

Camfield, F. W. *Revelation and the Holy Spirit: An Essay in Barthian Theology*. Foreword by John McConnachie. New York: Charles Scribner's Sons, 1934.

Casalis, Georges. *Portrait of Karl Barth*. Translated and Introduction by Robert McAfee Brown. Garden City: Doubleday & Co., 1963.

Clark, Gordon H. *Karl Barth's Theological Method*. Philadelphia: Presbyterian and Reformed Publishing Co., 1963.

Cochrane, Arthur C. "The Sermons of 1913 and 1914." In *Karl Barth in Re-View: Posthumous Works Reviewed and Assessed*, pp. 1–6. Edited by H. Martin Rumscheidt. Introduction by Eberhard Busch. Afterword by Hans Frei. Pittsburgh: Pickwick Press, 1981.

Come, Arnold B. *An Introduction to Barth's Dogmatics for Preachers*. Philadelphia: Westminster Press, 1963.

Cragg, Gerald R. *The Church and the Age of Reason: 1648–1789*. Grand Rapids: William B. Eerdmans Co., 1967.

Crawford, Robert. "The Theological Method of Karl Barth." *Scottish Journal of Theology* 25 (August 1972):320–36.

Crimmann, Ralph P. *Karl Barths frühe Publikationen und ihre Rezeption*. Bern: Peter Lang, 1981.

Dannemann, Ulrich. *Theologie und Politik im Denken Karl Barths*. Munich: Christian Kaiser Verlag, 1977.

Deschner, John. "Karl Barth as Political Activist." *Union Seminary Quarterly Review* 28 (Fall 1972):55–66.

Dillard, James Edgar. *We Southern Baptists: 1937–8*. Nashville: Executive Committee, Southern Baptist Convention, 1937–8.

Du Bose, Francis and Adams, Bob E. "Evangelization, Missions, and Social Action: A Southern Baptist Perspective." *Review and Expositor* 79 (Spring 1982): 351–66.

Earle, John R.; Knudsen, Dean D.; and Shriver, Donald W. *Spindles and Spires: A Re-Study of Religion and Social Change in Gastonia*. Atlanta: John Knox Press, 1976.

Fairweather, A. M. *The Word as Truth: A Critical Examination of the Christian Doctrine of Revelation in the Writings of Thomas Aquinas and Karl Barth*. London: Lutterworth Press, 1944.

Farrer, Austin. *A Rebirth of Images: The Making of St. John's Apocalypse*. Boston: Beacon Press, 1963.

Ford, D. F. "Barth's Interpretation of the Bible." In *Karl Barth: Studies of His Theological Method*, pp. 55–87. Edited by S. W. Sykes. Oxford: Clarendon Press, 1979.

Frei, Hans W. "Niebuhr's Theological Background." In *Faith and Ethics: The Theology of H. Richard Niebuhr*, pp. 9–64. Edited by Paul Ramsey. New York: Harper & Brothers, 1957.

Funk, Robert W. *Language, Hermeneutic, and Word of God: The Problem of Language in the New Testament and Contemporary Theology*. New York: Harper & Row, 1966.

Gadamer, Hans-Georg. *Philosophical Hermeneutics*. Edited and translated by David E. Linge. Berkeley: University of California Press, 1976.

Gaines, David P. *Belief of Baptists*. New York: R. R. Smith, 1952.

Gaustad, Edwin S. "The Backus-Leland Tradition." In *Baptist Concepts of the Church*, pp. 106–34. Edited by Winthrop Still Hudson. Chicago: Judson Press, 1959.

Gay, Peter. *The Enlightenment: An Interpretation. The Rise of Modern Paganism*. New York: Alfred A. Knopf, 1975.

Gilson, Etienne. *The Spirit of Medieval Philosophy*. Translated by A. H. C. Downes. New York: Charles Scribner's Sons, 1936.

Gollwitzer, Helmut. "Kingdom of God and Socialism in the Theology of Karl Barth." In *Karl Barth and Radical Politics*, pp. 77–120. Edited and translated by George Hunsinger. Philadelphia: Westminster Press, 1976.

Green, Clifford. "Liberation Theology? Karl Barth on Women and Men." *Union Seminary Quarterly Review* 29 (Spring & Summer 1974):221–31.

Gunnemann, Jon P. *The Moral Meaning of Revolution*. New Haven: Yale University Press, 1979.

Gunton, Colin E. *Becoming and Being: The Doctrine of God in Charles Hartshorne and Karl Barth*. Oxford: Oxford University Press, 1978; reprint ed. 1980.

Hamer, Jerome. *Karl Barth*. Translated by Dominic M. Maruca. Westminster, Md.: Newman Press, 1962.

Handy, Robert T. *A Christian America: Protestant Hopes and Historical Realities*. London: Oxford University Press, 1971.

————. Foreword to *Baptists in Transition: Individualism and Christian Responsibility*, by Winthrop S. Hudson. Valley Forge: Judson Press, 1979.

Harrison, Paul M. *Authority and Power in the Free Church Tradition: A Social Case Study of the American Baptist Convention.* Princeton: Princeton University Press, 1959.

Hart, Ray L. *Unfinished Man and the Imagination: Toward an Ontology and a Rhetoric of Revelation.* New York: Herder & Herder, 1968.

Hartwell, Herbert. Review of *Theologie und Sozialismus. Das Beispiel Karl Barths,* by Friedrich-Wilhelm Marquardt. *Scottish Journal of Theology* 28 (1975):63–72.

————. *The Theology of Karl Barth: An Introduction.* Philadelphia: Westminster Press, 1964.

Hastings, C. Brownlow. *Introducing Southern Baptists: Their Faith and Their Life.* New York: Paulist Press, 1981.

Hausmann, William John. *Karl Barth's Doctrine of Election.* New York: Philosophical Library, 1969.

Hays, Brooks and Steely, John E. *The Baptist Way of Life.* Macon: Mercer University Press, 1981.

Hazard, Paul. *The European Mind: The Critical Years (1680–1715).* Translated by J. Lewis May. New Haven: Yale University Press, 1953.

Henderson, Steven T. "Social Action in a Conservative Environment: The Christian Life Commission and Southern Baptist Churches." *Foundations* 23 (July–September 1980):245–51.

Hendry, George S. "The Freedom of God in the Theology of Karl Barth." *Scottish Journal of Theology* 31 (June 1978):229–44.

————. *The Holy Spirit in Christian Theology.* Philadelphia: Westminster Press, 1965.

Herzog, Frederick. *Justice Church: The New Function of the Church in North American Christianity.* Maryknoll: Orbis Books, 1980.

Heschel, Abraham J. *The Prophets.* New York: Harper & Row, 1962.

Hill, Samuel S., Jr. *The South and the North in American Religion.* Athens, Ga.: University of Georgia Press, 1980.

————. *Southern Churches in Crisis.* Boston: Beacon Press, 1967.

Hill, Samuel S., Jr.: Thompson, Edgar T.; Scott, Anne Firor; Hudson, Charles; and Gaustad, Edwin S. *Religion and the Solid South.* Nashville: Abingdon Press, 1972.

Hill, Samuel S., Jr. and Torbet, Robert G. *Baptists North and South.* Valley Forge: Judson Press, 1964.

Hinson, E. Glenn. "Southern Baptists: A Concern for Experiential

Conversion." *The Christian Century,* June 7–14, 1978, pp. 610–615.

Hobbs, Herschel H. *The People Called Southern Baptists* and *The Baptist Faith and Message.* Shawnee, Okla.: Oklahoma Baptist University, 1981.

Hood, R. E. "Karl Barth's Christological Basis for the State and Political Praxis." *Scottish Journal of Theology* 33 (1980):223–38.

———. "The Thorn of Liberalism in Karl Barth." *Anglican Theological Review* 44 (October 1962):403–14.

Hopper, Stanley Romaine. "The Modern Diogenes: A Kierkegaardian Crotchet." In *Religion and Culture: Essays in Honor of Paul Tillich.* Edited by Walter Leibrecht. New York: Harper & Bros., 1959.

Hordern, William. "Theologians of Our Time: IV. Karl Barth To-Day." *The Expository Times,* March 1963, pp. 177–80.

Hoyle, R. Birch. *The Teaching of Karl Barth: An Exposition.* London: Student Christian Movement Press, 1930.

Huber, Wolfgang. "The Barmen Theological Declaration and the Two Kingdom Doctrine." *Lutheran World* 24 (1977):30–44.

Hudson, Winthrop S. *Baptists in Transition: Individualism and Christian Responsibility.* Foreword by Robert T. Handy. Valley Forge: Judson Press, 1979.

———. "Shifting Patterns of Church Order in the Twentieth Century." In *Baptist Concepts of the Church,* pp. 196–218. Edited by Winthrop Still Hudson. Chicago: Judson Press, 1959.

Hunsinger, George. "Conclusion: Toward a Radical Barth." In *Karl Barth and Radical Politics,* pp. 181–233. Edited and translated by George Hunsinger. Philadelphia: Westminster Press, 1976.

———. "Karl Barth and Liberation Theology." *The Journal of Religion* 63 (July 1983):247–63.

———. "Karl Barth and Radical Politics: Some Further Considerations." *Studies in Religion* 7 (Spring 1978):167–91.

———, ed. and trans. *Karl Barth and Radical Politics.* Philadelphia: Westminster Press, 1976.

Jacobsen, Ingrid, ed. *War Barth Sozialist? Ein Streitgespräch Um Theologie und Sozialismus Bei Karl Barth.* Berlin: Verlag Die Spur, 1975.

Jennings, Theodore W., Jr. *Introduction to Theology: An Invitation to Reflection Upon the Christian Mythos.* Philadelphia: Fortress Press, 1976.

Jenson, Robert. *God After God: The God of the Past and the God of the Future, Seen in the Work of Karl Barth*. Indianapolis: Bobbs-Merrill Co., 1969.

Jersild, Paul. "Natural Theology and the Doctrine of God in Albrecht Ritschl and Karl Barth." *The Lutheran Quartery* 14 (August 1962):239–57.

Jones, Joe Robert. *Karl Barth and Informative Revelation: A Conceptual Analysis*. Ann Arbor, Mich.: University Microfilms, 1970.

Jüngel, Eberhard. *The Doctrine of the Trinity: God's Being Is In Becoming*. Grand Rapids, Mich.: William B. Eerdmans Co., 1976.

Keller, Adolf. *Karl Barth and Christian Unity: The Influence of the Barthian Movement Upon the Churches of the World*. Translated by Manfred Manrodt with Werner Petersmann. Introduction by Luther A. Weigle. New York: Macmillan Co., 1933.

Kelsey, George D. *Social Ethics Among Southern Baptists, 1917–1969*. Metuchen, N.J.: Scarecrow Press, 1973.

King, Martin Luther, Jr. "Letter from Birmingham Jail." In *Why We Can't Wait*, pp. 77–100. New York: Harper & Row, 1964.

———. *Strength To Love*. New York: Harper & Row, 1963.

———. *Stride Toward Freedom: The Montgomery Story*. New York: Harper & Bros., 1958.

———. *Why We Can't Wait*. New York: Harper & Row, 1964.

Klem, Arthur W. *Reinhold Niebuhr's Appraisal of Karl Barth*. Ann Arbor, Mich.: University Microfilms, 1967.

Klooster, Fred H. *The Significance of Barth's Theology: An Appraisal with Special Reference to Election and Reconciliation*. Grand Rapids: Baker Book House, 1961.

Küng, Hans. *Justification: The Doctrine of Karl Barth and a Catholic Reflection*. Philadelphia: Westminster Press, 1981.

Kuykendall, George Henry, Jr. *The Spirit and the Word: An Attempt to Develop A Post-Enlightenment Understanding of the Church*. Ann Arbor, Mich.: University Microfilms, 1972.

Lappin, Maitland M. *Baptists in the Protestant Tradition*. Toronto: The Ryerson Press, 1947.

Lee, Jung Young. "Karl Barth's Use of Analogy in His Church Dogmatics." *Scottish Journal of Theology* 22 (June 1969):129–51.

Lehmann, Paul L. "The Concreteness of Theology: Reflections on the Conversation Between Barth and Bonhoeffer." In *Footnotes To*

A Theology: The Karl Barth Colloquium of 1972, pp. 53–76. Edited and Introduction by Martin Rumscheidt. Corporation for the Publication of Academic Studies in Religion in Canada, 1974.

———. "Karl Barth, Theologian of Permanent Revolution." *Union Seminary Quarterly Review* 28 (Fall 1972):67–81.

Leith, John H., ed. *Creeds of the Churches: A Reader in Christian Doctrine from the Bible to the Present*. Atlanta: John Knox Press, 1977.

Livingston, James C. *Modern Christian Thought: From the Enlightenment to Vatican II*. New York: Macmillan Publishing Co., 1971.

Lobkowicz, Nicholas. *Theory and Practice: History of a Concept from Aristotle to Marx*. Notre Dame: University of Notre Dame Press, 1967.

Lotz, Denton. "Baptist Identity in Mission and Evangelism." *Foundations* 21 (January–March 1978):32–49.

Lumpkin, William L. *Baptist Confessions of Faith*. Chicago: Judson Press, 1959.

McClendon, James William, Jr. *Biography as Theology: How Life Stories Can Remake Today's Theology*. Nashville: Abingdon, 1974.

McConnachie, John. *The Significance of Karl Barth*. New York: Richard R. Smith, 1931.

McDaniel, George W. *The People Called Baptists*. Nashville: Sunday School Board of the Southern Baptist Convention, 1919.

McFague, Sallie. *Metaphorical Theology: Models of God in Religious Language*. Philadelphia: Fortress Press, 1982.

McKenzie, David. "Barth's *Anselm* and the Object of Theological Knowledge." *Foundations* 21 (July–September 1978):271–75.

Mackintosh, Hugh Ross. *Types of Modern Theology: Schleiermacher to Barth*. London: Nisbet and Co., 1945.

McLean, Stuart D. *Humanity in the Thought of Karl Barth*. Edinburgh: T. & T. Clark, 1981.

McNutt, William Roy. *Polity and Practice in Baptist Churches*. Foreword by Douglas Clyde MacIntosh. Philadelphia: Judson Press, 1948.

Maring, Norman H. and Hudson, Winthrop S. *A Baptist Manual of Polity and Practice*. Chicago: Judson Press, 1963.

Maring, Norman H. "The Individualism of Francis Wayland." In *Baptist Concepts of the Church*, pp. 135–69. Edited by Winthrop Still Hudson. Chicago: Judson Press, 1959.

Marquardt, Friedrich-Wilhelm. "Socialism in the Theology of Karl Barth." In *Karl Barth and Radical Politics*, pp. 47–76. Edited and translated by George Hunsinger. Philadelphia: Westminster Press, 1976.

Marquardt, Friedrich-Wilhelm. *Theologie und Sozialismus: Das Beispiel Karl Barths*. München; Kaiser, 1972.

Matczak, Sebastian A. *Karl Barth on God: The Knowledge of the Divine Existence*. New York: St. Paul Publications, 1962.

May, Henry F. *Protestant Churches and Industrial America*. New York: Harper & Bros., 1949.

Miller, Elizabeth. "Social Issues in the American Baptist Tradition." *Foundations* 24 (October–December 1981):359–71.

Moltmann, Jürgen. *Theology of Hope: On the Ground and the Implications of a Christian Eschatology*. New York: Harper & Row, 1967.

———. *The Trinity and the Kingdom: The Doctrine of God*. San Francisco: Harper & Row, 1981.

Mondin, Battista. *The Principle of Analogy in Protestant and Catholic Theology*. The Hague: Martinus Nijhoff, 1968.

Monsma, Peter Halman. *Karl Barth's Idea of Revelation*. Somerville, N.J.: Somerset Press, 1937.

Mose, Christopher. "Raising God's Eyebrows: Some Further Thoughts on the Concept of the *Analogia Fidei*." *Union Seminary Quarterly Review* 37 (Fall-Winter 1981–82):39–49.

Mueller, David L. *Karl Barth*. Waco, Tex.: Word Books, 1972.

Mullins, Edgar Y. *The Axioms of Religion*. Philadelphia: Griffith and Rowland Press, 1908.

Murchison, Duncan Cameron. *Theology and Hermeneutics: A Critical Study in the Thought of Karl Barth and Rudolph Bultmann*. Ann Arbor, Mich.: Univeristy Microfilms, 1974.

Niebuhr, Reinhold. "Barth's East German Letter." *The Christian Century*, February 11, 1959, pp. 167–8.

———. *Essays in Applied Christianity*. Edited by D. B. Robertson. New York: Meridian Books, 1959.

———. "The Quality of Our Lives." *The Christian Century*, May 11, 1960, pp. 568–72.

———. "Toward New Intra-Christian Endeavors." *The Christian Century*, December 31, 1969, pp. 1662–67.

Niebuhr, Richard R. *Resurrection and Historical Reason: A Study of Theological Method*. New York: Charles Scribner's Sons, 1957.

O'Grady, Colm. *The Church in Catholic Theology: Dialogue with Kar Barth*. London: Geoffrey Chapman, 1969.

———. *The Church in the Theology of Karl Barth*. Washington: Corpus Books, 1968.

Osborn, Robert T. "A 'Personalistic' Appraisal of Barth's Political Ethics." *Studies in Religion* 12 (Summer 1983):313–24.

———. "Positivism and Promise in the Theology of Karl Barth." *Interpretation* 25 (July 1971):283–302.

———. "Some Problems of Liberation Theology: A Polanyian Perspective." *Journal of the American Academy of Religion* 51 (March 1983):79–95.

Parker, T. H. L. "Barth on Revelation." *Scottish Journal of Theology* 13 (December 1960):366–82.

———. *Karl Barth*. Grand Rapids, Mich.: William B. Eerdmans, 1970.

Pauck, Wilhelm. *Karl Barth: Prophet of a New Christianity?* New York: Harper & Bros., 1931.

Payne, Ernest Alexander. *The Fellowship of Believers: Baptist Thought and Practice Yesterday and Today*. Foreword by H. Wheeler Robinson. London: Carey Kingsgate Press, 1952.

Pinson, William M., Jr. *Applying the Gospel: Suggestions for Christian Social Action in a Local Church*. Nashville: Broadman Press, 1975.

———. *The Local Church in Ministry*. Nashville: Broadman Press, 1973.

Pope, Liston. *Millhands and Preachers: A Study of Gastonia*. New Haven: Yale University Press, 1942.

Prenter, Regin. "Karl Barths Umbildung der traditionellen Zweinaturlehre in lutherischer Beleuchtung." *Studia Theologica* 11 (1957):1–88.

Pruden, Edward Hughes. *Interpreters Needed: The Eternal Gospel and Our Contemporary Society*. Philadelphia: Judson Press, 1951.

Ramsey, Ian T. *Religious Language: An Empirical Placing of Theological Phrases*. London: SCM Press. 1957.

Raynal, Charles Edward, III. *Karl Barth's Conception of the Perfections of God*. Ann Arbor, Mich.: Xerox University Microfilms, 1978.

Rifkin, Jeremy with Howard, Ted. *The Emerging Order: God in the Age of Scarcity.* New York: G. P. Putnam's Sons, 1979.

Roberts, R. H. "Karl Barth's Doctrine of Time: Its Nature and Implications." In *Karl Barth: Studies of His Theological Method,* pp. 88–146. Edited by S. W. Sykes. Oxford: Clarendon Press, 1979.

Robinson, H. Wheeler. *Life and Faith of Baptists: British Baptists.* New York: Arno Press, 1980.

———. "The Strength and the Weakness of the Baptists." In *A Baptist Treasury,* pp. 184–94. Edited by Sydnor L. Stealey. New York: Thomas Y. Crowell Co., 1958.

Robinson, James M. and Cobb, John B., Jr., ed. *The New Hermeneutic.* New York: Harper & Row, 1964.

Rumscheidt, H. Martin, ed. *Karl Barth in Re-View: Posthumous Works Reviewed and Assessed.* Introduction by Eberhard Busch. Afterword by Hans Frei. Pittsburgh: Pickwick Press, 1981.

———. *Revelation and Theology: An Analysis of the Barth-Harnack Correspondence of 1923.* Cambridge: University Press, 1972.

Runia, Klaas. *Karl Barth's Doctrine of Holy Scripture.* Grand Rapids, Mich.: William B. Eerdmans, 1962.

Rust, Eric C. "Theological Emphases of the Past Three Decades." *Review And Expositor* 78 (Spring 1981):259–70.

Sanders, W. Stephen. *The Socialist Movement in Germany.* Fabian Tract No. 169. London: Fabian Society, February 1913.

Sapp, W. David. "Southern Baptist Responses to the American Economy, 1900–1980." *Baptist History and Heritage* 16 (January 1981):3–12.

Schellong, Dieter. "On Reading Karl Barth from the Left." In *Karl Barth and Radical Politics,* pp. 139–57. Edited and translated by George Hunsinger. Philadelphia: Westminster Press, 1976.

Shadwell, Authur. *The Socialist Movement 1824–1924: Its Origin and Meaning, Progress and Prospects.* London: Philip Allen & Co., 1925.

Shaw, Bynum. *Divided We Stand: The Baptists in American Life.* Durham, N.C.: Moore Publishing Co., 1974.

Shestor, Lev. *Athens and Jerusalem.* Translated by Bernard Martin. Athens, Ohio: Ohio University Press, 1966.

Shinn, Roger L. "On Rendering to Caesar and to God." *Worldview* 2 (December 1959):10, 11.

Smart, James D. *The Divided Mind of Modern Theology: Karl Barth and Rudolph Bultmann 1903–1933*. Philadelphia: Westminster Press, 1967.

Smith, Ronald Gregor. *The Doctrine of God*. Philadelphia: Westminster Press, 1970.

Snyder, Dale Norman. *Karl Barth's Struggle with Anthropocentric Theology*. Boekhandel Wattez-'s-Gravenhage, 1966.

Stagg, Frank. "Eschatology: A Southern Baptist Perspective." *Review and Expositor* 70 (Spring 1982):381–95.

Stahl, Steven P. "The Concept of Revelation in the Theology of Karl Barth." *The Saint Luke's Journal of Theology* 23 (March 1980):116–32.

Stewart, Claude Y., Jr. *Nature in Grace: A Study in the Theology of Nature*. Macon, Ga.: Mercer University Press, 1983.

Stromberg, Roland N. *Religious Liberalism in Eighteenth-Century England*. London: Oxford University Press, 1954.

Stroup, George W., III. *Revelation and the Word of God: The Hermeneutics of the Christian Story*. Ann Arbor, Mich.: University Microfilms, 1974.

Sykes, S. W. "Barth On the Centre of Theology." In *Karl Barth: Studies of His Theological Method*, pp. 17–54. Edited by S. W. Sykes. Oxford: Clarendon Press, 1979.

————. "The Study of Barth." In *Karl Barth: Studies of His Theological Method*, pp. 1–16. Edited by S. W. Sykes. Oxford: Clarendon Press, 1979.

————, ed. *Karl Barth: Studies of His Theological Method*. Oxford: Clarendon Press, 1979.

Tempelman, Andrew D. "The Conditions of Intelligible Analogical God-Language in the Theologies of Paul Tillich, Eric Mascall and Karl Barth." Ph.D. dissertation, Divinity School of University of Chicago, 1972.

Thielicke, Helmut. *Theological Ethics*. Vol. II: *Politics*. Edited by William H. Lazareth. Philadelphia: Fortress Press, 1969.

Thurneysen-Barth. *Revolutionary Theology in the Making: Barth-Thurneysen Correspondence, 1914–1925*. Translated by James D. Smart. Richmond: John Knox Press, 1964.

Tiller, Carl W. *The Twentieth Century Baptist: Chronicles of Baptists in the First Seventy-five Years of the Baptist World Alliance*. Valley Forge: Judson Press, 1980.

Tillich, Paul. *Systematic Theology.* 3 vols. Chicago: University of Chicago Press, 1951–63. Vol. 2: *Existence and the Christ,* 1957.

Torrance, Thomas F. "Karl Barth." *Scottish Journal of Theology* 22 (March 1969):1–9.

———. *Karl Barth: An Introduction to His Early Theology, 1910–1931.* London: SCM Press, 1962.

Tribble, Harold W. *Our Doctrines.* Nashville: Sunday School Board of Southern Baptist Convention, 1936.

Watson, Gordon. "Karl Barth and St. Anselm's Theological Programme." *Scottish Journal of Theology* 30 (February 1977):31–45.

Wayland, Francis. *The Apostolic Ministry.* Rochester: Sage & Bros., 1853.

———. *Elements of Moral Science.* Boston: Gould and Lincoln, 1852.

———. *The Limitations of Human Responsibility.* Boston: Gould and Lincoln, 1838.

———. *Notes on the Principles and Practices of Baptist Churches.* New York: Sheldon, 1859.

———. *Sermon to the Churches.* New York: Sheldon, Blackerne & Co., 1858.

Wells, Harold G. "Karl Barth's Doctrine of Analogy." *Canadian Journal of Theology* 15 (1969):203–13.

West, Charles D. *Communism and the Theologians: Study of An Encounter.* London: SCM Press, 1958.

White, W. R. *Baptist Distinctives.* Nashville: Sunday School Board of Southern Baptist Convention, 1946.

Willey, Basil. *The Eighteenth Century Background: Studies on the Idea of Nature in the Thought of the Period.* New York: Columbia University Press, 1950.

———. *The Seventeenth Century Background: Studies in the Thought of the Age in Relation to Poetry and Religion.* New York: Columbia University Press, 1952.

Williams, R. D. "Barth on the Triune God." In *Karl Barth: Studies of His Theological Method,* pp. 147–93. Edited by S. W. Sykes. Oxford: Clarendon Press, 1979.

Willis, Robert E. *The Ethics of Karl Barth.* Leiden: E. J. Brill, 1971.

Wingren, Gustaf. *Theology in Conflict: Nygren, Barth, Bultmann.* Translated by Eric H. Wahlstrom. Philadelphia: Muhlenberg Press, 1958.

Winter, Gibson. *Liberating Creation: Foundations of Religious Social Ethics*. New York: Crossroad, 1981.

Wood, James E., Jr. "Baptist Thought and Human Rights." *Baptist History and Heritage* 13 (July 1978):50–62.

Wood, Presnell H. "Guest Editorial: Southern Baptist Responses to the Twentieth Century." *Baptist History and Heritage* 16 (January 1981): 1, 2.